American Culture in the 1970s

Twentieth-Century American Culture
Series Editor: Martin Halliwell, *Professor of American Studies, University of Leicester*

This series provides accessible but challenging studies of American culture in the twentieth century. Each title covers a specific decade and offers a clear overview of its dominant cultural forms and influential texts, discussing their historical impact and cultural legacy. Collectively the series reframes the notion of 'decade studies' through the prism of cultural production and rethinks the ways in which decades are usually periodised. Broad contextual approaches to the particular decade are combined with focused case studies, dealing with themes of modernity, commerce, freedom, power, resistance, community, race, class, gender, sexuality, internationalism, technology, war and popular culture.

American Culture in the 1910s
Mark Whalan

American Culture in the 1920s
Susan Currell

American Culture in the 1930s
David Eldridge

American Culture in the 1940s
Jacqueline Foertsch

American Culture in the 1950s
Martin Halliwell

American Culture in the 1960s
Sharon Monteith

American Culture in the 1970s
Will Kaufman

American Culture in the 1980s
Graham Thompson

American Culture in the 1990s
Colin Harrison

American Culture in the 1970s

Will Kaufman

Edinburgh University Press

In memory of my mother, Vickie Kaufman, and for my brothers, Mike and Steve, survivors of the seventies

Edinburgh University Press Ltd
22 George Square, Edinburgh

www.euppublishing.com

Typeset in 11/13 pt Stempel Garamond by
Servis Filmsetting Ltd, Stockport, Cheshire, and
printed and bound in Great Britain by
CPI Antony Rowe, Chippenham and Eastbourne

A CIP record for this book is available from the British Library

ISBN 978 0 7486 2142 2 (hardback)
ISBN 978 0 7486 2143 9 (paperback)

Published with the support of the Edinburgh University Scholarly Publishing Initiatives Fund.

Contents

Figures

Case Studies

Acknowledgements

When Martin Halliwell cornered me at an American Studies conference and asked me to contribute a book on the 1970s to his 'Twentieth-Century American Culture' series, I positively blanched. 'Come on,' he said. 'You know the references.' I'm still not sure what he meant. The seventies wasn't really my area, professionally – I was much more at home in the nineteenth century (the Civil War, Mark Twain) or, at the very latest, the 1930s (Woody Guthrie). My scholarly work on the seventies was limited to a few articles and chapters on Kurt Vonnegut and anti-Nixon satire. So, even now, I wonder if what Martin *really* meant was: 'Come on. You were there.'

If you can remember the 1960s, so the joke goes, you can't have been there. Well, I can certainly remember the seventies, and not always fondly. I entered my teens in 1971 – not a period of unalloyed happiness for many people. My mother was recently widowed, a low-paid secretary trying to support three boys through a string of job losses against a backdrop of high inflation and high unemployment: the previously unheard-of combination called 'stagflation'. For a brief period my mother had a paid job in the local office of the anti-war pressure group, SANE; consequently, I often found myself in the midst of turbulent demonstrations in the waning years of the Vietnam War, including the May Day march on Washington in 1971. The war was Nixon's, the battered economy was Carter's, and the comedy was Gerald Ford's (courtesy of Chevy Chase on *Saturday Night Live*). In my home town of Montclair, New Jersey, I was in the first class of children to be bussed across town to a school that neither of my older brothers knew anything about and for reasons I only barely understood. After gym class one day in 1974, the locker room reverberated to the wild chants of 'Ali! Ali! Ali!' I watched Anita Bryant get hit in the face with a pie on national television. The girl next door asked me what I thought of this guy Springsteen's new album, the one with the song about Rosalita on it. From Montclair Heights I watched the two skeletons of the World Trade Center gradually rise and overtake the Empire State Building, feeling vaguely affronted by the change to a familiar and beloved skyline. These and other 'references' have unavoidably fed into the writing of this book. I didn't understand their significance at the time. This is where the scholarship has come in.

I am grateful, first of all, to Martin Halliwell and to Nicola Ramsey at Edinburgh University Press for the opportunity to contribute this book and for their willing assistance throughout its composition. A number of colleagues and friends have pointed me to valuable material or honed my impressions through discussion. I'm grateful to Sämi Ludwig for his thoughts (and his work) on Toni Morrison; to Lynn Breeze for reminding me of the significance of the *Last Whole Earth Catalog*; to Nigel Wells for his gift of Sam Shepard's *Rolling Thunder Logbook*; to Nick Selby for material on the Language poets; to Donald Morse for presenting me with his authoritative study of Kurt Vonnegut; and to Zoltán Abádi-Nagy for sharing his critical wisdom about Vonnegut, Robert Coover and other seventies writers during a delightful drive across the Hungarian countryside. I am especially grateful to have received from the hand of Kasia Boddy a copy of her masterful *Boxing: A Cultural History* which illuminated so much about Norman Mailer and the Ali–Foreman 'Rumble in the Jungle'. My friends and, respectively, present and former colleagues, Jan Wardle and Heidi Macpherson, were always there when the work seemed to get on top of me. I appreciate the conference funding awarded by my department and faculty at the University of Central Lancashire. Finally, to my dear wife Sarah and our ace sons, Reuben and Theo . . . well, you know.

Chronology of
1970s American Culture

Date	Events	Criticism	Literature	Drama
1970	President Nixon announces a partial withdrawal from Vietnam while ordering troops into Cambodia. National Guardsmen kill student demonstrators at Kent State University, Ohio, and Jackson State University, Mississippi. Pro-war construction workers in hard hats attack anti-war demonstrators in lower Manhattan. Five thousand gay rights activists march in New York to commemorate the Stonewall riots. Chicano moratorium against the Vietnam War. Black Panthers' murder trial. First 'Earth Day' celebrated.	Garry Trudeau's *Doonesbury* cartoon strip debuts M. H. Abrams, *The Milk of Paradise* Dee Brown, *Bury My Heart at Wounded Knee* Hal Lindsay, *The Late, Great Planet Earth* Kate Millett, *Sexual Politics* Robin Morgan, ed., *Sisterhood Is Powerful* Charles Reich, *The Greening of America* Bobby Seale, *Seize the Time* Alvin Toffler, *Future Shock* Tom Wolfe, 'Radical Chic'	Richard Bach, *Jonathan Livingston Seagull* Jean Stafford, *Collected Stories* (Pulitzer prize) Anne Tyler, *A Slipping Down Life* John Updike, *Bech: A Book* Richard Vázquez, *Chicano* Eudora Welty, *Losing Battles* Richard Howard, *Untitled Subject* (Pulitzer) Denise Levertov, *Relearning the Alphabet* Maya Angelou, *I Know Why the Caged Bird Sings*	Ed Bullins, *The Duplex* and *It Bees Dat Way* Charles Gordone, *No Place to Be Somebody* (Pulitzer) John Guare, *House of Blue Leaves* Lanford Wilson, *Lemon Sky* and *Serenading Louie*

Film	Television	Popular Music	Visual Culture
Robert Altman, *M*A*S*H* Richard Fleischer et al., *Tora! Tora! Tora!* Arthur Hiller, *Love Story* Ralph Nelson, *Soldier Blue* Mike Nichols, *Catch-22* Arthur Penn, *Little Big Man* Bob Rafelson, *Five Easy Pieces* Joseph Sargent, *Colossus: The Forbin Project* Franklin J. Schaffner, *Patton* George Seaton, *Airport*	The Public Broadcasting System commences broadcasting Significant premieres: *Monday Night Football*, *All My Children*, *Mary Tyler Moore*, *The Flip Wilson Show*, *The Odd Couple*, *McCloud*, *The Partridge Family*	Jimi Hendrix and Janis Joplin die Diana Ross leaves the Supremes Black Sabbath inaugurates the 'heavy metal' genre Simon and Garfunkel release final album, *Bridge over Troubled Water* The Doobie Brothers form The Monkees disband Miles Davis, *Bitches' Brew* The Doors, *Morrison Hotel* Bob Dylan, *Self Portrait* Grateful Dead, *Workingman's Dead* Merle Haggard, 'The Fightin' Side of Me' Jackson Five, *ABC* Santana, *Abraxas* James Taylor, *Sweet Baby James* Neil Young, *After the Gold Rush* , 'Ohio' and 'Southern Man' Frank Zappa, *Weasels Ripped My Flesh*	Dan Graham, *Roll* Hans Haacke, *MoMA Poll* Alex Katz, *Vincent with Open Mouth* Isamu Noguchi, *Night Wind* Robert Smithson, *Spiral Jetty* Frank Stella, Museum of Modern Art retrospective

Date	Events	Criticism	Literature	Drama
1971	The *New York Times* publishes the *Pentagon Papers*. Twenty-nine inmates and ten others killed in a New York State Police assault on Attica prison rioters. Nixon normalises trade with Communist China and calls for Chinese admission to the United Nations. Two hundred thousand anti-war protesters march on Washington, resulting in mass arrests. Nixon devalues US dollar and uncouples it from the gold standard, unilaterally ending the 'Bretton Woods' system. Congress scraps Supersonic Transport project. Norman Mailer debates with prominent feminists at New York's Town Hall.	M. H. Abrams, *Natural Supernaturalism* Paul de Man, *Blindness and Insight* Erving Goffman, *Relations in Public* Fredric Jameson, *Marxism and Form* Elizabeth Janeway, *Man's World, Woman's Place* John Rawls, *A Theory of Justice*	William Peter Blatty, *The Exorcist* William Burroughs, *Wild Boys: A Book of the Dead* Don DeLillo, *Americana* E. L. Doctorow, *The Book of Daniel* Ernest M. Gaines, *The Autobiography of Miss Jane Pittman* John Gardner, *Grendel* Toni Morrison, *The Bluest Eye* Philip Roth, *Our Gang* John Updike, *Rabbit Redux* William S. Merwin, *Carrier of Ladders* (Pulitzer) Anne Sexton, *Transformations* Charles Simic, *Dismantling the Silence*	Philip Hayes Dean, *The Sty of the Blind Pig* David Mamet, *Duck Variations* David Rabe, *Sticks and Bones* and *The Basic Training of Pavlo Hummel* Steven Schwartz, *Godspell* Sam Shepard and Patti Smith, *Cowboy Mouth* Paul Zindel, *The Effect of Gamma Rays on Man-in-the-Moon Marigolds* (Pulitzer)

Film	Television	Popular Music	Visual Culture
Woody Allen, *Bananas*	Advertisement of	Jim Morrison dies	Diane Arbus dies
Robert Altman,	cigarettes banned on	The Eagles form as a	Vito Acconci, *Seedbed*
McCabe and Mrs	television	backing band for Linda	Alexander Calder,
Miller	Nixon imposes	Ronstadt	*WTC Stabile*
William Friedkin, *The*	embargo on news	The New York Dolls	Hans Haacke,
French Connection	coverage of illegal US	form	*Shapolsky et al.*
Stanley Kubrick, *A*	bombing campaign in	Allman Brothers, *Live*	
Clockwork Orange	Laos	*at the Fillmore East*	
Tom Laughlin, *Billy*	The Waltons first	The Carpenters, *The*	
Jack	appear in a special, *The*	*Carpenters*	
Mike Nichols, *Carnal*	*Homecoming: A*	Crosby, Stills, Nash	
Knowledge	*Christmas Story*	and Young, *Déjà Vu*	
Gordon Parks Sr,	Significant premieres:	Marvin Gaye, *What's*	
Shaft	*Masterpiece Theater,*	*Going On*	
Sam Peckinpah, *Straw*	*All in the Family, Soul*	Isaac Hayes, *Black*	
Dogs	*Train, The Electric*	*Moses* and *Shaft*	
Boris Sagal, *The*	*Company, Sonny and*	Carole King, *Tapestry*	
Omega Man	*Cher, McMillan and*	Bob Margouleff and	
Edward Sherrin,	*Wife, Columbo*	Malcolm Cecil,	
Valdez Is Coming	Final broadcasts of *The*	*Zerotime*	
Don Siegel, *Dirty*	*High Chaparral, The*	Joni Mitchell, *Blue*	
Harry	*Virginian, Hogan's*		
Melvin Van Peebles,	*Heroes* and *The Ed*		
Sweet Sweetback's	*Sullivan Show*		
Baadasssss Song			
Robert Wise, *The*			
Andromeda Strain			

Date	Events	Criticism	Literature	Drama
1972	Nixon visits Communist China. Equal Rights Amendment passes in the Senate. Nixon visits Soviet Union and signs nuclear limitations agreement. Shirley Chisholm becomes first African American woman presidential candidate. Nixon re-elected in landslide. Watergate scandal unfolds. Title IX of the Education Amendments Act outlaws sexual discrimination in federally funded school programmes. World Trade Center becomes world's tallest building. Igoe-Pruitt housing project demolished. *The Last Whole Earth Catalog* published.	*American Poetry Review* established Toni Cade Bambara, 'Black English' Stanley Fish, *Self-Consuming Artifacts* Thomas Harris, *I'm OK, You're OK* Fredric Jameson, *The Prison-House of Language* Lionel Trilling, *Sincerity and Authenticity* Robert Venturi et al., *Learning from Las Vegas* Sherley Ann Williams, *Give Birth to Brightness*	Rudolfo Anaya, *Bless Me, Ultima* Ira Levin, *The Stepford Wives* Bharati Mukherjee, *The Tiger's Daughter* Chaim Potok, *My Name Is Asher Lev* Ishmael Reed, *Mumbo Jumbo* Isaac Bashevis Singer, *Enemies: A Love Story* Wallace Stegner, *Angel of Repose* (Pulitzer) Hunter S. Thompson, *Fear and Loathing in Las Vegas* James Wright, *Collected Poems* (Pulitzer)	Women's Theater Council formed Frank Chin, *Chickencoop Chinaman* Hanay Geiogamah, *Body Indian* Miguel Piñero, *Short Eyes* Sam Shepard, *Tooth of Crime* Joseph Walker, *The River Niger* Tennessee Williams, *Small Craft Warnings*

Film	Television	Popular Music	Visual Culture
Robert Aldrich, *Ulzana's Raid* Woody Allen, *Everything You Always Wanted to Know about Sex but Were Afraid to Ask* John Boorman, *Deliverance* Francis Ford Coppola, *The Godfather* Gerard Damiano, *Deep Throat* Philip Kaufman, *The Great Northfield, Minnesota Raid* Ronald Neame, *The Poseidon Adventure* Gordon Parks Jr, *Superfly*	Nixon's visit to Beijing televised John Lennon and Yoko Ono guest host *The Mike Douglas Show* Significant premieres: *M*A*S*H*, *Sanford and Son*, *Maude*, *Kung Fu*, *The Waltons*, *Emergency*, *The Bob Newhart Show* Final broadcasts of *Bewitched* and *My Three Sons*	Mahalia Jackson dies Alice Cooper, *School's Out* John Denver, *Rocky Mountain High* The Eagles, *The Eagles* Roberta Flack, 'The First Time Ever I Saw Your Face' Don McLean, *American Pie* Curtis Mayfield, *Superfly* Johnny Nash, *I Can See Clearly Now* Lou Reed, *Transformer* Stevie Wonder, *Music of My Mind* and *Talking Book* Neil Young, *Harvest*	Diane Arbus retrospective, Museum of Modern Art James Turrell commences work reshaping Roden Crater, Arizona A.I.R. Gallery opens in SoHo, New York First retrospective of James Rosenquist at the Whitney Museum, New York Joan Jonas ('Organic Honey'), Funnel and Vertical Roll Helen Frankenthaler, *Coral Wedge*

Date	Events	Criticism	Literature	Drama
1973	Supreme Court sanctions abortion in *Roe* v. *Wade* decision. US and North Vietnam sign ceasefire agreement. OPEC commences oil embargo against US for support of Israel. Native American activists occupy Wounded Knee. Senate Watergate hearings commence. Amoco Building (Chicago) becomes world's tallest. Billy Jean King defeats Bobby Riggs in the tennis 'Battle of the Sexes'. *Our Bodies, Ourselves* published. *Ms.* magazine inaugurated. Phyllis Schlafly and Betty Friedan clash over the ERA.	Harold Bloom, *The Anxiety of Influence* Northrup Frye, *The Critical Path* Carolyn Heilbrun, *Toward a Recognition of Androgyny* Norman Holland, *Poems in Persons* Irving Howe, *The Critical Point* Anthony Sampson, *The Sovereign State of ITT*	Cormac McCarthy, *Child of God* Thomas Pynchon, *Gravity's Rainbow* Philip Roth, *The Great American Novel* Ronald Sukenick, *Out* Gore Vidal, *Burr* Kurt Vonnegut, *Breakfast of Champions* Eudora Welty, *The Optimist's Daughter* (Pulitzer) Maxine Kumin, *Up Country* (Pulitzer) Pedro Pietri, 'Puerto Rican Obituary' Tim O'Brien, *If I Die in a Combat Zone*	Asian American Theatre Workshop established in San Francisco David Mamet, *Squirrels* Jason Miller, *That Championship Season* (Pulitzer) Lanford Wilson, *Hot L Baltimore*

Film	Television	Popular Music	Visual Culture
Woody Allen, *Sleeper*	Senate Watergate	Gram Parsons dies	Nick Ut wins Pulitzer
Robert Clouse, *Enter*	hearings commence	Grand Ole Opry	Prize for photograph
the Dragon	Elvis Presley, *Aloha*	relocates from	of Kim Phuc and other
Michael Crichton,	*From Hawaii – Via*	downtown Nashville	napalmed children
Westworld	*Satellite*	to Opryland	Robert Indiana's
William Friedkin, *The*	Significant premieres:	CBGB opens in New	'LOVE' appears on
Exorcist	*Police Story, The*	York	8 cents postage stamp
Jack Hill, *Coffey*	*Young and the Restless,*	Richard Hell and Tom	First Whitney Biennial
Phil Karlson, *Walking*	*The $10,000 Pyramid,*	Verlain form	exhibition
Tall	*The Six Million Dollar*	Television. Kiss	Alexander Calder,
David Miller,	*Man, Kojak*	perform first concert	DC-8 'flying canvass'
Executive Action	Final broadcasts of	The Eagles, *Desperado*	William Eggleston, *The*
Sam Peckinpah, *Pat*	*Bonanza, Mission*	Roberta Flack, *Killing*	*Red Ceiling*
Garrett and Billy the	*Impossible, Rowan and*	*Me Softly*	Joan Jonas, *Songdelay*
Kid	*Martin's Laugh-In* and	Funkadelic, *Cosmic*	Roy Lichtenstein,
Martin Scorsese, *Mean*	*The Mod Squad*	*Slop*	*Artist's Studio, Look*
Streets		Johnny Russell, 'Red	*Mickey*
Jack Starrett, *Cleopatra*		Necks, White Sox, and	Andy Warhol, *Mao*
Jones		Blue Ribbon Beer'	*Zedong*
		Bruce Springsteen,	
		Greetings from Asbury	
		Park, N.J. and *The*	
		Wild, the Innocent, and	
		the E Street Shuffle	
		Tom Waits, *Closing*	
		Time	
		Eric Weissberg and	
		Steve Mandel, *Dueling*	
		Banjos	
		Stevie Wonder,	
		Innervisions	

Date	Events	Criticism	Literature	Drama
1974	Publishing heiress Patricia Hearst is kidnapped by, and subsequently joins, the Symbionese Liberation Army. Nixon resigns presidency over Watergate. Gerald Ford becomes president; Nelson Rockefeller becomes vice president. Eleven women are ordained as Episcopal priests in defiance of church law. OPEC oil embargo lifted. Sears Tower (Chicago) becomes world's tallest building. Muhammad Ali defeats George Foreman in the 'Rumble in the Jungle' in Zaire.	Daniel Bell, *The Coming of Post-Industrial Society* Wayne C. Booth, *The Rhetoric of Irony* and *Modern Dogma and the Rhetoric of Assent* Robert Pirsig, *Zen and the Art of Motorcycle Maintenance* Studs Terkel, *Working* Bob Woodward and Carl Bernstein, *All the President's Men*	Walter Abish, *Alphabetical Africa* Peter Benchley, *Jaws* Frank Chin, ed., *Aiiieeeee! An Anthology of Asian American Writers* Joseph Heller, *Something Happened* Erica Jong, *Fear of Flying* Stephen King, *Carrie* Robert Lowell, *The Dolphin* (Pulitzer) Joseph McElroy, *Lookout Cartridge* Toni Morrison, *Sula* Grace Paley, *Enormous Changes at the Last Minute* Charles Simic, *Return to a Place Lit by a Glass of Milk* Anne Tyler, *Celestial Navigation* Gore Vidal, *Myron* James Welch, *Winter in the Blood* Anne Sexton commits suicide; *The Death Notebooks* published posthumously	Steppenwolf Theatre Company founded in Chicago Paul Carter Harrison, *The Great MacDaddy* Terrence McNally, *The Ritz* David Mamet, *Sexual Perversity in Chicago* David Rabe, *In the Boom Boom Boom*

Film	Television	Popular Music	Visual Culture
Francis Ford Coppola, *The Conversation*	On prime-time television, Nixon announces he has 'nothing to hide' with the release of White House tapes transcripts (19 April) and subsequently announces his resignation (8 August)	The Ramones form The Bottom Line opens in New York City	Robert Morris, sado-masochist poster exhibition at Castelli Gallery, New York
John Guillerman and Irwin Winkler, *The Towering Inferno*		Debbie Harry and Blondie form	William Eggleston, *14 Pictures*
Jack Hill, *Foxy Brown*		Talking Heads form	Paul McCarthy, *Painting, Wall Whip*
Tobe Hooper, *The Texas Chainsaw Massacre*	*The Autobiography of Miss Jane Pittman* (TV movie)	Beach Boys, *Endless Summer*	Gordon Matta-Clark, *Window Blow-Out*
Alan J. Pakula, *The Parallax View*		The Eagles, *On the Border*	Richard Serra, *Boomerang*
Roman Polanski, *Chinatown*	First US broadcast of *Monty Python's Flying Circus*	Lynyrd Skynyrd, 'Sweet Home Alabama'	Frank Stella, *Tuftonboro*
Mark Robson, *Earthquake*	Significant premieres: *Happy Days, Good Times, Rhoda, Little House on the Prairie, The $25,000 Pyramid, Chico and the Man, The Rockford Files, Police Woman*	Joni Mitchell, *Court and Spark*	
Martin Scorsese, *Raging Bull*		Patti Smith, 'Hey Joe'	
Michael Winner, *Death Wish*		Steely Dan, *Pretzel Logic*	
	Final broadcasts of *The Brady Bunch, The Secret Storm, Love American Style, Room 222, The F.B.I.* and *The Newlywed Game*	Stevie Wonder, *Fulfillingness' First Finale*	

Date	Events	Criticism	Literature	Drama
1975	South Vietnam overrun by invading North Vietnamese troops; US evacuates all forces. Assassination attempt on President Ford. New York City on verge of bankruptcy; Ford refuses a Federal rescue package. CIA formally implicated in overthrow of Allende government in Chile. Muhammad Ali v. Joe Frazier in 'The Thrilla in Manila', the Philippines.	Harold Bloom, *A Map of Misreading* and *Kabbalah and Criticism* Geoffrey Hartman, *The Fate of Reading and Other Essays* Norman Holland, *5 Readers Reading* Norman Mailer, *The Fight* Karl Shapiro, *The Poetry Wreck*	Edward Abbey, *The Monkey Wrench Gang* E. L. Doctorow, *Ragtime* Judith Rossner, *Looking for Mister Goodbar* Michael Shaara, *The Killer Angels* (Pulitzer) John Ashbery wins all major US poetry prizes for 'Self-Portrait in a Convex Mirror' Miguel Agarín and Miguel Piñero, eds, *Nuyorican Poetry: An Anthology of Puerto Rican Words and Feelings*	Edward Albee, *Seascape* (Pulitzer) Amiri Baraka, *The Motion of History* Leslie Lee, *The First Breeze of Summer* David Mamet, *American Buffalo* Ntozake Shange, *for colored girls who have considered suicide/when the rainbow is enuf* Charlie Smalls and William F. Brown, *The Wiz* Lanford Wilson, *The Mound Builders*

Film	Television	Popular Music	Visual Culture
Woody Allen, *Love and Death* Robert Altman, *Nashville* Charles Bail, *Cleopatra Jones and the Casino of Gold* Bryan Forbes, *The Stepford Wives* Stanley Kubrick, *Barry Lyndon* Steven Spielberg, *Jaws*	Home Box Office (HBO) commences cable broadcasting Significant premieres: *Saturday Night Live*, *The Jeffersons*, *One Day at a Time*, *Wheel of Fortune*, *Baretta*, *Barney Miller*, *Welcome Back, Kotter*, *Good Morning America* Final broadcasts of *Gunsmoke*, *Ironside*, *The Odd Couple* and *Kung Fu*	Iron Maiden form Joan Baez, *Diamonds and Rust* The Bee Gees, *Jive Talkin'* Alice Cooper, *Welcome to My Nightmare* Bob Dylan, *Rolling Thunder Review*, *Blood on the Tracks* and *The Basement Tapes* (with the Band) The Eagles, *One of These Nights* Funkadelic, *Let's Take It to the Stage* Joni Mitchell, *The Hissing of Summer Lawns* The Ramones, 'Blitzkreig Bop' Gil Scott-Heron, *The Revolution Will Not Be Televised* Paul Simon, *Still Crazy after All These Years* Patti Smith, *Horses* Bruce Springsteen, *Born to Run* Steely Dan, *Katy Lied*	Andy Warhol publishes *The Philosophy of Andy Warhol* Vito Acconci, *Plot* Robert Mapplethorpe, cover photo for Patti Smith's *Horses* Gordon Matta-Clark, *Day's End* and *Conical Intersect*

Date	Events	Criticism	Literature	Drama
1976	Supreme Court declares death penalty unconstitutional. US celebrates bicentennial on 4 July. Georgia governor Jimmy Carter defeats Gerald Ford in presidential election.	M. H. Abrams, 'The Deconstructive Angel' Daniel Bell, *The Cultural Contradictions of Capitalism* Harold Bloom, *Poetry and Repression* Peter Brooks, *The Melodramatic Imagination* Stanley Fish, 'Interpreting the Variorum' Morton Halerpin et al., *The Lawless State* Tom Wolfe, 'The Me Decade and the Third Great Awakening'	Saul Bellow wins Nobel Prize for Literature and Pulitzer for *Humboldt's Gift* Raymond Carver, *Will You Please Be Quiet, Please?* Raymond Federman, *Take It or Leave It* Maxine Hong Kingston, *The Woman Warrior* Gore Vidal, *1876* Kurt Vonnegut, *Slapstick* Alice Walker, *Meridian*	Amiri Baraka, *What Was the Relationship of the Lone Ranger to the Means of Production?* Michael Bennet, Marvin Hamlisch et al., *A Chorus Line* (Pulitzer) John Guare, *Rich and Famous* Larry Neal, *The Glorious Monster in the Bell of the Horn* Marsha Norman, *Getting Out* David Rabe, *Streamers* Sam Shepard, *Suicide in B Flat*

Film	Television	Popular Music	Visual Culture
Robert Altman, *Buffalo Bill and the Indians*	Museum of Broadcasting opens in New York City	Journalist Caroline Coon first employs the genre designation, 'punk'	Alexander Calder dies Man Ray dies Vito Acconci, *The Red Tapes*
Michael Anderson, *Logan's Run*	Mini-series: *Captains and the Kings*, *Rich Man, Poor Man*	The Sex Pistols' *Anarchy in the UK* released in USA	William Eggleston, Museum of Modern Art exhibition
John G. Avildsen, *Rocky*	Significant premieres: *The Bionic Woman*,	The Eagles win the first ever platinum	Joan Jonas, *The Juniper Tree*
Richard Donner, *The Omen*	*Laverne and Shirley*, *Charlie's Angels*, *Mary*	record for *Their Greatest Hits*	Robert Ryman, *Untitled*
Milos Forman, *One Flew Over the Cuckoo's Nest*	*Hartman*, *Wonder Woman*, *Quincy, M. E.*, *The Muppet Show*	Bob Dylan, the Band, and others perform *The Last Waltz*	
Sidney Lumet, *Network*	Final broadcasts of *Marcus Welby, M.D.*	George Clinton and Parliament-Funkadelic,	
Alan J. Pakula, *All the President's Men*	and *Medical Center*	P-Funk/Rubber Band Earth Tour	
Martin Scorsese, *Taxi Driver*		Bob Dylan, *Desire* The Eagles, *Hotel California*	
		Steve Miller Band, *Fly Like an Eagle*	
		Joni Mitchell, *Herjira*	
		Modern Lovers, *Modern Lovers*	
		Donna Summer, *A Love Trilogy*	
		Stevie Wonder, *Songs in the Key of Life*	

Date	Events	Criticism	Literature	Drama
1977	Gay rights ordinance rejected in Miami referendum after fierce campaign led by opponent Anita Bryant. US signs Panama Canal treaty surrendering American sovereignty and control of the canal. President Carter appears in the first of his televised 'fireside chats'. Mass arrests of anti-nuclear power protesters in New Hampshire. Blackout cripples New York City.	Shoshana Felman, 'To Open the Question' Judith Fetterley, *The Resisting Reader* Robert Jowett and John Shelton Lawrence, *The American Monomyth* J. Hillis Miller, 'The Critic as Host'	Robert Coover, *The Public Burning* Marilyn French, *The Women's Room* Alex Haley, *Roots* (special Pulitzer) Larry Heinemann, *Close Quarters* Michael Herr, *Dispatches* Cyra McFadden, *The Serial* James Merrill, *Divine Comedies* (Pulitzer) Philip Roth, *The Professor of Desire* Leslie Marmon Silko, *Ceremony*	Michael Cristofer, *The Shadow Box* (Pulitzer) John Guare, *Landscape of the Body* David Mamet, *The Water Engine* Arthur Miller, *The Archbishop's Ceiling* Tennessee Williams, *Vieux Carre*

Film	Television	Popular Music	Visual Culture
Woody Allen, *Annie Hall*	*Roots* (mini-series)	Elvis Presley dies	Stanley Forman wins Pulitzer Prize for
Robert Altman, *Three Women*	Significant premieres: *Three's Company,* *Soap, The Love Boat,*	Ronnie Van Zant and other members of Lynyrd Skynyrd die in	photograph, 'The Soiling of Old Glory'
John Badham, *Saturday Night Fever*	*Lou Grant, ChiPs* Final broadcasts of *Sanford and Son, Mary*	plane crash Studio 54 disco opens in New York	Alexander Calder posthumously awarded Presidential Medal of
Donald Cammell, *The Demon Seed*	*Tyler Moore, McCloud* and *McMillan and*	*Saturday Night Fever* soundtrack released	Freedom Sherrie Levine, Cindy
Wes Craven, *The Hills Have Eyes*	*Wife*	The B-52s debut Jackson Browne,	Sherman and Jack Goldstein stage
George Lucas, *Star Wars*		*Running on Empty* Fleetwood Mac,	'Pictures' exhibition at Artists Space in New
Terence Malick, *Days of Heaven*		*Rumours* Richard Hell and the	York Starr Kempf constructs
Steven Spielberg, *Close Encounters of the Third Kind*		Voidoids, *Blank Generation* Iggy Pop, *Lust for Life*	his first steel 'wind sculpture' Cindy Sherman
		Billy Joel, *The Stranger* Meat Loaf, *Bat Out of*	commences *Untitled Film Stills*
		Hell Donna Summer, 'I Feel	Museum of Modern Art, *American Art*
		Love' Talking Heads, *Talking*	*since 1945* exhibition First appearance of
		Heads: 77 Television, *Marquee*	Jenny Holzer's *Truisms* Walter De Maria, *The*
		Moon	*Lightning Field* Donald Judd, *Untitled*
			(Meter Box) Gordon Matta-Clark,
			Jacob's Ladder Wayne Thiebauld, *24th*
			Street Intersection

Date	Events	Criticism	Literature	Drama
1978	'Affirmative Action' upheld but compromised in the Supreme Court *Bakke* decision. Tax revolt in California leads to statewide passage of 'Proposition 13' against real estate tax. Ratification deadline for Equal Rights Amendment extended by Senate. Mass suicide of over nine hundred followers of the self-styled Reverend Jim Jones at Jonestown, Guyana. Fifteen thousand Vietnamese refugees, so called 'boat people', admitted to US. Cleveland, Ohio, declares bankruptcy.	John Gardner, *On Moral Fiction* Christopher Lasch, *The Culture of Narcissism* Edward Said, *Orientalism*	Isaac Bashevis Singer wins Nobel Prize Ann Beattie, *Secrets and Surprises* John Irving, *The World According to Garp* James Alan McPherson, *Elbow Room* (Pulitzer) Janice Mirikitani, *Awake in the River* Howard Nemerov, *Collected Poems* (Pulitzer) Tim O'Brien, *Going after Cacciato* Ishmael Reed, *Flight to Canada* Gerald Vizenor, *The Darkness in Saint Louis Bearheart* First issue of *L=A=N=G=U=A=G=E*	Donald L. Coburn, *The Gin Game* (Pulitzer) Beth Henley, *Crimes of the Heart* Sam Shepard, *Curse of the Starving Class* Lanford Wilson, *Fifth of July*

Film	Television	Popular Music	Visual Culture
Hal Ashby, *Coming Home* John Carpenter, *Halloween* Michael Cimino, *The Deer Hunter* Francis Ford Coppola, *The Godfather, Part II* Michael Crichton, *Coma* Martin Scorsese, *The Last Waltz*	First appearance of the Blues Brothers on *Saturday Night Live* First broadcast of the Super Bowl on CBS The Smithsonian Institution receives Archie and Edith Bunker's chairs from the set of *All in the Family* Mini-series: *Centennial, The Bastard, Holocaust* Significant premieres: *Fantasy Island, Dallas, Taxi, Mork and Mindy, Battlestar Galactica* Final broadcasts of *The Six Million Dollar Man, Police Woman, The Bob Newhart Show, Maude, Columbo, Rhoda* and *Chico and the Man*	The Dead Kennedys form Blondie, *Parallel Lines* Bob Dylan, *Street Legal* Parliament, *Funkentelechy vs the Placebo Syndrome* and *The Motor-Booty Affair* Kenny Rogers, 'The Gambler' Bruce Springsteen, *Darkness on the Edge of Town*	Gordon Matta-Clark dies Norman Rockwell dies Dan Flavin, *Untitled (to the Real Dan Hill)* Helen Frankenthaler, *Cleveland Symphony Orchestra* Jenny Holzer, *Inflammatory Essays* Roy Lichtenstein, *Lamp* Dennis Oppenheim, *Cobalt Vectors: An Invasion* George Segal, *Abraham and Isaac* Tom Wesselmann, *Bedroom* paintings

Date	Events	Criticism	Literature	Drama
1979	US and China formally establish diplomatic relations. Near-meltdown at Three Mile Island nuclear plant in Pennsylvania. US and Soviet Union sign Salt II treaty. OPEC levies second oil embargo. The federal Department of Energy established. Carter makes his 'crisis of confidence' speech. Islamist fundamentalists seize US embassy in Tehran, initially taking sixty-six hostages.	Harold Bloom et al., eds, *Deconstruction and Criticism* Wayne C. Booth, *Critical Understanding* Jonathan Culler, *Structuralist Poetics* Joan Didion, *The White Album* Sandra Gilbert and Susan Gubar, *The Madwoman in the Attic* Gerald Graff, *Literature Against Itself* Fredric Jameson, *Fables of Aggression* Paul de Man, *Allegories of Reading* Elaine Showalter, 'Towards a Feminist Poetics'	John Barth, *LETTERS* John Cheever, *Stories of John Cheever* (Pulitzer) Gustav Hasford, *The Short-Timers* Joseph Heller, *Good as Gold* Ruth Beebe Hill, *Hanta Yo: An American Saga* Norman Mailer, *The Executioner's Song* Bernard Malamud, *Dubin's Lives* Philip Roth, *The Ghost Writer* Gilbert Sorrentino, *Mulligan Stew* Kurt Vonnegut, *Jailbird* Robert Penn Warren, *Now and Then* (Pulitzer)	John Guare, *Bosoms and Neglect* David Henry Hwang, *FOB* Sam Shepard, *Buried Child* (Pulitzer) Lanford Wilson, *Talley's Folly*

Film	Television	Popular Music	Visual Culture
Woody Allen, *Manhattan* James Bridges, *The China Syndrome* Francis Ford Coppola, *Apocalypse Now* Stuart Rosenberg, *Amityville Horror* Ridley Scott, *Alien*	C-SPAN, ESPN and the Movie Channel (cable channels) are launched Mini-series: *The Rebels*, *Roots: The Next Generations*, *Backstairs at the White House* Significant premieres: *Archie's Place*, *The Dukes of Hazzard*, *Trapper John, M.D.*, *Benson*, *Knot's Landing* Final broadcasts of *All in the Family*, *Battlestar Galactica*, *Good Times*, *Welcome Back, Kotter* and *Wonder Woman*	Disco Demolition Nite at Comiskey Park, Chicago Ry Cooder's *Bop Till You Drop* is the first all-digital recording The Clash open their first American tour (San Francisco) with 'I'm So Bored with the USA' Bob Dylan, *Slow Train Coming* Funkadelic, *Uncle Jam Wants You!* The Knack, 'My Sharona' Rickie Lee Jones, *Rickie Lee Jones* Joni Mitchell, *Mingus* Donna Summer, *Bad Girls* The Village People, *Go West* Stevie Wonder, *Journey Through the Secret Life of Plants*	Roy Lichtenstein, *Pow Wow*

The Intellectual Context

A number of problems immediately occur when one attempts to conceptualise 'the seventies'. The first is the apparent arbitrariness of 'the decade' as a meaningful periodising marker. A major historian of the 1970s, Bruce J. Schulman, is aware of this problem, admitting: 'It is easy to mock the overwrought chronologies that lay such heavy weight on years that end with zero.'[1] Others would appear to agree. Why privilege 'decade markers', Stephen Rachman asks, when equally we 'take our temporal cures from political transitions like changes in administration'?[2] Music historian Grcil Marcus is most dismissive of the arbitrary 'decade marker':

> As the formal end of the 1960s approached, in some circles dread over the supposed event was as great as the nagging feeling that upon the dawning of the first day of the year 2000 the world will be rendered unrecognizable, assuming it still exists. The notion was that as the clock struck midnight on January 31, 1969, some spirit of invention and resistance peculiar to the time would magically disappear . . .[3]

In the light of such scepticism over the value of placing interpretive weight on years beginning or ending in 0, some cultural critics and historians have opted for other strategies. At one extreme, for instance, Stephen Paul Miller takes his cue from Foucault, breaking down the decade into smaller components: 'Michel Foucault's *The Order of Things* (1967) uses the term "episteme" to describe an era's prevailing mindset, its epistemological horizons . . . Epistemes graduate through micro-periods without losing their dominant discursive characteristics. For instance, roughly speaking, I micro-periodise the 1970s into 1970–1, 1972–4, 1975–7, and 1978–9'.[4] Thus, while still paying fealty to the 0-ending 'decade marker', Miller places more significance on particular

periods within the decade. At the other extreme, dismissing the concept
of the ten-year marker outright, Schulman prefers to elasticise the
period, opting for a cultural analysis based on what he calls 'the long
1970s, fifteen malaise- and mayhem-filled years, from 1969 to 1984',
during which 'the United States experienced a remarkable makeover. Its
economic outlook, political ideology, cultural assumptions and fundamental social arrangements changed.'[5] Schulman thus seizes on a
number of significant events and processes that demonstrate to him
'how during the Seventies, the tides of American life turned', including,
notably, the 'great shift' of 'political power, economic dynamism, and
cultural authority' from the northern centres to the southern Sunbelt.[6]

Other recent scholars have played equally fast and loose with the
ironclad 'decade marker'. For Edward D. Berkowitz, the 1970s lasted
from 1973 to 1981 – from the end of United States military action in
Vietnam to the inauguration of Ronald Reagan – between which events
the ground was prepared for the social and economic conservatism of
the 1980s.[7] Mark Hamilton Lytle's time frame is even more slippery:
as the subtitle of his cultural history indicates, the seventies were actually subsumed into a 'Sixties Era' that lasted 'from Elvis to the Fall of
Richard Nixon'.[8] In his extremely dark assessment of the 1970s, Philip
Jenkins maintains:

> The year 1970 is an especially implausible candidate for marking the end
> of an era, because so much of the unrest of the 1960s was peaking in that
> year, while critical events we think of as characterizing sixties liberalism
> actually occurred afterward. Though these historical markers are sym-
> bolic rather than real, I will argue that 'the sixties' began with the assas-
> sination of John Kennedy in 1963 and ended with the resignation of
> Richard Nixon in 1974.[9]

The concept of a 'great shift' underlies another significant reading
of the 1970s, that of J. David Hoeveler Jr, who argues that the decade
marked – or was marked by – the transition from modernism to postmodernism, what he calls 'the postmodernist turn':

> The recurrent motif in 1970s culture is the dismantling of inherited
> forms, descriptive norms, sharp and inclusive modes of categorization;
> instead, we have the blurring of distinctions, the mixing of forms, a
> discomfort with preciseness in signification and representation . . . The
> 1970s arrived to its place of recognition in American intellectual history
> by a series of undermining acts.[10]

These characteristics of Hoeveler's 'postmodernist turn' were, to some extent, identified and critiqued (with considerable dismay) by one of the decade's most influential sociologists, Daniel Bell, who, in the midst of the 1970s, concluded that American society had experienced its own irrevocable turn, or shift, from the 'industrial' to the 'post-industrial' mode. For the most part, Bell uses the term 'post-industrial' to describe changes in the economy, the labour market (or 'occupational system') and the arena of technological development.[11] However, as Bell argued in two highly polemical treatises – *The Coming of Post-Industrial Society* (1974) and *The Cultural Contradictions of Capitalism* (1976) – 'post-industrial society' has its cultural corollary, which is 'post-modernism'. Bell lamented what he perceived as 'a widening disjunction' between modern social structures and the culture – 'the symbolic expression of meanings' – generated by, or along with, them.[12] Social structures, Bell felt, were ruthlessly rational and efficient, while culture, sadly, was fixated on the self rather than on the community at large. Bell's alarming description of the rupture between culture and society preludes a devastating cultural critique:

> What I find striking today is the radical disjunction between the social structure (the techno-economic order) and the culture. The former is ruled by an economic principle defined in terms of efficiency and functional rationality, the organization of production through the ordering of things, including men as things. The latter is prodigal, promiscuous, dominated by an anti-rational, anti-intellectual temper in which the self is taken as the touchstone of cultural judgments, and the effect on the self is the measure of the aesthetic work of experience.[13]

Thus, in Bell's sour estimation, culture is devoted to sensation rather than contemplation, to raw experience rather than value – in short, to 'hedonism, the idea of pleasure as a way of life'.[14]

Such a blanket dismissal of American – or any – culture is, of course, sloppy and untenable. It seems to indicate, however, a desire on the part of cultural critics to encapsulate, to 'nail down' the tenor of a decade or, indeed, of an age. This is Graham Thompson's major objection to Miller's controlling definition of the 1970s as the decade in which 'surveillance and self-surveillance' became dominant American tropes.[15] Thompson argues: 'Producing a narrative of a decade that seeks to establish overarching definitions and to analyse specific cultural products and cultural production itself in light of these definitions is to mistake American narratives for totalising narratives about America'.[16] While heeding Thompson's advice against the temptation to totalise about something as multivalent and, perhaps, arbitrarily marked as a 'decade', we can still identify a variety of moments, processes and narratives worth exploring. Schulman, for one, does just this in his discussion of how the 1970s 'reshaped' a host of American 'landscapes' – 'race relations, religion, family life, politics, and popular culture':

> One year alone, 1973, witnessed the end of American intervention in Vietnam, the U.S. Supreme Court decision in *Roe v. Wade*, the exposure of the Watergate conspiracies, the Indian occupation of Wounded Knee, and the first Arab oil shock. Billie Jean King won the Battle of the Sexes, *The Godfather* swept the Academy Awards, and a young evangelical preacher named Jim Bakker appeared on the airwaves, intent on creating 'God's television'.[17]

Particular events thus carry their own weight in helping to define a decade. For music critic Tony Parsons, transitions between decades can occur in a particular arena – due to a signal event – regardless of developments elsewhere. Reviewing the 1990 reissue of the New York Dolls' first album (1973), Parsons wrote: 'Until *The New York Dolls* a hangover from the sixties had permeated the music scene. That album was where a new decade began, where a contemporary version of the essence of rock 'n' roll emerged to kick out the tired old men and clear the way for the New Order.'[18] This seems to imply that, while it might still be the 1960s in, say, the political or economic sphere, it may already be the 1970s in music. Arguably, this way madness lies.

One thing is certain: there are enough key cultural and historical moments to confound the conventional or stereotypical impression of the 1970s as the 'undecade' or as merely 'the aftermath of the sixties'[19] – 'an eminently forgettable decade', the decade of 'bad clothes, bad hair, and bad music impossible to take seriously'.[20] Such impressions threaten to overwhelm our sense of what precisely made the 1970s the *seventies*, as one of many recent cultural products indicates. The Fox Network's long-running sitcom, *That Seventies Show* (1998–2006) situates its characters in a small Wisconsin suburb in the years 1976–9. What is it in particular that makes it a '70s show', given that its teenage characters undergo crises and rites of passage that would be experienced by teens in other decades as well – sexual exploration, 'hanging out', family relationships, balancing school and after-school demands? Granted, the characters do play with such periodised topics as political scepticism and disenchantment with the Gerald Ford and Jimmy Carter administrations, the oil crises and petrol rationing, the impact of second-wave feminism and drug use. But even more important are the visual and aural elements – fashion, hair styles, technological props (for example the Pong video game), period slang and diction. As Sherrie Inness argues, the show relies on the sort of '1970s iconography' that informs larger trends in cultural nostalgia for the decade of the Bee Gees, *Saturday Night Fever*, 'lava lamps, suede rugs, and beanbag chairs . . . polyester leisure suits' – in short, the trappings of 'a fantasy, but one that has had a strong impact on the United States'.[21]

To a large extent, as Derek Kompare suggests, the 'rising cultural interest in the recent American past in the 1970s' is due largely to what he calls 'the *television heritage*' prompted in no small part by the programming of reruns of actual seventies shows.[22] Moving beyond the realms of parody, caricature or nostalgia, however, it is more useful to approach the 1970s – as Shelton Waldrep does – as 'a period [that] exists in several parallel dimensions. It is a zone of generational memory, a boundary between times of political excess, a period of still underexamined cultural production that marks the beginning of a new plurality' characterised by 'popular and artistic diversity'.[23] Approaching the decade thus will not only offer new and valuable readings of cultural texts and practices, but it will also offer ways in which to challenge the critical and intellectual negativity of Bell and like-minded thinkers who reduce the culture of the 1970s to a collective expression of narcissism, hedonism and solipsism.

The 'Me Decade'?

There were indeed cultural developments in the 1970s that must share some responsibility for the overarching misapprehensions of the decade as the decade of narcissism. It is, for example, easy to target a variety of 'New Age' or 'personal awareness' movements as the signal narcissistic expressions of the 1970s – 'Est, Esalen, Rolfing, Zen, yoga, Arica, channelling, transactional psychology' among them.[24] Towards the end of the decade, Cyra McFadden, in her novel *The Serial* (1977), could look back at the previous few years to construct a cast of Marin County, California, self-obsessives who take 'getting in touch with themselves' to the heights of caricature:

Figure I.1 Seventies Pad (c.1975). Three Lions/Getty Images.

Now Rita lived out in Woodacre with her old man, some other conge-
nial freaks and a kiln. Deeply involved with the human-potential movement, she had like *mutated* over the years through Gurdjieff, Silva Mind
Control, actualism, analytical tracking, parapsychology, Human Life
Styling, postural integration, the Fischer-Hoffman Process, hatha and
raja yoga, integral massage, orgonomy, palmistry, Neo-Reichian body-
work and Feldenkrais functional integration. Currently she was com-
muting to Berkeley twice a week for 'polarity balancing manipulation',
which, she reported through her annual mimeographed Christmas letter,
produces 'good thinking'.[25]

McFadden's parody has a critical counterpoint in an essay by Tom
Wolfe, 'The Me Decade and the Third Great Awakening', first published in the *New York Magazine* of 23 August 1976. For better or
worse, this essay – known generally as, simply, 'The Me Decade' – has
influenced many people's perceptions of the 1970s (and is the original
source of the popular catchphrase that is so often used to describe the
decade). As Wolfe writes: 'The new alchemical dream is: changing
one's personality – remaking, remodelling, elevating, and polishing
one's very *self* . . . and observing, studying, and doting on it. (Me!)'[26]
Wolfe's essay propelled the subject of American narcissism into the
popular arena, but he was not alone in seizing on narcissism as the

spirit of the age. Jim Hougan, Peter Marin, Edwin Schur and Richard Sennett all analysed the corrosive impact of narcissism on American society.[27] Leading the discussion by far, and with the greatest force, was the cultural historian Christopher Lasch whose *The Culture of Narcissism* (1978) remains a key critical examination of America in the 1970s.

The Culture of Narcissism (1978)

Lasch sees narcissism in general as 'a metaphor for the human condition',[28] but he also situates it in a particular time frame. Narcissism is the 'personality of our time', (31) related to specific social developments:

> Hardly more than a quarter-century after Henry Luce proclaimed 'the American century' [1941], American confidence has fallen to a low ebb. Those who recently dreamed of world power now despair of governing the city of New York. Defeat in Vietnam, economic stagnation, and the impending exhaustion of natural resources have produced a mood of pessimism in higher circles, which spreads through the rest of society as people lose faith in their leaders. (xiii)

Lasch argues that in consequence the American people have turned 'the pursuit of happiness to the dead end of a narcissistic preoccupation with the self' – 'the apotheosis of individualism' by which 'strategies of narcissistic survival . . . present themselves as emancipation'. (xv, 66) The narcissistic 'strategies' that Lasch singles out – whether 'the cult of expanded consciousness, health [or] personal "growth" ' – are, to him, symptoms of profound despair and they have no doubt contributed to succeeding caricatures of the 1970s in popular culture and criticism: 'Having no hope of improving their lives in any of the ways that matter, people have convinced themselves that what matters is psychic self-improvement: getting in touch with their feelings, eating health food, taking lessons in ballet or belly-dancing, immersing themselves in the wisdom of the East, jogging, learning how to "relate", overcoming the "fear of pleasure" '. (4)

For Lasch, all such strategies have led, in the first place, to 'the trivialization of personal relations'. (187) The importance of child-rearing is eclipsed by eroticism, yet it is an eroticism in which 'sex' is separated from 'feeling': 'The progressive ideology of "nonbinding commitments" and "cool sex" makes a virtue of emotional disengagement' while 'at the same time, people demand from personal relations the richness and intensity of a religious experience'. (194, 200)

Lasch establishes an explicit connection between 'the cult of personal relations' at an individual level and a receding 'hope of political solutions' at the social level. (51) The 'banality of pseudo-self-awareness', he argues, is reflected in a 'theatrics of politics' without substance. (71) Politics thus becomes an empty exercise in therapy; American preoccupations have thus descended 'from politics to self-examination': 'Having displaced religion as the organizing framework of American culture, the therapeutic outlook threatens to displace politics as well, the last refuge of ideology. Bureaucracy transforms collective grievances into personal problems amenable to therapeutic intervention'. (13–14) Even at the existing political level, Lasch argues, the preoccupation with the self is paramount. Politics has become a game of 'self-promotion through "winning images"'; (56) success – political or otherwise – must be 'ratified by publicity' (60) and truth thus takes a back seat to mere credibility:

> When politicians and administrators have no other aim than to sell their leadership to the public, they deprive themselves of intelligible standards by which to define the goals of specific policies or to evaluate success or failure. It was because prestige and credibility had become the only measure of effectiveness that American policy in Vietnam could be conducted without regard to the strategic importance of Vietnam or the political situation in that country. (78)

Politicians and administrators thus become both victims and agents of 'the atrophy of competence' and 'the eclipse of achievement'. (59, 127) The professional and managerial elite, including politicians, may well be America's 'ruling class', (221) but they have debased themselves in the corrupt pursuit of publicity:

> In a society in which the dream of success has been drained of any meaning beyond itself, men [sic] have nothing against which to measure their achievements except the achievements of others. Self-approval depends on public recognition and acclaim . . . Today men seek the kind of approval that applauds not their actions but their personal attributes. They wish to be not so much esteemed as admired. They crave not fame but the glamour and excitement of celebrity. (59)

Such criticisms are by now all too familiar in an age that has coined a term – 'spin' – to define the process that Lasch identified and critiqued in 1978; but one of Lasch's most impressive contributions to the analysis is his situation of image-pursuit – of what we now call 'spin' – in its broad historical frame:

> In an earlier stage of capitalist development, industrialization reduced the artisan or peasant to a proletarian, stripped him of his land and tools, and stranded him in the marketplace with nothing to sell but his labour power. In our time, the elimination of skills not only from manual work but from white-collar jobs as well has created conditions in which labour power takes the form of personality or intelligence. Men and women alike have to project an attractive image and to become simultaneously role players and connoisseurs of their own performance. (92)

Many will no doubt find fault with Lasch's merciless – and perhaps sweeping – generalisation; but many, too, will acknowledge the prevalence of the ills he first identified in the 1970s and which have persisted to the present: the 'propaganda of commodities' through which consumption is held up as 'the answer to the age-old discontents of loneliness, sickness, weariness [and] lack of sexual satisfaction', but which itself 'creates new forms of discontent peculiar to the modern age' ('Is your job boring and meaningless? Does it leave you with feelings of futility and fatigue? Is your life empty? Consumption promises to fill the aching void'). (71–3) Lasch's concern with 'education as a commodity' (151) will also ring true for many, even if their conclusion is less damning: 'Sweeping social changes, reflected in academic practice, thus underlie the deterioration of the school system and the consequent spread of stupidity'. (127) Certainly, too, Lasch's identification of 'the dread of old age' – reflected in the proliferation of 'sciences and pseudo-sciences' such as 'geriatrics, gerontology, thanatology, cryonics [and] "immortalism"' (207) – will carry some weight for those familiar with the plethora of products and processes that remove wrinkles, hide age-spots and replace sagging skin. 'The denial of age in America', Lasch writes, is yet another symptom of the culture of narcissism; 'the prolongevity movement, which hopes to abolish old age altogether', is less 'a cult of youth' than 'a cult of the self', expressing 'in characteristic form the anxieties of a culture that believes it has no future'. (217)

In spite of such a dire conclusion (the tenor of which drives his whole book), Lasch holds out a thread of hope which actually deserves more prominence in any assessment of the American 1970s – the ground-swell of grass-roots activism, prompted by 'the inadequacy of solutions dictated from above':

> In small towns and crowded urban neighborhoods, even in suburbs, men and women have initiated modest experiments in cooperation, designed to defend their rights against the corporation and the state. The 'flight from politics', as it appears to the managerial and political elite, may signify the citizen's growing unwillingness to take part in the political system as a consumer of prefabricated spectacles. It may signify, in other words, not a retreat from politics at all but the beginnings of a general political revolt. (xv)

As will be discussed below, Lasch was quite observant in his speculation on grassroots activism, even if he gave less credit to these 'modest experiments' than they rightfully deserved.

The narcissism that Bell, Wolfe and Lasch variously identify may be seen in a number of instances in which individuals in the 1970s appeared oblivious to the dangers of following certain quests for 'self-improvement' or 'self-awareness'. Cults like L. Ron Hubbard's Church of Scientology, which had begun to attract significant numbers in the 1970s, continue to invite critical derision even in the present decade; but more threatening was the Korean missionary Sun Myung Moon's Unification Church – 'the Moonies' – whose recruitment of college-age adherents often relied on deceptive, highly orchestrated brainwashing campaigns. More sinister still, to a tragic degree, was the blindness of over nine hundred acolytes of the self-styled 'Reverend' Jim Jones, a delusional demagogue who, in 1978, led his followers through a ritual of mass suicide in the jungles of Guyana.

At the other, more prosaic, extreme, technological developments conspired to turn people away from each other and into solitary consumers of culture. David A. Cook has explored the impact of the Sony Betamax and, latterly, the VHS-format video cassette recorder (VCR), a development he describes as an 'historic shift':

> At the beginning of the 1970s, the movies were primarily a collective experience – something seen regularly on large screens in specially designed theatres with masses of other people. By the decade's end they had become something that could also be carried around in a briefcase or shopping bag for video playback at home.[29]

Just as we now know, however, that the invention of the VCR in no way signalled the death knell of the collective cinema experience, we can also look back at the 1970s for substantial evidence with which to confound Bell, Wolfe and Lasch. Peter N. Carroll has argued passionately for the need to rehabilitate the reputation of the 1970s in the wake of such negative assessments:

> The times were not narcissistic; only certain people were. And by using them as the benchmark of the decade, writers like Wolfe diminished the value of those who lived otherwise . . . Such attitudes allowed little room for alternatives, for protest. Instead, the Me Decade became the standard by which normal behavior would be measured.[30]

Miller likewise concludes that the 1970s deserves a better press than that given by Bell, Wolfe and Lasch, especially in view of the social advances that the decade witnessed:

> Of course, the seventies was a crucial period, if only because during this decade initiatives from the sixties in the women's movement, civil and voting rights enforcement, affirmative action, and environmental regulation were established. Progressive forces brought into play in the sixties had their effect at national and grassroots levels.[31]

Added to this list would of course be the massive public activism against the Vietnam War, hardly a narcissistic enterprise.

It is in the context of such social and political developments that the intellectual and cultural contexts of the 1970s dovetail into one another. This cultural and intellectual integration can be observed, for instance, in the relationship between Vietnam, Watergate and expressions of popular criticism, as Miller argues: 'The war and the scandal [are] related phenomena that enunciate relevant discourses related to government and the populace's response to its workings.'[32] Thus, there was more than merely a causal chain between the publication of the leaked *Pentagon Papers* by the *New York Times* in 1971 – exposing Defense Department corruption since the war's onset – and the break-in at the Watergate offices of the Democratic National Committee in 1972, which ultimately led to President Nixon's resignation in 1974. There was also a critical chain examining what political commentators called the 'credibility gaps' of the Nixon administration, a chain extending from the congressional debating halls to protest rallies to the comic-strip pages in the newspapers. What David Wyatt says about Vietnam – that it is both America's 'wound' and a 'great and terrible resource'[33] – can also be applied to Watergate which, while it is a shameful story of corrupt power politics, is also the inspiration for some of the decade's most important examples of political and cultural critique as well as investigative journalism. In this, Bob Woodward and Carl Bernstein's *All the President's Men* (1974) shares a critical edge with Garry Trudeau's *Doonesbury* comic strip which, as Howard Sounes observes, was pointedly shifted by the *Washington Post*'s editors from the comics page to the editorial page with the explanation that 'Trudeau had crossed the line from comic artist to political commentator'.[34] The Watergate story may well be an example of the political narcissism of Richard Nixon, so evidently obsessed with the 'enemies' out to get *him*, regardless of the health of the body politic; but the wealth of cultural critiques spawned by Watergate indicates a determination to expose and condemn such narcissism.

Facing the Limits of American Power

Other events throughout the decade – political and economic – generated new areas of intellectual and cultural criticism. Watergate and the defeat in Vietnam occurred in the context of other crises that combined to demonstrate America's economic vulnerability and political limitations. In October 1973, the Arab members of OPEC – the Organization of Petroleum Exporting Countries – placed an embargo on oil exports to the United States in retaliation against Washington's pro-Israel bias. Petrol shortages, rationing and mile-long petrol station queues were the result – a situation that returned with a second OPEC oil embargo in the summer of 1979. President Nixon's decision in August 1971 to uncouple the dollar from the gold standard, allowing its value to float freely against that of other currencies, resulted in wild global currency fluctuations. This, combined with a surge in domestic borrowing, marked a decline in American manufacturing, and global crop shortages resulted in mid-decade economic stagnation and lengthening unemployment lines. At the same time, rocketing prices – inflation – combined with joblessness to produce an economic scenario never before seen in America, 'stagflation', which particularly bedevilled the Ford and Carter administrations. 'For the first time since the Great Depression,' Schulman observes, 'talk of limits and diminishing expectations filled presidential addresses and dinner table conversations.'[35] Daniel Bell's mid-decade assessment appears, in retrospect, desperately hopeful and, in some respects (with the benefit of hindsight), misjudged:

> It is all too soon to write off Western economic power. By the end of the decade, the dependence of the Western countries on Middle East oil may be largely reduced; there will be new and different sources and kinds of energy. For a period of time, there may be large-scale shift of capital to the Middle East countries, but the basic economic lead of the West is in high technology and management, and this is bound to reassert itself.[36]

The second OPEC embargo of 1979 put paid to Bell's suggestion that 'the end of the decade' would see a large reduction of American dependence on Arab oil; but he was right in his conclusion: 'What the international economic events of the 1970s revealed was a failure of political will to match the economic urgencies, and this is a different and more disturbing aspect of the instability of the international order'.[37] The Iranian seizure of over fifty American Embassy personnel in Teheran in November 1979 – and their 444-day captivity that ended on the day of Ronald Reagan's inauguration in January 1981 – can only have confirmed the sense of an unstable international order, at least for those prepared to assume that a stable international order subject to American dominance could ever be understood as the norm.

Indeed, major critical treatises of the 1970s – academic as well as popular – suggest that assumptions of such a 'norm' were being challenged even as they were being proposed. Telford Taylor's *Nuremberg and Vietnam: An American Tragedy* (1970) outlined the extent to which American involvement in Vietnam infringed aspects of international law, a charge broadened to include concerted American destabilisation efforts in Latin America and elsewhere in an exposé by Morton Halerpin and others called *The Lawless State* (1976). Anthony Sampson's *The Sovereign State of ITT* (1973) argued that, in any event, the power of multinational corporations had begun to outstrip and transcend that of nation-states, including the United States. Robert Jowett and John Shelton Lawrence's *The American Monomyth* (1977) situated American adventurism around the globe in the context of a cultural myth of America's messianic capacity. In his *Theory of International Politics* (1979), the political scientist Kenneth Waltz proposed that the governing principle of international relations is in fact 'anarchy'; American global dominance thus could not be construed as the norm. Examples such as these indicate a critical tendency to examine not only the workings but also the limits of American power and influence in the world.

Among the most important and revolutionary of these interrogations of American power came not from the field of political science or international relations, but rather literary criticism: Edward Said's *Orientalism* (1978). Although its primary focus is on European colonialism's construction of the East as 'other', *Orientalism* raises a host of questions about American assumptions of a 'stable' world order and the place of the United States in that order. For those who have experienced the rise of Middle Eastern anti-Americanism and of Islamist fundamentalism in the late twentieth and early twenty-first centuries, Said's *Orientalism* offers many signposts on the road to that pass.

Orientalism (1978)

Said, a Palestinian-American professor of English and Comparative Literature at Columbia University, set out in *Orientalism* to theorise Western conceptions of the East, or 'the Orient', in what became a truly momentous study. 'The Orient', he writes, 'was almost a European invention, and had been since antiquity a place of romance, exotic beings, haunting memories and landscapes, remarkable experiences.'[38] Crucial to Said's theory was the perception that the Western project of 'Orientalism' – 'a way of coming to terms with the orient that is based on the orient's special place in European Western experience' – actually reflects as much, if not more, upon Western identity as upon the East itself: 'The orient has helped to define Europe (or the West) as its contrasting image, idea, personality, experience.' (1–2) The impact of such a belief system was the construction of a severe, politically charged 'vision of reality' based on a perceived 'difference between the familiar (Europe, the West, "us") and the strange (the Orient, the east, "them")'. (44) Underpinning this binary 'vision' are real power structures with immense influence:

> None of this Orient is merely imaginative. The Orient is an integral part of European *material* civilization and culture. Orientalism expresses and represents that part culturally and even ideologically as a mode of discourse with supporting institutions, vocabulary, scholarship, imagery, doctrines, even colonial bureaucracies and colonial styles. (2)

Most of Said's study is devoted to European Orientalism spearheaded by the French and British colonialists; but the United States attracts increasing attention, Said argues, as 'the vastly expanded American political and economic role in the Near East (the Middle East) makes great claims on our understanding of that Orient'. (2) America's relatively late interest in the East, Said claims – barring the odd expressions of interest by individuals such as Melville and Twain, or a handful of Transcendentalists and theologians and members of the American Oriental Society established in 1842 – was due to the fact that 'the American frontier, the one that counted, was the westward one'. (290) By the end of World War II, however, 'the shift from British and French to American hegemony' was secured; (25) the United States fitted itself 'quite self-consciously – in the places excavated by the two European powers' and now dominates and approaches both Orientalism and the orient 'as Britain and France once did'. (4, 17) Said makes clear one further link between earlier European and later American Orientalism: 'For a European or American studying the orient there can be no disclaiming the main circumstances of *his* actuality: that he comes up against the orient as a European or American first, as an individual second.' (11) Given that 'political societies impart to their civil societies a sense of urgency . . . where and whenever matters pertaining to their imperial interests abroad are concerned', (11) in the case of the United States that 'urgency' is wrapped up in the security of the consumer economy:

> The Arab and Islamic world as a whole is hooked into the Western market system. No one needs to be reminded that oil, the region's greatest resource, has been totally absorbed into the United States economy. By that I mean not only that the great oil companies are controlled by the American economic system; I mean also that Arab oil revenues, to say nothing of marketing, research, and industry management, are based in the United States. (324)

The cultural ramifications of this 'one-sided' market relationship are enormous; it is not simply that 'the Western market economy and its consumer orientation' has underwritten 'a class of educated people whose intellectual formation is directed to satisfying market needs'. (325) More broadly, the reception of American culture in the Middle East is also a question of market dominance:

> There is a vast standardization of taste in the region, symbolized not only by transistors, blue jeans, and Coca-Cola but also by cultural images of the orient supplied by American mass media and consumed unthinkingly by the mass television audience. The paradox of an Arab regarding himself as an 'Arab' of the sort put out by Hollywood is but the simplest result of what I am referring to. (324–5)

Thus, 'the Arab world today is an intellectual, political, and cultural satellite of the United States. . . The Arab and Islamic world remains a second-order power in terms of the production of culture, knowledge, and scholarship.' (322–3) Even though 'the powerful current of anti-imperialist Third World ideas that has gripped the region since the early 1950s has tempered the Western edge of the dominant culture', (323) the structures of knowledge and culture are firmly dominated by the West. This is true even in the case of Arab studies:

> There is no major journal of Arab studies published in the Arab world today, just as there is no Arab educational institution capable of challenging places like Oxford, Harvard, or UCLA in the study of the Arab world, much less in any non-Oriental subject matter. The predictable result of all this is that oriental students (and oriental professors) still want to come and sit at the feet of American Orientalists, and later to repeat to their local audiences the clichés I have been characterizing as Orientalist dogmas. (323–4)

The 'clichés' of which Said writes are not merely those of Western television and cinema wherein 'the Arab is associated either with lechery or bloodthirsty dishonesty': 'He appears as an oversexed degenerate, capable, it is true, of cleverly devious intrigues, but essentially sadistic, treacherous, low. Slave trader, camel driver, moneychanger, colourful scoundrel . . .' (286–7) They are clichés also prompted by the turbulence of realpolitik, in which a hollowed-out part is allowed to stand for the complex whole:

> Most accounts of Arab oil equate the oil boycott of 1973–4 (which principally benefited Western oil companies and a small ruling Arab elite) with the absence of any Arab moral qualification for owning such vast oil reserves. Without the usual euphemisms, the question most often being asked is why such people as the Arabs are entitled to keep the developed (free, democratic, moral) world threatened. From such questions comes the frequent suggestion that the Arab oil fields be invaded by the marines. (286)

As befits a major scholar in Western literature, Said observes that the champions of Orientalism in the United States since the 1950s – in government agencies and think tanks dominated by pretensions to objective social science – have not availed themselves of material which might combat the clichés, stereotypes and 'ideological fictions' (321) that make Orientalism such an intellectually corrupt enterprise:

> One of the striking aspects of the new American social-science attention to the Orient is its singular avoidance of literature. You can read through

reams of expert writing on the modern near East and never encounter a
single reference to literature. What seem to matter far more to the regional
expert are 'facts', of which a literary text is perhaps a disturber. The net
effect of this remarkable omission in modern American awareness of the
Arab or Islamic Orient is to keep the region and its people conceptually
emasculated, reduced to 'attitudes', 'trends', statistics: in short, dehu-
manized. (291)

Said's unfortunate gender bias in this instance (the equation of dehu-
manisation with emasculation) should not obscure the gravity of the situation he describes, particularly with regard to the corrosive impact of
Orientalist assumptions and influence on Easterners themselves. 'Cultural
domination is maintained', Said writes, 'as much by Oriental consent as by
direct and crude economic pressure from the United States'. (324) This fact
is in itself a 'reason for alarm': 'the pages of books and journals in Arabic
(and doubtless in Japanese, various Indian dialects, and other oriental lan-
guages) are filled with second-order analyses by Arabs of "the Arab mind",
"Islam", and other myths'. (322)

As Said makes clear, mythologising is a fundamental aim of Orientalist
discourse; but the impact of Orientalism is far from mythological: the
'Orient' – whatever that may be – 'is now less a myth perhaps than a place
criss-crossed by Western, especially American, interests'. (26) As the
Iranian revolution of 1979 was to prove, these interests would be increasingly and vigorously challenged.

Said's *Orientalism* is rightly credited with inaugurating postcolonial
criticism. But, in its exposition of negotiations between knowledge,
description and power, it also illuminates the workings of oppositional
processes that were taking place in the United States well before its publication. Such progressive processes as feminist and gay/lesbian activism
undoubtedly contributed to conservative backlash and to the nostalgia
for a 'stable' social order at home. It is significant that when President
Carter, in the first of his televised 'Fireside Chats' (1 February 1977),
hammered home to Americans that there was indeed an energy crisis
and that their habits of consumption would have to change, he both
hearkened back to and strategically updated the cosy radio broadcasts
of Franklin D. Roosevelt in the midst of the Depression. Carter sat
before the cameras, dressed in a cardigan (soon described by media
wags as a 'cartergan') in a room warmly furnished with bookshelves and
colonial-era oak furniture – and told Americans that the times, as well
as their standard of living, had irrevocably changed.[39]

Two years later, on 15 July 1979, Carter appeared again on television to inform the public of the 'almost invisible' threat that he had
perceived in the country:

It is a crisis of confidence. It is a crisis that strikes at the very heart and soul and spirit of our national will. We can see this crisis in the growing doubt about the meaning of our own lives and in the loss of a unity of purpose for our nation. The erosion of our confidence in the future is threatening to destroy the social and the political fabric of America.[40]

Carter's speech was, he said, inspired by some of the 'voices of America' to which he had listened at a Camp David gathering. As he was told by a cross section of Americans: 'Some of us have suffered from recession all our lives'; 'Some people have wasted energy, but others haven't had anything to waste'; 'Our neck is stretched over the fence and OPEC has a knife.'[41] These vox pop enunciations might well justify Schulman's perception of the 1970s as a malaise-filled decade. These expressions of powerlessness, however, if taken as the decade's benchmark, belie the determination and the hard-won (if incomplete) advances made on a number of social fronts.

Grass-roots Activism

On 23 June 1972, Title IX of the Education Amendments Act went into effect, declaring: 'No person in the United States shall, on the basis of sex, be excluded from participation in, be denied the benefits of, or be subjected to discrimination under any education program or activity receiving Federal financial assistance.'[42] While this achievement is typically discussed in terms of its impact on girls' and women's participation in school and collegiate sports, it actually represents a far broader feminist victory in terms of equality of opportunity across the educational sector. Title IX was perhaps the most visible indication of advances made by feminists also campaigning for equal opportunities in the workplace, in the health sector and in pay; and, given the persistence of unequal pay in the American workplace, the adoption of Title IX can be considered, at best, a partial victory. In the same year as its adoption, the Equal Rights Amendment to the Constitution (ERA) was introduced in Congress, with its opening provision: 'Equality of rights under the law shall not be denied or abridged by the United States or by any State on account of sex.'[43] Since that date, the ratification battle over this version of the ERA has continued, with a dogged reintroduction of the statute taking place in every subsequent Congressional session (the latest, as of the time of writing, being 27 March 2007). While the continued failure of three-quarters of the states to ratify the amendment has remained a source of immense frustration to the women's movement, 1972 marked a watershed in that the amendment was finally adopted by the Senate and recommended to the separate states; it had taken forty-nine years even to reach the Senate floor. The following year, the Supreme Court's highly controversial decision to legalise a woman's right to abortion – *Roe v. Wade* – was made, not on the grounds of a woman's right to choose, but rather on a woman's 'right of personal privacy'.[44] Again, this continuously challenged Supreme Court provision indicates a feminist advance across a highly contested battlefield, the end of which is not yet in sight.

Other important martial signals were sent out at the beginning of the decade, one of the most important being the feminist anthology edited by Robin Morgan, *Sisterhood Is Powerful* (1970). With over fifty ground-breaking essays by feminist activists in medicine, publishing, television, the military, academe, journalism, office administration, psychology, psychiatry and the sex industry, and with testimonies from across the racial and political canvas, the anthology is, as Morgan argues, both a call to arms and 'an action' reflecting other actions in the highly charged public sphere:

> It is now the spring of 1970. During the past few months, wildcat strikes by women workers at General Electric, Bendix, and the New York Bell Telephone Company surprised both management and labor; the women felt they had been sold out by the union which was more concerned about its male members. The first serious woman jockey was pelted by rocks before a major race . . . Instead of delivering her expected grateful goodbye speech on television, the outgoing Miss USA exposes the commercial way in which she has been used, and denounces her exploiters. Women are marching, picketing, and mounting a variety of actions against abortion laws in every state. Boycotts have been started against billionaire corporations like Procter & Gamble or Lever Brothers, which manipulate women as consumers but are blatantly discriminatory in their own hiring and salary practices.[45]

The project of second-wave feminism to demystify social relationships that may have for decades appeared 'the norm', but which are in fact staunchly defended patriarchal positions, extended – as the debate over abortion demonstrated – to women's ownership of their own bodies. Miller describes the 'exhilarating sense of exploration' with which 'women demystified their bodies', citing as a crucial marker the publication of a still-revolutionary women's health guide, *Our Bodies,*

Ourselves (1973), by the Boston Women's Health Book Collective.[46] This frank project to wrest women's health care from the control of the male-dominated medical profession met with fierce opposition from conservative forces.

Our Bodies, Ourselves (1973)

In 1969, participants at a women's conference in Boston gathered to discuss their experiences *as* women. For many of them, it was the first time that they had done so. They were, in their own words, 'both a very ordinary and a very special group, as women are everywhere':

> Our ages range from twenty-five to forty-one, most of us are from middle-class backgrounds and have had at least some college education, and some of us have professional degrees. Some of us are married, some of us are sep-arated, and some of us are single. Some of us have children of our own, some of us like spending time with children, and others of us are not sure we want to be with children.[47]

As the group encounter progressed, the women realised that they shared a 'similar feeling of frustration and anger toward specific doctors and the medical maze in general'; they all 'wanted to do something about those doctors who were condescending, paternalistic, judgmental and non-informative'. (11) Knowledge of women's bodies – their own bodies – was, they had found, the jealously guarded preserve of mostly male 'experts' whose guardianship of that knowledge conferred upon them an almost tyrannical power. Collectively, the women agreed what each of them had felt separately: 'Our bodies are the physical bases from which we move out into the world; ignorance, uncertainty – even at worst, shame – about our physical selves create in us an alienation from ourselves that keeps us from being the whole people that we could be.' (13)

The women agreed to meet over a period of ten to twelve sessions, finding all the while that they could 'discuss, question and argue with each other in a new spirit of cooperation rather than competition' with medical experts. (11) In 1973, as the Boston Women's Health Book Collective, they published the results of their sessions, the groundbreaking *Our Bodies, Ourselves: A Book by and for Women*. Part practical guide, part political manifesto and part intellectual statement, *Our Bodies, Ourselves* con-tained essays on a range of topics – anatomy, physiology, sexuality, repro-duction, nutrition, childbearing, menopause. More defiantly, chapters on abortion, rape, birth control, venereal disease, self-defence and lesbianism challenged any assumption that women should remain passive objects at the mercy of microbes or men. Women's anger – and their right to be angry – were explicitly justified and defended: 'We have been asked why this is exclusively a book about women, and why we have restricted our course to women. Our answer is that we are women and, as women, do not consider ourselves experts on men (as men through the centuries have presumed to be experts on us).' (12)

Underlying the Collective's anger was a situation that could not have been shared by men, as one of the book's most resounding passages implies:

> Picture a woman trying to do work and to enter into equal and satisfying rela-
> tionships with other people – when she feels physically weak because she
> has never tried to be strong; when she drains her energy trying to change her
> face, her figure, her hair, her smells, to match some ideal norm set by mag-
> azines, movies and TV; when she feels confused and ashamed of the men-
> strual blood that every month appears from some dark place in her body;
> when her internal body processes are a mystery to her and surface only to
> cause her trouble (an unplanned pregnancy, or cervical cancer); when she
> does not understand or enjoy sex and concentrates her sexual drives to
> aimless romantic fantasies, perverting and misusing a potential energy
> because she has been brought up to deny it. (13)

Out of the shared realisation, the anger and the concerted effort to research and to pool their experiences in the development of a 'critique', the Collective reflected upon their 'crucial and formative experiences', sensing their 'potential power as a force for political and social change'. (13) It is this correct assumption that makes *Our Bodies, Ourselves* one of the most important documents of the American 1970s. As one of the many poems interspersed with the essays declares: 'Our anger is changing our faces, our bodies. / Our anger is changing our lives' (15)

The practical and political activism begins with an evaluation of 'the institutions that are supposed to meet our health needs – the hospitals, clinics, doctors, medical schools, nursing schools, public health depart-ments, Medicaid bureaucracies and so on'. (13) The doctors in particular come in for a stringent re-evaluation – one ultimately leading to an adjust-ment in power relations:

> Understanding the medical terminology means that we now can understand
> the things the doctors say. Knowing their language makes medical people
> less mysterious and frightening. We now feel more confident when asking
> questions. Sometimes a doctor has been startled to find us speaking 'his' lan-
> guage. 'How do you know that? Are you a medical student?' we heard again
> and again. 'A pretty girl like you shouldn't be concerned about that'. (25)

The re-evaluation – and the seizure of knowledge – was profound: 'For some of us it was the first time we had looked critically, and with strength, at the existing institutions serving us'. (13) The project thus culminated in a series of practical, viable alternatives for women, underpinned by a 'Model Patients' Bill of Rights' (355) and a series of models for grass-roots organising (fund-raising, mutual help groups, self-help groups, a home-birth and birth-centres movement), all intended to fight against 'the inhu-mane legal restrictions, the imperfections of available contraceptives, the poor sex education, the highly priced and poorly administered health care that keep too many women from having this crucial control over their bodies'. (13)

One of the most significant aspects of *Our Bodies, Ourselves* is the voice it gives to the previously silenced, whose reflections run throughout the book:

> *I wanted to be a doctor, but I was told in direct and indirect ways that my ultimate ambition should be marrying a doctor and raising a family. I gave up my dream.* (18)

> *Every time my husband has free time he sits down and reads a book. We both have a sense that this is really important. When I have free time I sit and crochet or read, and it feels as if I am doing nothing.* (19)

> *I went with other women on a trip south almost two years ago. This was the first time I had gone on a trip without my husband. Several things went wrong with the car on the trip. When I came back to Boston I decided that I really wanted to learn how to take care and be in control of a car myself. I learned about auto mechanics. It required a lot of work and discipline. In a way, I identify with the car. There is a connection between my feelings of wanting to take care and control of my life and the feelings of wanting to take care and control of my car.* (22)

The publication of *Our Bodies, Ourselves* prompted a massive outcry from conservative and reactionary Americans. As Carroll explains:

> The issue of sexual censorship touched directly on feminist concerns. Historically, conservatives had used obscenity laws to prevent dissemination of birth control information, and in 1978 a Montana school district banned the feminist health publication *Our Bodies, Ourselves*. 'I'm sick and tired of hearing the cry of censorship,' stated a Helena prosecutor. 'We've genuflected at the altar of free speech for too long.'[48]

But the reactions were clearly prompted by more than the frank discussions of birth control, masturbation, abortion and rape. As the Collective declared: 'This kind of body education has been liberating for us and may be a starting point for the liberation of many other women.' (12) This was not good news for the reactionary old guard, also flexing their muscles in the 1970s.

The concerted cultural assertion of the women's movement was matched by the activism of other American victims of discrimination throughout the decade. In June 1970, five thousand gay men and women marched to commemorate the first anniversary of the Stonewall riots in New York. The previous year, police officers had raided a gay bar, the Stonewall Inn in Greenwich Village, prompting days of pitched battles on the streets. As Miller explains:

> Police often surveyed homosexual bars, but if a gay or lesbian frequenter of a bar such as Stonewall observed codes of sexual nuance and invitation, he or she was somewhat safe. However, in 1969, when numerous

arrests were made at the Stonewall bar, it seemed as if even the obser-
vance of this code in the confines of a gay bar was little guarantee against
the police's interpretation of acceptable sexual communication and the
rights of a certain group to assemble. Backed, in a manner of speaking,
to the stone wall, 'Stonewall' began to connote not as much a shield
against unwarranted inquiry as a stand for self-identity in the public
realm.[49]

The Stonewall Riots are thus still remembered as a turning point in the
struggle for civil rights among gays and lesbians; after all, as Michael
Bronski recalls, 'in the early 1960s, homosexuals were interviewed on
television seated behind potted palms to hide their identities. In 1972,
Jill Johnston, *Village Voice* dance critic, announced her lesbianism on
the *Dick Cavett Show*, flashed a big smile, and waved "Hi Mom!" '[50]
The watershed that was Stonewall 'established a homosexual militancy
and identity in the public imagination that was startling and deeply
threatening' to preservationists of an older order, who now had to
accept the existence of the Gay Liberation Front.[51]

Gay rights and feminist activism combined in the early 1970s to
prompt interrogations of masculinity, spawning what Schulman
describes as 'a vast, self-conscious men's movement', beginning with
the establishment in 1970 of the country's first centre for men in
Berkeley, California, and developing into such practices as 'men's
forums and consciousness-raising groups', 'weekend retreats in the
woods, men's studies sections in bookstores' and other signals in
response to this apparent crisis of male identity – a perceived 'shift
from John Wayne to Alan Alda . . . from the strong, silent type to the
sensitive New Age male'.[52] Contributing to the nascent 'men's movement' were such tracts as Herb Goldberg's *The Hazards of Being
Male* (1976), a psychological study, and James Hillman's *Puer Papers*
(1979), an anthropological study on the archetype of the 'eternal
boy'.

In addition to women's and gay rights militancy, and spawning
similar reactive trends, ethnic assertion in the 1970s marked a further
arena of grass-roots activism. In East Los Angeles, Chicanos
(Americans of Mexican descent) began the decade – in August 1970 –
with a moratorium and a march of thirty thousand strong, not only to
protest against the Vietnam War but also to emphasise the connections
between the war abroad and racism at home. The 'Brown Berets', as
the students in the vanguard of the moratorium called themselves,
evoked a militant activism shared by other ethnic groups such as the

American Indian Movement (AIM), whose strategies throughout the 1970s included the mass seizure of Federal facilities that had begun with the occupation of Alcatraz Island in 1969, and climaxed with the occupation of Wounded Knee, South Dakota, in 1973.

Militant groups such as these took some of their cues from the Black Panthers who, by 1970, had shifted from the project of black internationalism (spearheaded by co-founders Bobby Seale and Huey Newton) to that of 'Black Power'. The militant activism of the Panthers at the end of the 1960s, exacerbated by shoot-outs among themselves and against the FBI and the police, resulted in a series of high-profile murder trials which, in turn, attracted a curious rash of celebrity attention. Tom Wolfe, Gail Sheehy and other journalists took note of the Panthers' celebrity and the 'Radical Chic' that fed it. The phrase comes from Wolfe's 1970 essay for *New York Magazine* describing a fund-raising event for the Panthers hosted by the composer and orchestra conductor, Leonard Bernstein:

> The Field Marshal of the Black Panther Party has been sitting in a chair between the piano and the wall. He rises up; he has the hard-rock look, all right; he is a big tall man with brown skin and an Afro and a goatee and a black turtleneck much like Lenny's, and he stands up beside the piano, next to Lenny's million-dollar *chatchka* flotilla of family photographs. In fact, there is a certain perfection as the first Black Panther rises within a Park Avenue living room to lay the Panthers' ten-point program on New York Society in the age of Radical Chic.[53]

As Michael E. Staub observes, the 'demonizing rhetoric' that characterised public discussion of the Panthers eventually shifted to 'trivializations [that] would finally present the Black Panther member more as oversexed media sweetheart than violence-prone social menace'.[54] But it is important not to let such dramatic events (and their highly stylised coverage) obscure perhaps more significant events, such as the first presidential candidacy of an African American woman, Shirley Chisholm, in 1972, four years after she had become the first African American woman elected to Congress. Until the candidacy of Hillary Clinton in 2007, no other woman – black or white – had come closer to securing the nomination of the Democratic Party, which Chisholm ultimately lost to Senator George McGovern.

All these developments indicate that diverse identity markers were being firmly posited, defended and advanced in the 1970s. But almost inevitably, as gender, sexuality and ethnicity emerged as subjectivities to be claimed and reinvented, in the midst of this drastic reformation of a culture out to foreground 'diversity', agents of reactionary conservatism rallied to defend their own conceptions of normality. As Staub argues, during the 1960s 'sophisticated anti-Left strategies were already being tested and refined, and these trends intensified at the turn of the seventies'.[55] Moreover, the decade saw the firm coupling of reactionary conservatism with Christian fundamentalism, setting in train an alliance that remains politically and culturally potent to this day.

Christian Fundamentalism and Neoconservatism

In 1970, Hal Lindsay published the book that would outsell all other non-fiction books in the United States in the 1970s, *The Late, Great Planet Earth*. With the book of Revelations as his primary road map, Lindsay offered a host of geopolitical predictions leading to the conclusion that 'some time in the future there will be a seven-year period climaxed by the visible return of Jesus Christ' – a seven-year period that 'couldn't begin until the Jewish people re-established their nation in their ancient homeland of Palestine'.[56] Such fundamentalist belief has underpinned conservative American support for the defence of Israel consistently championed by such powerful American evangelists as Pat Robertson, Jerry Falwell and Billy Graham, all of whom have claimed that Christians are better friends of the Jewish state than are most American Jews. As Falwell said, 'It's my belief that the Bible Belt in America is Israel's only safety belt.'[57] Schulman has reviewed 'the mounting influence of evangelical Christianity' in the 1970s:

> In 1976, Jimmy Carter, a born-again Baptist, became president of the United States. In 1980, revivalist Billy Graham's newspaper, *Decision*, reached a circulation of 24 million. Religious radio stations numbered over a thousand, broadcasting the good news along with more than one hundred Christian television stations. The so-called televangelists – Jim Bakker, Pat Robertson, Jimmy Swaggart, Oral Roberts – became national figures, and later figures of national scandal. Polls revealed that nearly half of Americans regarded the Bible as the actual word of God. A sizeable majority claimed they had 'no doubts' Jesus would return to earth, and 80 percent expressed the belief that they would appear before God on Judgment Day.[58]

Even the denizens of the left were not immune: the 1970s was the decade of Bob Dylan's conversion to fundamentalist Christianity, culminating in his Christian-themed album, *Slow Train Coming* (1979), which Sounes calls 'one of the most extreme career changes of any mainstream rock star of the decade'.[59]

Fundamentalist Christianity was one of the strongest forces to fill the vacuum left by the disintegration of what political theorists have called the post-war 'liberal consensus'. In spite of the dominance of anti-Communism and Cold War hostility, liberal voters had managed to secure the election of a New Deal Democrat – Lyndon Johnson – over the Republican Barry Goldwater in 1964. While Johnson's presidency was overshadowed by the escalation of the Vietnam War, he is rightly credited with advancing much of the New Deal agenda into the 1960s and beyond through his 'Great Society' programme. The Civil Rights and the Voting Rights acts, the 'War on Poverty', Medicare, Medicaid, the national endowments for the arts and humanities and public broadcasting are all part of Johnson's legacy.

Reacting against what they perceived as left-wing social engineering, increasingly conservative critics, such as Irving Kristol, began to challenge the dominance of liberal policymakers as the 'Great Society' took hold. In 1965, Kristol had founded the journal *The Public Interest* which joined William F. Buckley's ten-year-old *National Review* as the second major platform for what would develop into the neoconservative movement of the next two decades. By 1970, these two journals were leading the way in articulating the major themes of American conservatism. In addition to concerns about the morality of 'social engineering', as Jerome Himmelstein argues, conservatives in the 1970s identified 'a cornucopia of social issues on which to build', many of them growing out of the grass-roots initiatives discussed above – gay rights, women's rights, sexual liberation, affirmative action and race.[60] Schulman provides the panorama surveyed throughout the 1970s by voters and activists within the 'nascent' neoconservative movement that was 'waiting in the wings' for its moment of ascendancy – which turned out to be the election of Ronald Reagan in 1980:

> White backlash against civil rights and taxes revealed mounting resentment among previously loyal members of the liberal Democratic party coalition. For years, urban white ethnics had expressed discontent with the changing faces of their neighborhoods – the seeming encroachment of minority communities, the construction of housing projects and garbage dumps, the rising crime rates and disrespect for police. Often they had punished liberal politicians in local elections, gravitating

toward law-and-order candidates who combined a conservative social agenda with a working-class touch.[61]

American society was thus a vigorously contested battleground, and it produced a range of cultural expressions that were no less fraught with contest. Fiction and poetry, television and drama, film and visual culture, popular music and style, public space and public spectacle – these were the sites of cultural agitation that made the 1970s one of the most turbulent decades of the post-war period. A critical examination of each of these areas must undermine any easy assumption that this was, simply and totally, the 'Me Decade'. Hence the direction of the following chapters, each of which engages with the cultural work in a particular arena, designed to build – and to build upon – a critical momentum that openly challenges the dismissive generalisations of Bell, Lasch, Wolfe and others who apparently saw so little of cultural value in the 1970s. If anything, the seventies demonstrated that the conventional arenas of cultural work (literature, television, drama, film, art and music) could not in the end contain the enormous amount of energy devoted to them. For this reason, Chapter 5 – 'Public Space and Spectacle' – explores what at times appears to be an overspill, or an avalanche, of cultural energy pouring into the American landscape, skyscape and public arena. The concluding obligation is a complete 're-thinking' of the decade – not only the historical period (marked throughout the rest of this book as 'the 1970s') but also the cultural period and its retrospective construction (designated as 'the seventies'). If this book succeeds in its objective, then the 1970s – and 'the seventies' – will never look the same again.

Chapter 1

Fiction and Poetry

In 'Some Notes on Time in Fiction' (1973), the novelist and short-story writer, Eudora Welty implied a near-physiological compulsion – if not a holy obligation – for American writers to look backward and retain their hold on the past:

> Remembering is so basic and vital a part of staying alive that it takes on the strength of an instinct of survival, and acquires the power of an art. Remembering is done through the blood, it is a bequeathment, it takes account of what happens before a man is born as if he were there taking part. It is a physical absorption through the living body, it is a spiritual heritage. It is also a life's work.[1]

Welty's declaration is particularly resonant in the context of the 1970s, when both the literary and the critical fields increasingly took on the appearance of unfamiliar and uncharted territory. The decade displayed a sometimes fraught conversation between the practice of fiction and poetry on the one hand and literary criticism on the other. Both areas revealed concomitant urges to look backward and forward – to retain a hold on the security of the known and to give way to the experimental drive. Moreover, literature and criticism shared a journey beyond the formal and textual concerns of postmodernism into a ground-swell of ethnic assertion in which a plurality of marginalised voices emerged to transform, once and for all, the face of the American canon.

The Critical Context

In spite of its reputation for centripetal critical tendencies – the development of theories blithely confirming how 'things fall apart', how

'the centre cannot hold' (to quote Yeats's poem 'The Second Coming')
– the decade witnessed an apparent rearguard effort to reaffirm the
social relevance of literary criticism and practice against the growing
tendency to view the world as a linguistic and textual gameboard.
Established critics such as Northrop Frye in *The Critical Path: An
Essay on the Social Context of Literary Criticism* (1973) and Irving
Howe in *The Critical Point* (1973) argued that the object of criticism,
regardless of current fashion, is first and foremost to explain the social
implications of all textual expression. The final work of Lionel Trilling,
Sincerity and Authenticity (1972) likewise warned against the tendency
to give in to the tide of critical irrelevancy. As A. Walton Litz explains,
Trilling's last plea was uttered against what he perceived as the 'uncon-
trolled self-expression and social chaos in the late 1960s and early
1970s'; thus, mapping 'a historical movement from the responsible to
the irresponsible self', Trilling's last work 'is tinged with an almost
tragic sense of loss – the loss of that glory of the "modern spirit", the
individual who can balance his inner needs against his external
responsibilities'.[2]

The difficulty in striking that balance is exemplified by two of the
decade's runaway popular successes: Richard Bach's short, juvenile
allegory about a nonconformist bird cast out from his society,
Jonathan Livingston Seagull (1970), which captivated a generation of
high-school and college-age readers with the prospect of unlimited
individual achievement, and Robert Pirsig's *Zen and the Art of
Motorcycle Maintenance* (1974), an introspective treatise in keeping
with the arrival of other consciousness-expanding movements such
as Transcendental Meditation. In Bach's fable, Jonathan Livingston
Seagull's spiritual journey towards fulfilment through a gradually
transcendent self-knowledge seemed, to its most severe critics, 'the Me
Decade' encapsulated. As the narrator says of the book's eponymous
freewheeling soarer: 'What he had once hoped for the Flock, he now
gained for himself alone; he learned to fly, and was not sorry for the
price that he had paid.'[3] The book's popular impact was so resounding
that in China, as Zhu Hong writes, the worried Communist authori-
ties cited *Jonathan Livingston Seagull* as 'representative "poisonous
material"' from the United States, 'literary apologia for a dying
monopoly system' in which naked individualism obliterates the social
and the political conscience.[4] Closer to home, Philip Slater drew a
straight line from the self-righteous, can-do optimism of Jonathan
Livingston Seagull – circling ever higher and higher above the collective body politic – to the debacle of American hubris in Vietnam. Slater

condemned the implicit self-absorption propounded in the fable: 'In place of feedback from others, the individualistically programmed person inserts self-feedback. In place of increasingly fine mutual tuning, each individual mechanically obeys his own program, following his own closed self-circuitry until he spins himself into oblivion.'[5]

In somewhat similar vein to Bach's allegory, Pirsig's *Zen and the Art of Motorcycle Maintenance* proposed a route to self-knowledge through the American road trip, infusing – in the combined spirit of Jack Kerouac's *The Dharma Bums* (1958) and the counter-cultural film *Easy Rider* (1969) – the motorcycle subculture with a watered-down, Americanised version of Buddhist spiritualism: 'The Buddha, the Godhead, resides quite comfortably in the circuits of a digital computer or the gears of a cycle transmission as he does at the top of a mountain or in the petals of a flower. To think otherwise is to demean the Buddha, which is to demean oneself.'[6] Thus, in the context of such New Age popularity, it is clear that Trilling might well have been speaking equally of critics and literary practitioners, for what most concerned him and other members of the so-called 'New York Intellectuals' still operating in the 1970s (including Saul Bellow, Daniel Bell and Irving Howe) was the social, cultural and political relevance of both literature and criticism.

Critical fashion appeared to offer a practice increasingly divorced from social reality, from the humanist project, from the American critical tradition and from the communicative norms and objects of language itself. As J. David Hoeveler summarises:

> Literary theory provided a key focus for the cultural politics of the 1970s. The subject became a contested ground, one on which the French presence in particular gave it an international setting and a cosmopolitan air. Even undergraduates of American colleges and universities found themselves mastering a new vocabulary. 'Structuralism', 'poststructuralism', and 'deconstruction' signalled the new modes of understanding and interpretation. Others like 'semiotics', 'diachronic', 'aporia', and 'binary oppositions' gave resplendence, if not esoterica, to the academic discourse.[7]

It was French structuralism that first began the erosion of the prevailing American critical base that had been grounded in New Criticism and the Myth and Symbol school. The late 1960s and early 1970s saw this infiltration of Continental theory with the semiological concepts of the linguist Ferdinand de Saussure filtered through the writings of later theorists – Roland Barthes, Tzvetan Todorov, Gérard Genette – and worked into the American field by the likes of Jonathan Culler. The fusion of Noam Chomsky's concept of 'linguistic competence' with imported structuralist theory in Culler's *Structuralist Poetics* (1979) was not sufficient to put an American stamp on the assumptions of French theory. The shift from the New Critics' time-honoured focus on literary symbolism to something so apparently mechanical and 'pragmatic', as Richard Ruland and Malcolm Bradbury note, proved 'wholly unacceptable to a large segment of the literary community' in the United States.[8]

Immediately on the heels of structuralism, as it were, came its threatened undoing in the form of deconstruction, a critical approach that took hold in the mid-1970s and was dominated by the so-called 'Yale School' of critics: Geoffrey Hartman, Paul de Man, J. Hillis Miller, Stanley Fish and Harold Bloom. As Stephen Paul Miller describes it, deconstruction was akin to a 'mechanistic Jaws within literary criticism, displaying an ambivalence toward unity by confining all literature to a semiotic and textual realm while questioning the nature of the sign and the existence of unified texts'.[9] Deconstructionist scepticism over the validity of totalising interpretations was 'a revolution in thought', in Ruland and Bradbury's words, signalling a move 'from a world of determinable truth to one of multiple, often conflicting interpretation'.[10] But this scepticism was only one source of wider critical hostility: Fish's pluralist theories of 'interpretive communities', Hartman's proclamation of the death of elite culture (a slap in the faces of modernist icons like Pound, Eliot and Yeats) and Bloom's Freudian insistence on psychological repression and an 'anxiety of influence' driving literary innovation (as though all writers were engaged in an Oedipal struggle to overthrow rather than absorb the insights of their predecessors) were all highly challenging positions.[11] Equally provocative was the sense that critics had chosen only to talk with each other rather than with society at large. This sense of 'literary criticism as a dialogue among critics', as Litz describes, implied that readers were no longer 'confronted with contemporary writers of such overwhelming power that they command[ed] the critic's attention. The result . . . is a self-regarding criticism that can easily become an end in itself.'[12]

It would, of course, be a mistake to conclude that no valuable analytical approaches came out of the deconstructionist movement: identifying silences, contradictions and a plurality of voices in a text is one of the richest and most fruitful objects of critical practice. But Bloom's designation of his own study, *The Anxiety of Influence* (1973) as 'a

poem' in itself, or Hartman's claim that he and his fellow deconstruc-
tionists were 'the unacknowledged poets of our time', did little to
counter the impressions of 1970s criticism as a self-regarding enterprise riding on the coat-tails of – and ostentatiously ignoring – the
dynamic literary practice occurring at the time.[13]

   In 1974, one critic, at least, was certainly prepared to acknowledge
the practice of fiction as he reviewed the contemporary novel for the
scholarly journal, *Contemporary Literature*. In his mock guide, 'How
to Construct a Novel That Will Be Critically Fashionable', Earl Rovit
sarcastically advised:

1. Never make the mistake of telling a story . . .
2. Eschew the coin of *realism* as if it were laundered Mexican currency . . .
3. Draw caricatures instead of characters and relate anecdotes rather
   than bothering with a sequential narrative line . . .
5. Cut the ground from under the reader's feet as he moves along. Forget
   about a message, attack the medium! Make it perfectly clear that
   fiction is artifice, is artificial, is an elaborate nonsensical game . . .
6. Avoid passion. This is a dangerous emotion which presupposes a
   human commitment . . .
8. And last and most important, take a violent stance against the slightest suspicion of bourgeois morality and mores.[14]

It is clear that Rovit's argument must have, in reality, been more against
the critics than the novelists, for the 'contemporary novel' as he wrote
was not exclusively the province of clever postmodern experimentalists.
In fact, established writers who had cut their teeth as early as the 1920s
were still producing important works in the 1970s across all the genres.

Seventies Poetry: Continuum and Watershed

The 1970s hosted the continuation of an established poetic fellowship.
Muriel Rukeyser, the radical feminist already known for her
Depression-era work and her writings on the Spanish Civil War, saw
her *Collected Poems* published in 1971, in the midst of her anti-
Vietnam War activism. Howard Nemerov, who had produced a strong
body of work throughout the 1950s and 60s, saw his *Collected Poems*
win the Pulitzer Prize in 1977, four years after Robert Lowell won the
same award for his final engagement with the sonnet, *The Dolphin*
(1973). Denise Levertov published five important collections in the
seventies, beginning with *Relearning the Alphabet* (1970) and ending

with *Life in the Forest* (1978), while W. D. Snodgrass, who had won the Pulitzer Prize for poetry in 1959, continued into the seventies with *The Remains* (1970), a family history, and *The Fuehrer Bunker: A Cycle* (1977), a dramatic verse history based on dialogue between members of the Nazi upper echelon. Anne Sexton, the confessional poet who committed suicide in 1974, saw through the publication of *Transformations* (1971), a comic feminist revisiting of the Brothers Grimm fairy tales, followed by *The Book of Folly* (1972) and, laden with mortal premonition, her two posthumous collections, *The Death Notebooks* (1974) and *The Awful Rowing Toward God* (1975). Other long-established American poets still publishing in the 1970s were Josephine Miles, Donald Justice, May Swenson, Robert Creeley, Lawrence Ferlinghetti, Elizabeth Bishop, Robert Penn Warren, Richard Wilbur, Richard Eberhart, James Dickey, W. S. Merwin, Galway Kinnell and A. R. Ammons.

At the same time, the seventies marked a transitional watershed in American poetry, seeing the emergence of highly experimental groups, such as the Deep Image poets led by Robert Bly and James Wright, who seized on the resonance of natural images, infusing the American landscape with mythic potency. The so-called New York School of poetry, grounded in urban images and connections with abstract expressionist painters and jazz musicians as far back as the 1940s – and represented in the writings of Frank O'Hara, Kenneth Koch and James Schulyer – saw its fourth eminent alumnus, John Ashbery, emerge to win all three major American poetry prizes in 1975 with his magisterial 'Self-Portrait in a Convex Mirror'. Few works of poetry could be better placed to confound the impression of the poet Karl Shapiro, who lamented in his essay collection, *The Poetry Wreck* (1975) that American poetry had irrevocably descended from the heights of complex intensity to the saccharine banalities of Rod McKuen. The same could be said for the body of poetry emerging from a disparate group of experimentalists on both sides of the country, whose fusion of poetry, politics and theory was destined to transform the face of American poetry. Their operative word was 'Language' and it was far from a mere statement of the obvious. Rather, the work of the Language Poets amounted to a collective praxis aimed at placing the awareness of language at the centre of perception and political activism. For the Language Poets, reading and writing were highly disruptive, revolutionary acts with far-reaching social consequences.

Language Poetry

In the mid-1970s, a relatively unfamiliar and puzzling form of poetry began to attract critical notice:

> the polka beets serene
> whimper out of dominion starve
> steer under crenellated literature
> crinkle sweet lips
> sedimentary paste   an Elk
> eyeballing destiny
> chines thereof   chimes from chimes
> sole of the foot planting   reference
> to event is ghost[15]

Apparently eschewing any kind of grammatical sense or thematic articulation, this was the work of a loosely gathered group of 'theoretically militant' poets emerging simultaneously in New York and the San Francisco Bay area.[16] Eventually critics began to speculate over whether this group might 'be actually capable of bringing about a major shift of attention in American poetry and politics'.[17] Here was a poetry stridently to challenge the forty-year-old poetic establishment represented by such individuals and collectives as W. H. Auden, the Beats, the 'Confessional Poets' (Sylvia Plath, Anne Sexton, Robert Lowell et al.), Kenneth Rexroth and others in the 'San Francisco Renaissance', the New York School, the Black Mountain School and all those towering figures held up as examples in poetry workshops across the United States and in such influential anthologies as Donald Allen's *The New American Poetry* (1960).[18]

This group of avant-garde arrivistes was first described by one of their number, Ron Silliman, in the ethnopoetics journal *Alcheringa* in 1975: '9 poets out of the present, average age 28 . . . Called variously "language centered", "minimal", "non-referential formalism", "diminished referentiality", "structuralist". Not a *group*, but a *tendency* in the work of many.'[19] Whether a 'group' or a 'tendency', the poets and their work were given a formal designation with the first issue of the journal *L=A=N=G=U=A=G=E* (February 1978) under the editorship of Bruce Andrews and Charles Bernstein. Geoff Ward argues: 'As a matter of historical fact, *L=A=N=G=U=A=G=E* was the first published, collective evidence of the impact of what university literature departments now summarise as "theory" on the practise of poetry in America.'[20] Looking back from a vantage point of two decades later, one of the so-called Language Poets, Bob Perelman, recalled that there was never 'a uniform literary program' followed by the group, which eventually included, among many others, Silliman, Bernstein, Andrews, Clark Coolidge, Lyn Hejinian, Robert Grenier and Diane Ward: 'But there was a loose set of goals, procedures, habits, and verbal textures: breaking the automatism of the poetic "I" and its naturalized voice; foregrounding textuality and formal devices; using or alluding to Marxist or poststructuralist theory in order to open the present and to critique and change.'[21] The Language Poetry movement was – and remains – both 'a collective project to write and to analyze poetry in relation to the impact of European theory' and 'a project for massive social change', as Ward argues; the emergence of Language Poetry thus marked 'a critical moment for the whole post-1945 period in American poetry'.[22]

One of the most significant theoretical facets of Language Poetry has been its scepticism, bordering on contempt, for the privileging of the individual, unified subject – for the notion of poetry (or for that matter language itself) as the product of the singular 'I', the Author-as-God dethroned by Roland Barthes in 'The Death of the Author'. As Bernstein has argued: 'It's a mistake, I think, to posit the self as the primary organizing feature of writing. As many others have pointed out, a poem exists in a matrix of social and historical relations that are more significant to the formation of an individual text than any personal qualities of the life or voice of an author.'[23] For Perelman, the fetishisation of the author had led to an institutionalised illusion over the generation of meaning: 'All it leads up to is the pathetic fallacy of "I could hear the wilderness listen" . . . The poet is firmly in the driver's seat, "*I* could hear the wilderness," and firmly in control of all the meaning, "*I* thought hard for us all" . . . Here, the I is in a privileged position unaffected by the words.'[24]

The product of such a 'fallacy', as Silliman argued in similar fashion, could only be 'language that passed itself off as a mockup of consciousness'.[25] Aiming to shatter this 'mockup', the Language Poets set out to divorce language completely from imposed references, to expose the lie of 'faked and traditional coherence' and to break apart the false god of 'the unified subject'.[26] This amounted to 'a polemical reversal of the now traditional model of relations between poem, poet and reader', as Ward observes; the reader was now openly called upon 'to participate in the production of meaning'.[27]

In practice, the dethroning of the poetic 'I' and the empowerment of the reader meant spotlighting and examining language strictly for its 'mediatory function'.[28] As Silliman argued (against the conventionally applauded poetic egotism of Walt Whitman): 'We do not contain multitudes so much as we are the consequence of a multitude of conflicting and overdetermined social forces, brought to us, and acted out within us, as language.'[29] Thus, for the Language Poets, as Stephen Fredman explains, 'the critical activity of deconstruction, of investigating a text as an endless play of subtexts, is a means of poetic creation'.[30] Andrews and Bernstein argued that the shared aim of the Language Poets – whatever their individual differences – was to develop and lay bare 'a spectrum of writing that places its attention primarily on language and ways of making meaning, that takes for granted neither vocabulary, grammar, process, shape, syntax, program or subject matter'.[31]

The group's focus on the workings of language must inevitably underlie what Ward identifies as 'the political implications of an extremist use of language' and the revelation of the self as 'basically a construct of social networks, no free agent, but rather a living and breathing point of intersection for various social and historical pressures or codes'.[32] The analysis of both linguistic expression and poetic form as socially and politically implicated came at a highly pressurised moment. As Perelman recalled, 'Language writing coalesced as American involvement in Vietnam was nearing its bankrupt conclusion: this was a significant cause of the unaccommodating nature of its poetics.'[33] Other members of the Language group issued various forms of manifesto, freighted with the revolutionary language of that highly charged period. Silliman claimed as his object: '(1) recognition of the historic nature and struggle of referentiality, (2) placing the issue of language, the repressed element, at the center of the program, and (3) placing the program into the context of conscious class struggle'.[34] Steve McCaffery's explanation equated linguistics with economics by way of analogy: 'Grammar is a huge conciliatory machine assimilating elements into a ready structure. This grammatical structure can be likened to profit in capitalism, which is reinvested to absorb more human labor for further profit. Classical narrative structure is a profit structure.'[35] Overall, as Andrews and Bernstein maintained, the Language group's intention was to prevent 'turning language into a commodity for consumption' and 'repossessing the sign through close attention to, and active participation in, its production'.[36]

   In sum, and in practice, the Language group attempted to execute what Ward describes as 'a combined theory of poetry, economics and revolution'.[37] Members of the group continue to take advantage of expressive opportunities for radical collaboration provided by the Internet – in particular the poetics listserv hosted by the Electronic Poetry Center at SUNY Buffalo, lending further credence to Ward's claim that 'Language writing at its best actually uncovers unexplored resources in American poetry of the postwar period.'[38]

In addition to the Language poets, younger poets consolidated their presence in the 1970s: the blue-collar, anarchist poet, Philip Levine; Stephen Berg, founder of the *American Poetry Review* in 1972; Mark Strand, the Borges-influenced surrealist; James Merrill, whose *Divine Comedies* won the Pulitzer in 1977; Mona Van Duyn, who earned the National Book Award for *To See, To Take* (1971); and Marvin Bell, also in the front line of teaching poetry as college composition. All of these poets confounded Shapiro's impression that American poetry had become a degraded form. Moreover, the 1970s marked the emergence of two particularly important immigrant poets from Eastern Europe: the Yugoslavian-born Charles Simic whose large body of work reflected the experience of uprooting and resettlement, in particular the collections *Dismantling the Silence* (1971) and *Return to a Place Lit by a Glass of Milk* (1974), and the Russian-born Joseph Brodsky, destined to become the United States Poet Laureate in 1991.

Seventies Fiction: From Realism to Postmodernism and Beyond

American fiction in the 1970s was, like poetry, marked by the sustained presence of established authors and the emergence of radical experimentalists. Eudora Welty's longest novel, *Losing Battles*, appeared in 1970 and she won the Pulitzer Prize for *The Optimist's Daughter* in 1972. Gore Vidal published not only his sequel to the gender-bending *Myra Breckinridge* (1968) – *Myron* – in 1974, but also the first two titles of his five-volume novel series on American history and politics, *Burr* (1973) and *1876* (1976). James Baldwin published his last two novels, *If Beale Street Could Talk* in 1974 and *Just Above My Head* in 1979, and William Burroughs explored police-state repression in the futuristic *Wild Boys: A Book of the Dead* (1971). Vladimir Nabokov published the last novel of his lifetime, *Look at the Harlequins!* (1974), while his American stories were collected in *Nabokov's Dozen* (1971) and *Details of a Sunset* (1976). The mid-decade saw Saul Bellow winning both the Pulitzer Prize for *Humboldt's Gift* (1975), based partially on the anguished life of the poet, Delmore Schwartz, and the Nobel Prize for Literature in 1976. John Updike's novelistic output reflected the rude health of socially engaged, realist fiction in the 1970s, beginning with the publication of *Bech: A Book* (1970), introducing his anti-heroic author figure, Henry Bech, and *Rabbit Redux* (1971), in which Harry Angstrom, Updike's 'unheroic protagonist' from *Rabbit, Run* (1960), 'begins to take on mythic proportions' as a stand-in for an America 'trying unsuccessfully to come to terms' with contemporary social developments.[39] Updike also offered trenchant depictions of sexual and marital crises with the stories collected in *Museums and Women* (1972), *Problems* and *Too Far to Go* (both 1979). John Cheever, like Updike carrying strong associations with short fiction in *The New Yorker*, engaged with family, alcoholism and domestic ritual in *The World of Apples* (1973) and won both the Pulitzer Prize and a National Book Critics Circle Award for his collected *Stories of John Cheever* (1979).

The 1970s proved a most prolific decade for the novelist and short-story writer Joyce Carol Oates who began the decade with the collection *The Wheel of Love* (1970) and a National Book Award in 1970 for her novel, *them* (1969); a corpus of Gothic Americana followed in the form of seven novels, one novella, nine short-story collections and one play, as well as one volume of poetry and three volumes of criticism. Emerging novelists, such as Anne Tyler, with *A Slipping Down Life*

(1970) and *Celestial Navigation* (1974), were perpetuating the craft of realism, as were such short-story writers as Ann Beattie (*Distortions*, 1976; *Secrets and Surprises*, 1978), Gail Godwin (augmenting her novelistic output with the collection, *Dream Children*, in 1976) and Grace Paley, whose *Enormous Changes at the Last Minute* (1974) re-introduced for the new decade the socially, sexually and politically engaged characters of her 1959 collection, *The Little Disturbances of Man*. In the realm of the short story, the decade saw the emergence of one of the twentieth century's most important American practitioners, Raymond Carver, whose *Will You Please Be Quiet, Please?* (1976) helped lay the groundwork for the intensely minimalist style that would come to be known as 'Dirty Realism'.

Will You Please Be Quiet, Please? (1976)

By the mid-1980s it was almost a cliché for book reviewers and blurb writers to describe Raymond Carver as 'the American Chekhov', chiming with Kim A. Herzinger's sense that among American writers it was Carver who had most perceptibly inherited the Russian short-story master's 'tone and temper'.[40] This was no small inheritance, as William L. Stull makes clear:

> Before Chekhov, there were fables, tales, and sketches. But there were no short stories, no 'plotless' evocations of human subjectivity on the threshold of perception. Chekhov created the modern story in the 1880s, partly out of journalistic necessity, by fusing realistic detail and romantic lyricism. The result was a lambent mode of fabulation that teases out the mysteries of 'normal' life.[41]

Kasia Boddy's definition of Carver and Chekhov as 'Companion-Souls of the Short Story' is yet one further indication of the American writer's stature as well as his acknowledged debt to his main literary influence.[42] Indeed, Carver's homage to Chekhov went beyond his attention to detail and his refusal to moralise in his stories; his final work of short fiction, 'Errand', was a lyrical, microscopically detailed account of Chekhov's death and its immediate aftermath, winning for Carver one of the greatest prizes for American short fiction, the O. Henry Award.[43]

Carver's nuanced attention to the details of everyday life accounted for his inclusion in the fellowship of 'Dirty Realists' so named by *Granta* editor Bill Buford in 1983. Carver's short fiction – like that of Richard Ford, Tobias Wolff, Bobbie Ann Mason, Elizabeth Tallent and Jayne Ann Phillips – was 'not a fiction devoted to making the large historical statement,' Buford observed:

> It is instead a fiction of a different scope – devoted to the local details, the nuances, the little disturbances in language and gesture – and it is entirely

appropriate that its primary form is the short story and that it is so conspic-
uously part of the American short story revival. These are strange stories,
unadorned, unfurnished, low-rent tragedies about people who watch
daytime television, read cheap romances or listen to country and western
music. They are waitresses in roadside cafes, cashiers in supermarkets, construction workers, secretaries and unemployed cowboys. They play bingo,
eat cheeseburgers, hunt deer and stay in cheap hotels. They drink a lot and
are often in trouble: for stealing a car, breaking a window, pickpocketing a
wallet. They are from Kentucky or Alabama or Oregon, but, mainly, they could
just about be from anywhere: drifters in a world cluttered with junk food and
the oppressive details of modern consumerism.

This is a curious, dirty realism about the belly-side of contemporary
life . . .[44]

Carver's minimalist depictions of working-class and lower-middle-class
Americans – introduced in his first collection, *Will You Please Be Quiet, Please?*
– show them mocked and taunted by a good life ever just out of reach. They are
grounded by the realities of a straitened economy and a diminishing of high
post-war expectation. As Carver made clear in an interview: 'None of my stories
have ever really happened, but stories don't just come out of thin air. They have
to come from somewhere . . . They have some reference points in the real
world.'[45] The 'real world' of his characters is often introduced through veiled references to the economy or the job market:

Earl Ober was between jobs as a salesman. But Doreen, his wife, had gone
to work nights as a waitress at a twenty-four-hour coffee shop at the edge of
town.[46]

Jack got off work at three. He left the station and drove to a shoe store
near his apartment. He put his foot up on the stool and let the clerk unlace
his work boot.[47]

My marriage had just fallen apart. I couldn't find a job. I had another girl.
But she wasn't in town.[48]

I was out of work. But any day I expected to hear from up north.[49]

Thus, the characters represent, as Carver described them, 'the very desperate, very populous substratum of American life. The people who can't
meet their financial and moral obligations and responsibilities.'[50] For his
part, Carver always maintained that his characters were 'survivors' –
people who 'have to pull up their socks and go on'.[51] Yet in the light of such
glacial, almost imperceptible movement forward or upward on the part of
Carver's characters, Alan Wilde argues that '*catatonic*' is the best way to
describe them 'and the strategies that interpret them', since

in the face of frustration and misery, the eroding of pleasure and the all too
evident spectacle of the waste of their lives, [they] demonstrate a terrible
blankness that suspends the activities of the self and, except in fantasy or
violence, betrays its effective lack of control: its inability to do other than
mirror what his characters experience as the insensateness of the world.[52]

In particular, in *Please Will You Be Quiet, Please?* there seems to be an inextricable linkage between love and aborted expression – between desire and strangled speech. Amid Carver's depictions of failed and failing marriages and doomed couplings, love appears – in Kirk Nesset's words – as 'a darkly unknowable and irreversible force, a form of sickness not only complicating but dominating the lives of characters. Characters are alternately bewildered, enraged, suffocated, diminished. Isolated, and entrapped by love . . . rarely do they actually recognize their individual circumstances as such.'[53] Thus, with the darkening of love, 'as love begins to eat through them, and they find themselves either betraying or betrayed, or trapped in a kind of sexuality they cannot understand – they become partakers of sexual politics, which not only bring on love's sicknesses but aggravate them as well'.[54] Hence such weighted, disturbing passages as that in the title story of the collection, as Marian lightheartedly goads her husband, Ralph, about a brief encounter of years ago:

> And they both laughed abruptly together and abruptly she said, 'Yes'. She said, 'He did kiss me a few times'. She smiled.
> He knew he should try to match her smile, but he could not. He said, 'You told me before he didn't. You said he only put his arm around you while he was driving. So which is it?'
> *'What did you do that for?' she was saying dreamily. 'Where were you all night?' he was screaming, standing over her, legs watery, fist drawn back to hit again. Then she said, 'I didn't do anything. Why did you hit me?' she said.*
> 'How did we ever get onto this?' she said.
> 'You brought it up', he said.[55]

Nesset convincingly argues that 'the individual failures of the characters' lives' – in particular 'the ailing and broken marriages' – are reflected or 'recapitulated' in their failures at communication: 'Thus, another constant in *Will You Please Be Quiet, Please?* – as its title suggests – is the issue of language and its limitations . . . [T]his issue is developed in the stories as inarticulateness, or brooding silence, on the part of the characters.'[56] The pervasive silence or tendency towards elision is an early Carver hallmark:

> That's a funny story, Rita says, but I can see she doesn't know what to make of it.
> I feel depressed. But I won't go into it with her. I've already told her too much.
> She sits there waiting, her dainty fingers poking her hair.
> *Waiting for what?* I'd like to know.[57]

Consequently, an enormous interpretive burden is often placed upon the reader. The effect that Arthur Bethea describes with reference to Carver's first-person narrators is frequently experienced in third-person narration as well: 'Whether the cause is indifference to introspection, linguistic and cognitive limitations, inexperience, self-induced numbness, or fear', Carver's narrators 'perceive and narrate their experiences in ways that call for reader correction.'[58]

> Thus it is here, in the space for 'reader connection' opened up by the silences of both first-person and third-person narrators, that it is possible to discern the implications behind Carver's rendering of 'the local details' that Buford identifies. As Nesset argues, 'For Carver's lovers, ultimately, the politics of sex reflect a kind of larger politics . . . Residing in the form of hardscrabble domesticity, Carver's marriages are thus scaled-down models representing larger, rather more terrifying politics – or anti-politics.'[59] In this regard, Carver's stories are stunning reflections of the power struggles increasingly bared throughout the decade that began with the declaration that 'the personal is political'.[60]

In spite of the resilience of realism, avant-garde literary experimentation did come to the fore in the 1970s, much of it preoccupied with the nature of textuality and the sense of imprisonment within the linguistic (as opposed to the social or political) frame. One of the most striking examples of this preoccupation is Walter Abish's *Alphabetical Africa* (1974), in which each chapter is composed of words beginning with the same letter of the alphabet; thus, Chapter One, devoted to 'A', commences: 'Albert arrives, alive and arguing about African art, about African angst, and also, alas, attacking Ashanti architecture, as author again attempts an agonizing alphabetical appraisal.'[61] Abish's short-story collections, *Minds Meet* and *In the Future Perfect* (both 1975), as well as his poetry collection *Dual Site* (1970) all focus attention, as Marc Chénetier observes, on 'the possibilities of signifiers making sense autonomously' through texts that are 'at once programmed and unpredictable'.[62] Equally striking in its experimental, textually focused force is Ronald Sukenick's *Out* (1973) which, on the one hand, does have a political edge to it (the action is focused on a group of radical, militant activists moving westwards across America) but whose unconventional typography reflects the dominance of the textual. As the book progresses, fuelled by situations of conspiracy and psychedelia, the blank spaces on the page grow larger and larger until the language itself disappears.[63] Similarly, Eugene Wildman's *Montezuma's Ball* (1970) focuses on the materiality of the text through the strategic insertion of coloured pages between the white leaves and, across a ten-page section, the 'ultimate hyperbolic demonstration' in which the print disappears altogether, leaving 'a sequence of empty pages'.[64] Lack of presence is likewise a preoccupation of Joseph McElroy's *Lookout Cartridge* (1974) in which the facts of history are called into question through the loss of a possibly non-existent film cartridge, leaving behind only a suspect diary. As John Johnston argues, 'con-

sciousness itself' in *Lookout Cartridge* is thus 'always a matter of
mediality', requiring 'different media of perception and recording for
its articulation'; consciousness 'arises in the gap between what is registered on the film and what is registered in memory, or between what
is on the film and what is in the diary, or in the discontinuities between
different narrative accounts'.[65]

Such increasingly intense focus on textuality – on the *process* of
description as opposed to the *object* of description – led almost
inevitably to what John Barth had called 'The Literature of Exhaustion'
in a 1967 essay for *The Atlantic*. As Barth argued, 'By "exhaustion" I
don't mean anything so tired as the subject of physical, moral or intellectual decadence – only the used-upness of certain forms or the felt
exhaustion of certain possibilities.'[66] This 'felt exhaustion' became the
subject of Gilbert Sorrentino's novel, *Mulligan Stew* (1979) which, as
Jerome Klinkowitz argues, is 'a deliberate deconstruction and eventual
destruction of virtually every innovative technique 60s and 70s fiction
produced'.[67] As the novel's idealist artist-figure, Lamont, chides the
fashionable hack writer, Trellis: 'The idea of a novel about a writer
writing a novel is truly old hat. Nothing further can be done with the
genre, a genre that was exhausted at the moment of its conception.'[68] As
if to compound this argument, Barth produced in the same year
LETTERS (1979), a highly self-reflexive novel in which Barth, as a
character, encounters characters from his previous novels. This strategy
was shared by Kurt Vonnegut in *Breakfast of Champions* (1973), in
which Vonnegut confronts his own fictional alter ego, the science-
fiction writer Kilgore Trout. Such experiments reflect a wider concern
among writers who sense that their very identities *as* writers are, as
Klinkowitz observes, 'completely textual'.[69]

Thus, when William Gass argued in 1970, 'Reality is not a matter of
fact, it is an achievement,' he was suggesting in part that attention to
the process of construction may be the closest one can come to a
glimpse of the real.[70] One of the greatest worries among critics over
this perception is the apparent blitheness or playfulness with which
postmodern writers tended to confront this representational crisis.
The novelist Raymond Federman referred to his *Take It or Leave It*
(1976) as 'an exaggerated second hand tale', as though such unorigi-
nality were an artistic accomplishment, but equally galling to the
socially minded critic would be the readiness with which such post-
modernists eschewed all earnestness.[71] Federman suggested in a discussion with Sukenick that postmodern fiction was 'always amusing,
always full of laughter . . . [and] playful for the sake of playfulness'.[72]

And when not meeting crisis with hilarity, Daniel Bell argued, post-modernist fiction set out to concern itself with 'consumption styles' as its subject, as though that were the closest that contemporary fiction could come to a real social critique.[73] One can indeed identify novelists emerging in the 1970s whose work seemed to fit Bell's description, notably Don DeLillo, whose first novel, *Americana* (1971) inaugurated his preoccupation with the politics of consumerism. Subsequent novels, such as *End Zone* (1972), about the public's obsession with American football as a commodity, and *Great Jones Street* (1973) in which the main character seeks redemption through a rock star's lifestyle, likewise took consumerism as their subject. Bell was mistaken in implying, however, that contemporary fiction was uniformly amoral, devoid of social critique or divorced from the chain of history. Even when foregrounding experimental form, novels such as William Gaddis's *J. R.* (1975) carried highly salutary warnings – in this case, through the story of an eleven-year-old boy who becomes a corrupt capitalist wizard by following to the letter the logic of the American Dream. One of the decade's greatest popular successes, John Irving's *The World According to Garp* (1978), presented as its ultimately tragic subject a self-destructive writer unable to resist the seduction of contemporary sexual and economic temptations.

One of the most striking concerns of postmodern novelists was the relationship between text and history. Thomas Pynchon's *Gravity's Rainbow* (1973) – 'the exemplary Postmodern text' as Ruland and Bradbury describe it[74] – attempts to map London during the German rocket onslaught of 1944 in order to explore representations of paranoia and conspiracy. Robert Coover's *The Public Burning* (1977) reflected similar preoccupations through the comedic mouthpiece of his narrator, Richard Nixon, re-writing the Rosenberg trial and the McCarthyite witch-hunts in what Leo Braudy calls 'a sweeping Brueghel-like vision of all of 1950s culture'.[75] Kurt Vonnegut's *Jailbird* (1979) likewise presented Nixon's rise and fall as more akin to a farcical 'musical comedy' than as history.[76] (This was in fact very close to Nixon's own description of Watergate as 'a comedy of errors'.)[77] E. L. Doctorow's two works of history-as-fiction, *The Book of Daniel* (1971) – once again examining the aftermath of the Rosenbergs' executions – and *Ragtime* (1975) also injected a strong element of theatricality to the unfolding of public events. In this regard, the Vietnam War proved to be a catalyst for important explorations of the slippage between fiction and history, notably in Michael Herr's *Dispatches* (1977) which tested the boundaries between autobiography and novel, and such works as Gustav Hasford's semi-autobiographical *The Short-timers* (1979, the basis for Stanley Kubrick's 1987 film, *Full Metal Jacket*), Tim O'Brien's *If I Die in a Combat Zone* (1973) and *Going after Cacciato* (1978), Robert Stone's *Dog Soldiers* (1974), Larry Heinemenn's *Close Quarters* (1977, partially the basis of Oliver Stone's 1986 film, *Platoon*), and one of the few novels exploring the African American experience in Vietnam, John Williams's *Captain Blackman* (1972). Further problematising of the boundary between textual and public events came to the fore in such New Journalistic works as Norman Mailer's *The Executioner's Song* (1979) and in the 'Gonzo Journalism' of Hunter S. Thompson's *Fear and Loathing on the Campaign Trail* (1972) and his autobiographical novel drawing strongly on similar techniques, *Fear and Loathing in Las Vegas* (1972).

The decade's apparent postmodern preoccupations with form and surface coverage led critics, such as Daniel Bell, and practitioners, such as John Gardner, both to preach and to practice against the prevailing tide, turning towards presumably bygone ages of literary grandeur for sustenance – in Gardner's case to ancient Greece in *Wreckage of Agathon* (1970) and to Anglo-Saxon England in his updating of the Beowulf legend, *Grendel* (1971). Gardner's novels of conflict and resolution in modern American settings, such as *Sunlight Dialogues* (1972), *Nickel Mountain* (1973) and *October Light* (1976) are also to some degree corollaries of his manifesto against postmodernism, *On Moral Fiction* (1978), which caused a great storm in its accusations of amorality in contemporary fiction. Gardner's critical compatriot, Bell, also looked ruefully backwards as he argued:

> The literature of modernity – the literature of Yeats, Lawrence, Joyce, and Kafka – was a literature which, as Lionel Trilling put it, took 'to itself the dark power which certain aspects of religion once exercised over the human mind'. It was, in its private way, concerned with spiritual salvation. But its successors seem to have lost concern with salvation itself.[78]

Such accusations, as Miller notes, contributed to 'the lasting impression we have of the seventies as a vapid decade that could not fulfil the social visions of the sixties, even though much of America experienced the sixties during the seventies'.[79]

Nothing can better refute the charge of the seventies as 'vapid', however, than the flowering of a rich literature of cultural and racial pluralism in the wake of sixties activism. Peter N. Carroll encapsulates this outpouring:

During the late 1960s, the cry 'Black Power' – a protest against white cultural supremacy by black militants – forced racial outsiders to question the desirability of assimilation. By the early 1970s, the pride of ethnic identity had spread to other nonwhite groups as well as to white ethnics, rural whites, and gays of all backgrounds. Simultaneously, the emergence of the women's movement introduced cultural identity questions that transcended categories of race and ethnicity. Thus, instead of defining the national culture in terms of homogenized social categories of class and economic position, the new sensibility demanded consideration of cultural categories that included ethnicity and gender.[80]

Miller's assertion that 'much of America experienced the sixties during the seventies' can thus be taken with a grain of salt. In the area of literature, at least, it is perhaps more correct to say that the seventies saw the multicultural agitation of the previous two decades come to a striking fruition. Jewish American, African American, Native American, Asian American and Latino writing all witnessed a positive explosion in the 1970s.

Jewish American Writing

Jewish American fiction had come to the fore in the 1950s and 1960s, yet major figures such as Bernard Malamud, Philip Roth and Isaac Bashevis Singer continued to produce important work in the seventies. Malamud's *The Tenants* (1971) is one of the few novels dealing with the ongoing crisis in Black–Jewish relations, while *Dubin's Lives* (1979) engages with the connections between lived lives and biography. Roth's seventies output began with his bitter satire of Richard Nixon, *Our Gang* (1971) and, following several more novels including *The Great American Novel* (1973), *My Life as a Man* (1974) and *The Professor of Desire* (1977), culminated with the introduction of his semi-autobiographical character, Nathan Zuckerman in *The Ghost Writer* (1979). Roth's epic figure would continue to reflect upon the vicissitudes of American life and literature until his death in the ninth Zuckerman book, *Exit Ghost* (2007). Singer, winner of the Nobel Prize for literature in 1978, produced his only novel with an American setting – *Enemies: A Love Story* – in 1972, followed by *Shosha* in 1978 as well as his third volume of memoirs, with a title declaring that this Polish immigrant was, by 1979, *Lost in America*.

Other significant Jewish writers included Meyer Levin, who had first published *The Reporter* in 1929 and who in the seventies was still focusing on Jewish American identity in *The Settlers* (1972), *The Obsession* (1973), *The Spell of Time* (1974) and *The Harvest* (1978). The rabbi-turned-novelist, Chaim Potok, built upon his 1960s output with *My Name Is Asher Lev* (1972) and *In the Beginning* (1975). Jerome Charyn in *Blue Eyes* (1975) and *Marilyn the Wild* (1976) melded ethnic representation with the hard-boiled crime genre through his Jewish police detective, Isaac Sidel. Stanley Elkin's *The Dick Gibson Show* (1971), *The Franchiser* (1976) and *The Living End* (1979) treated issues such as personal loss and terminal illness with a hilarious absurdity born of the traditions of eastern European Jewish humour that reflected resilience under oppression. Joseph Heller, perhaps America's reigning comic absurdist in the wake of his monumental *Catch-22* (1961), returned with *Something Happened* in 1974 and *Good as Gold* in 1979. Both Heller's seventies novels uncover the problems of communicative entropy that also preoccupied the more experimental postmodern novelists during the decade. Thus, the narrative of Bob Slocum in *Something Happened* is not simply 'one long narrative about the self', as Bell mistakenly objected.[81] It is rather a sobering evocation of death-in-life through comic absurdity, as Slocum implies in the narrative:

> In my middle years, I have exchanged the position of the fetus for the position of a corpse. When I go to sleep now, it is no longer on my side with my knees tucked up securely against my abdomen, and my thumb near my mouth. I lie on my back with my hands clasped across my chest decorously like a cadaver and my face pointed straight up toward the ceiling.[82]

In *Good as Gold*, the focus on communicative entropy continues on a more farcical plane. At one point the Jewish protagonist Bruce Gold, coming to grips as an outsider in the exclusively WASPish Washington DC, is told:

> Now these Commission meetings tomorrow morning can be of great importance to you, Bruce, because they're of no importance to anyone else. Do whatever you want as long as you do whatever we want. We have no ideas, and they're pretty firm. Seize control. The Administration will back you all the way until it has to.'[83]

It is thus not without reason that 'You're boggling my mind!' becomes the book's catchphrase, as the communicative illogic so memorably foregrounded in *Catch-22* returns with a renewed force.

Jewish American short fiction in the seventies is no less focused on disjunctions between an individual's Jewish sensibility and the dominant culture. Bernard Malamud extended his exploration of this sensibility with his short-story collection, *Rembrandt's Hat* (1973), while Cynthia Ozick transplanted Jewish religious figures from Moses onwards into contemporary American settings in the stories of *The Pagan Rabbi* (1971). Equally bizarre and comic were the fatalistic characters of Stanley Elkin's *Searches and Seizures* (1973) and, in particular, Isaac Bashevis Singer's collections *A Friend of Kafka* (1970), *A Crown of Feathers* (1973) and *Passions* (1975). All of these writers create characters who, as Gilbert Muller observes, are 'physically removed from the threat of cataclysm but still marked by the wounds of the Holocaust experience':

> Their dark night of the soul clashes with postwar American euphoria, forcing the juxtaposition of buoyant national experience against apocalyptic experience that in turn produces cultural representations of a new epoch that is, as Singer suggests by the title of a posthumous novel, *meshugah* – crazy, senseless, insane.[84]

The comedy of Jewish American fiction thus reflects a sensation of a presumably stable order being undermined, of the world having broken loose from its anchorage in reality. To some degree this is in keeping with earlier historical periods in which shifts of cultural expectation and challenges to dominant agendas appear to conservatives as 'the world turned upside down'. Carroll's exploration of 'identity politics' in the 1970s indicates one such cultural upheaval: 'Since the 1970s, the noun "American" is more frequently preceded by descriptive adjectives – racial, ethnic or geographical. For most citizens today, a presumed white middle class no longer defines public life.'[85] Leading the attack on white middle-class norms was the cultural activism of African American writers and critics who matched the political commitment of the streets with that of the page.

African American Writing

The 'Black Aesthetic' movement of the early seventies, reflected in the eponymous critical volume by Addison Gayle Jr and the early criticism of the black feminist Claudia Tate, sought to theorise the processes of black cultural nationalism and the 'Black Arts Movement'.[86] Toni Cade Bambara's manifesto on 'Black English' proposed an alternative linguistic value system, while Sherley Ann Williams's *Give Birth to Brightness* (1972), subtitled 'A Thematic Study in Neo-Black Literature', focused on heroic representations in African American literature, music and other cultural arenas.[87]

An explosion of militant African American autobiography by such writers as Bobby Seale, George Jackson, Donald Reeve and Angela Davis gave voice to some of the most oppositional figures of the turbulent decade.[88] Autobiography also problematised rigid expectations of fiction, with Maya Angelou's *I Know Why the Caged Bird Sings* (1970) and Alex Haley's *Roots* blurring the boundaries between (on the one hand) family history and (on the other hand) novelistic conventions. Poets such as Don L. Lee (later Haki Madhubuti), the members of the proto-rap group The Last Poets and feminists Nikki Giovanni, Audre Lorde, Mari Evans and Sonia Sanchez brought a new militancy to African American poetry, while Ishmael Reed, Jay Wright, Michael S. Harper and Lucille Clifton all drew on black vernacular and folk sources to establish connections between the oral and literary traditions.

But it was African American fiction which most visibly experienced the 'boom' in the 1970s described by Robert Stepto, 'comparable to that more readily acknowledged in Latin American letters' and 'capable of attracting an international audience'.[89] The fellowship of major African American novelists emerging in this milieu included Ishmael Reed, playing with history and postmodernism in *Mumbo Jumbo* (1972), *The Last Days of Louisiana Red* (1974) and his epic parody of the slave narrative, *Flight to Canada* (1978); John Edgar Wideman, interrogating black modernism in *Hurry Home* (1970) and revolutionary black nationalism in *The Lynchers* (1973); Ernest M. Gaines yoking together Emancipation, Reconstruction and the Civil Rights movement in *The Autobiography of Miss Jane Pittman* (1971), and Alice Walker with her first two novels, *The Third Life of Grange Copeland* (1970) and *Meridian* (1976). Other major novelists consolidating their presence included Lucille Clifton, Gayl Jones, John Williams, William Melvin Kelley and Leon Forrest. In the short-story genre, Toni Cade Bambara, Ann Petry, Jayne Anne Phillips and the Pulitzer Prize-winning James Alan McPherson all situated race in a variety of contexts – class, gender, national identity.

Of all the fiction writers emerging in the 1970s, however, it was Toni Morrison who most visibly established the trajectory for the international acclaim that would culminate in the award of the Nobel

Prize for Literature in 1993. Her novels *The Bluest Eye* (1971) and *Sula* (1974) established her reputation for sustained, trenchant fiction, while her exploration of the African American oral tradition, *Song of Solomon* (1977), has earned the status of one of the most important American novels of the twentieth century.

Song of Solomon (1977)

From the beginning of the novel, as a crowd gathers to see whether a forlorn black man on the roof of a Michigan hospital will jump to his death or – as he says – 'fly away on my own wings', Morrison is engaged in a complex anthropological and linguistic exercise.[90] As Michael Awkward notes, *Song of Solomon* has two main 'functions': '(1) to preserve the traditional Afro-American folktales, folk wisdom, and general cultural beliefs, and (2) to adapt to contemporary times and needs such traditional beliefs by infusing them with "new information" and to transmit the resultant amalgam of traditional and "new" to succeeding generations'.[91] Thus, the novel's main plot line – about a young, northern, middle-class black man's journey southwards into the land and history of his family – reflects the mid-seventies zeitgeist most spectacularly captured by the book and film of Haley's *Roots*. But, as Michael Rothberg argues, Morrison's engagement with 'contemporary legacies of traumatic memory' is far from an exercise in faddishness: 'What the novel calls "posthumous communication" can serve as a site for rethinking the relationship among written texts, between written and oral memory, and between historical occurrences and literary invention.'[92]

The prime conflict in the novel lies not so much between individual characters as between the oral and written traditions. As Joyce Irene Middleton argues: '*Song of Solomon* illustrates the oral tradition as a conveyor of cultural values, ideas, heroes and accomplishments that are often in direct conflict with schooling and literate training, where the written word renders African American history invisible.'[93] Morrison herself has explained:

> I agree with John Berger that peasants don't write novels because they don't need them. They have a portrait of themselves from gossip, tales, music, and some celebrations. That is enough. The middle class at the beginning of the industrial revolution needed a portrait of itself because the old portrait didn't work for this new class. Their roles were different; their lives in the city were new. The novel served this function then, and it still does. It tells about the city values, the urban values. Now my people, we 'peasants', have come to the city, that is to say, we live with its values. There is a confrontation between old values of the tribes and new urban values.[94]

Hence the centrality of music and song in Morrison's novel, as well as the implicit critique of formal literary values at the expense of folk knowledge. Morrison maintained:

There has to be a mode to do what the music did for blacks, what we used to be able to do with each other in private and in that civilization that existed underneath the white civilization. I think this accounts for the address of my books. I am not explaining anything to anybody. My work bears witness and suggests who the outlaws were, who survived under what circumstances and why, what was legal in the community as opposed to what was legal outside it. All that is in the fabric of the story in order to do what the music used to do. The music kept us alive, but it's not enough anymore. My people are being devoured.[95]

There is an inescapable irony in Morrison's attempt to restore and preserve an African American oral tradition through the medium of the novel, and this irony is inscribed in the conflict between the protagonist, nicknamed 'Milkman' Dead, and his father, Macon Dead, so named through the inheritance of a written mistake in a Reconstruction-era ledger book:

Macon focused his eyes on his son. 'Papa couldn't read, couldn't even sign his name. Had a mark he used. They tricked him. He signed something, I don't know what, and they told him they owned his property. He never read nothing. I tried to teach him, but he said he couldn't remember those little marks from one day to the next. Wrote one word in his life – Pilate's name; copied it out of the Bible. That's what she got folded up in that earring. He should have let me teach him. Everything bad that ever happened to him happened because he couldn't read. Got his name messed up cause he couldn't read.' (53)

In contrast with his father, Milkman gradually learns the value of another mode of communication and the transmission of knowledge exemplified by an epiphany he experiences during a bobcat hunt with his newfound distant relatives in Virginia. The dogs and the hunting men are, he realises, 'talking to each other' and 'saying distinctive, complicated things' in a primal call-and-response mode:

It was all language. [. . .] No, it was not language; it was what there was before language. Before things were written down. Language in the time when men and animals did talk to one another, when a man could sit down with an ape and the two converse; when a tiger and a man could share the same tree, and each understood the other; when men ran *with* wolves, not from or after them. And he was hearing it in the Blue Ridge Mountains under a sweet gum tree. And if they could talk to animals, and the animals could talk to them, what didn't they know about human beings? Or the earth itself, for that matter. (278)

What connects modes of knowledge transmission to broader, political issues in Morrison's work are what Sämi Ludwig identifies as 'logical snares of representation' at work in American culture:

They have to be pointed out because they dominate the media, the political debates and agendas, and they are abused for reasons of power, racism, and, sometimes, sheer ignorance. Moreover, many of these images also determine our internalized discourses, our own thinking, writing, reading. It is at this cognitive core of mental human agency where Morrison is most political . . .[96]

There is thus a corollary between Macon Dead's wholesale adoption of literate values and account-book exactitude and his contempt for his sister Pilate's embracing of folk knowledge and orality. This corollary is reflected, moreover, in Macon's embracing of middle-class individualism and acquisitiveness as the prime indicators of achievement. As he tells Milkman:

'Boy, you got better things to do with your time. Besides, it's time you started learning how to work. You start Monday. After school come to my office; work a couple of hours there and learn what's real. Pilate can't teach you a thing you can use in this world. Maybe the next, but not this one. Let me tell you right now the one important thing you'll ever need to know: own things. And let the things you own own other things. Then you'll own yourself and other people too.' (55)

In contrast, as Milkman learns in extremis in the midst of the bobcat hunt:

His watch and his two hundred dollars would be of no help out here, where all a man had was what he was born with, or had learned to use. And endurance. Eyes, ears, nose, taste, touch – and some other sense that he knew he did not have; an ability to separate out, of all the things there were to sense, the one that life itself might depend on. (277)

Thus, the initial catalyst for Milkman's southern journey – the search for a legendary horde of family treasure – becomes in reality a search for fool's gold. But what he finds in its place is a much more valuable inheritance: a link to a family, a place and a history of which he had had no knowledge:

'Well, I'll be.' Reverend Cooper took off his glasses. [. . .] 'I know your people!'
Milkman smiled and let his shoulders slump a little. It was a good feeling to come into a strange town and find a stranger who knew your people. All his life he'd heard the tremor in the word: 'I live here, but my *people*. . .' or: 'She acts like she ain't got no *people*', or: 'Do any of your *people* live there?' But he hadn't known what it meant: links (229).

The euphoria with which Milkman encounters ever stronger levels of family connection is compromised by many of the embarrassments and mis-steps that make up a *Bildungsroman* – a novel of education in which a cocky, foolish youth progresses towards self-awareness and wider knowledge. Milkman eventually concludes that 'the consequences of [his] own stupidity would remain, and regret would always outweigh the things he was proud of having done' (335). The acquisition of valuable, useful knowledge is a process bedevilled with pitfalls – in Milkman's case, these are as much of a linguistic nature as they are ethical or political. Although he eventually pieces together the fragments of folk tales and songs that reveal to him his family lineage, it is not before he has acquired the painful knowledge of language as a trap. A cold, pompous letter of thanks as a means of breaking off his relationship with Pilate's daughter, Hagar, leads to her psychotic breakdown and her half-hearted attempts to murder him:

> And he did sign it with love, but it was the word 'gratitude' and the flat-out coldness of 'thank you' that sent Hagar spinning into a bright blue place where the air was thin and it was silent all the time, and where people spoke in whispers or did not make sounds at all, and where everything was frozen except for an occasional burst of fire inside her chest that crackled away until she ran out into the streets to find Milkman Dead (99).

Thus, one of Milkman's most important lessons is to know when to trust language and when to be wary of it. As a boy, he had failed to heed Pilate's warning:

> 'Saying something is pitch black is like saying something is green. What kind of green? Green like my bottles? Green like a grasshopper? Green like a cucumber, lettuce, or green like the sky is just before it breaks loose to storm? Well, night black is the same way. May as well be a rainbow.' (41)

Language is thus a maze to be negotiated, a sensitive field subject to trip-wire reaction. So too are family relations and relations between the sexes. Milkman learns this after Hagar's death and after being brained by a bottle-wielding Pilate, who imprisons him in a cellar in order to teach him to read the signals:

> Milkman rolled his head back and forth on the cellar floor. It was his fault, and Pilate knew it. She had thrown him in the cellar [. . .] Something of Hagar's must be nearby. Pilate would put him someplace near something that remained of the life he had taken, so he could *have* it. She would abide by this commandment from her father herself, and make him do it too. 'You just can't fly on off and leave a body.' (332)

Milkman's journey towards cultural, personal and ethical awareness posits *Song of Solomon* as, yet again, one of the most potent examples to counter the charge of 1970s culture as a repository of simple, narcissistic impulses.

Native American, Asian American and Latino Writing

The ethnic renaissance in 1970s literature was so pronounced and far reaching as to suggest that multiculturalism had in fact become the American mainstream. Writers from other ethnic groups emerged from the margins to claim visible territory. In Native American fiction, Leslie Marmon Silko explored the crisis of assimilation in *Ceremony* (1977), while James Welch depicted the economic and social harshness of reservation life in *Winter in the Blood* (1974) and the conflict between contemporary urban and traditional tribal values in *The Death of Jim Loney* (1979). Gerald Vizenor's *Darkness in Saint Louis Bearheart* (1978) is based on a quest for ritual understanding, as is Janet

Figure 1.1 Toni Morrison (1977), author of *Song of Solomon.* © Helen Marcus.

Campbell Hale's *Owl Song* (1974). Popular fiction saw the emergence of the Seneca del Sur-Yaqui, Martin Cruz Smith, who would become world renowned with the publication in 1981 of his best-selling thriller, *Gorky Park*; in 1977, he published the mystery novel *Nightwing*, with its protagonist a well-travelled, disaffected Native American. Also high on the bestseller list was Ruth Beebe Hill's massive potboiler, *Hanta Yo: An American Saga* (1979); its first draft was written in English, translated into Lakota, and ultimately published in English as a translation from the Lakota. The short-story genre saw the publication of three important collections in 1978: Simon Ortiz's *The Howbah Indians*, Peter Blue Cloud's *Back Then*

Tomorrow and Gerald Vizenor's *Wordarrows*. In poetry, Leslie Marmon Silko began her writing career with the publication of *Laguna Woman* (1974), Paula Gunn Allen published *The Blind Lion* in the same year, James Welch began the decade with *Riding the Earthboy 40* (1971) and N. Scott Momaday pre-dated his autobiographical *The Way to Rainy Mountain* with two verse collections, *Angle of Geese* (1971) and *The Gourd Dancer* (1976). Simon Ortiz, Joy Harjo, Linda Hogan and Barney Bush also emerged as important Native American poets in the 1970s.

Asian American writers likewise contributed to the decade's flowering of ethnic literatures. Maxine Hong Kingston's *The Woman Warrior* appeared in 1976, problematising not only the relationship between traditional Chinese and mainstream American values but also that between fiction and autobiography. Bharati Mukherjee prefigured her novel *Jasmine* (1989) with two novels depicting an Indian woman's encounter with contemporary American culture: *The Tiger's Daughter* (1972) and *Wife* (1975). Shawn Wong's novel *Homebase* (1979) saw the protagonist, Rainsford Chan, searching for the elusive Californian town after which he was named, while short-story collections by Jeffery Paul Chan (*Jackrabbit* and *The Chinese in Haifa*, both 1974) and Richard Kim (*Last Names*, 1971, and *Lost Souls*, 1974) respectively explored the Chinese and Korean experience in America. The wealth of Asian American poetry was reflected in Janice Mirikitani's collection *Awake in the River* (1978), in collections by two Hawaiian poets – Eric Chock's *Ten Thousand Wishes* and Geraldine Kudaka's *Numerous Avalanches at the Point of Intersection* (both 1978) – in Fay Chiang's *In the City of Contradictions* (1979) and in the publication of Frank Chin's groundbreaking *Aiiieeeee! An Anthology of Asian American Writers* (1974).

The output of Latino literature was equally significant in the 1970s, in particular Chicano and Puerto Rican writing. Chicano poetry and fiction reflected both the pride and, at times, the militancy of a group aware of its gathering power and influence in the American body politic. Just as the Chicano Moratorium of 1970 marked the largest consolidated protest against the Vietnam War by a given ethnic group, so did literary expression reflect a powerful collective consciousness. Richard Vázquez's novel *Chicano* (1970) inscribed contemporary Mexican-American civil rights activism into the story of the Sandoval family, fleeing from war-torn revolutionary Mexico to a new, complicated life in the United States. Tomás Rivera's *y no se lo tragó la tierra – And the Earth Did Not Devour Him* (1971) – and Rolando Hinojosa-Smith's

Estampas del valle – Sketches of the Valley (1972) – brought the California and Texas Chicano experiences, respectively, to the short story form. Bernice Zamora's *Restless Serpents* (1976) and Gary Soto's *The Elements of San Joaquin* (1977) and *The Tale of Sunlight* (1978) were important early poetry collections in the careers of these two writers, while Rudolfo Anaya's first novel, *Bless Me, Ultima* (1972), would soon become a classic of Chicano literature. Some of the most lively output came from the Chicano attorney and activist, Oscar Zeta Acosta – the model for 'Dr Gonzo' in Hunter S. Thompson's *Fear and Loathing in Las Vegas* – whose novel, *The Revolt of the Cockroach People* (1973) was based on the Chicano Moratorium of 1970.

On the East Coast, Puerto Rican writing was contributing to the reconstitution of the American literary canon. In 1973, a highly influential movement was inaugurated with the founding of the Nuroyican Poets' Café in New York's East Village by Miguel Agarín, Miguel Piñero, Bimbo Rivas, Lucky Cienfuegos and Pedro Pietri, among other notable artists. With the Puerto Rican diaspora centred in the New York metropolitan area, this café became a locus for the monumental activity eventually reflected in Algarín and Piñero's groundbreaking *Nuyorican Poetry: An Anthology of Puerto Rican Words and Feelings* (1975). Pietri's epic poem, 'Puerto Rican Obituary' (1973), the poems of Victor Hernández Cruz in his collections *Mainland* (1973) and *Tropicalization* (1976) and Tato Laviera's novel, *La Carreta Made a U Turn* (1976) all swelled the corpus of Puerto Rican writing. The novellas and short stories of the New York-born Nicholasa Mohr further expanded the range of Puerto Rican expression in *El Bronx Remembered* (1976) and *In Nueva York* (1977). Mohr's writing for adolescents – in particular, the novels *Nilda* (1974) and *Felita* (1979) – won acclaim at a time when the bolstering of ethnic group consciousness increasingly became a school curricular issue for Latino as well as African American cultural activists.

In its entirety, the rich outpouring of American literature proved beyond doubt that the 1970s could hardly be called the decade where 'nothing happened' and where 'vapid' narcissism ruled. Further proof was revealed in the arenas of television and drama, film and visual culture, popular music and the public space, all of which situate the seventies as a vibrant decade demanding renewed critical scrutiny.

Chapter 2

Television and Drama

The small screen and the dramatic stage were highly charged sites in the American 1970s. While television programmers took great strides in order to wrestle with sensitive political and social issues, television's domination by network officials and corporate sponsors threatened to keep it a hobbled and gagged medium throughout the decade. Situation comedies like *M*A*S*H* and *All in the Family* were certainly politically engaged, and the groundbreaking comedy review *Saturday Night Live* carried a late-night edge that gave hints of political daring; but the corporate restrictions of 1970s programming meant that the most politically momentous 'series' may well have been, in the end, the televised Senate Watergate Hearings of 1973–4. Nonetheless, certain televisual milestones such as the mini-series, *Roots*, are today remembered by adults as highly formative experiences.

Television demonstrated a great capacity to influence because of its mass audience. The same could not be said for American drama of the 1970s or any other decade; but the relative lack of a mass audience does not mean that drama is a negligible cultural arena. On the contrary, 1970s drama demonstrated a capacity to engage with menace and controversy with a depth and immediacy that were not often shared by network television throughout the decade. This chapter pairs television and drama precisely for their illuminating contrasts: the one controlled by corporate interests, 'standards and practices' offices and the ratings game, more often than not wedded to tested forumulas; the other relatively unpoliced, unfettered and freely experimental. Together they reflect the broad spectrum of critical engagement and evasion, entertainment and polemic, formula and experiment. Moreover, both cultural arenas demonstrate that, as in literature, race and ethnicity had become inescapable – if not central – factors.

1970s Television: Engagement or Evasion?

John Fiske argues that 'the world of television is clearly different from
our real social world, but just as clearly related to it in some way';
rather than representing 'the manifest actuality' of a society, television
programmes reflect, 'symbolically, the structures of values and relationships beneath the surface'.[1] Beyond such visually and aurally
iconic musical review programmes as *The Osmonds* and *The Jackson
Five*, 1970s television can, for many, be conjured up in recollections of
genre shows that somehow *do* relate to life on the streets or in the
workplace or in the home – the police drama (*The F.B.I.*, *Kojak*,
Ironside, *The Mod Squad*); the medical drama (*The New Doctors*,
Medical Center, *Marcus Welby, M.D.*); the family sitcom (*The Brady
Bunch*, *The Partridge Family*, *All in the Family*). Some will recall the
seventies as the decade in which 'made-for-TV movies' such as *The
Autobiography of Miss Jane Pittman* first proliferated on the screen
(with over a hundred broadcast on the three major networks by 1972);
others will think of the advent of the 'mini-series' (*Roots*, *Rich Man,
Poor Man*, *Centennial*).[2] Like the weekly television series, television
films and mini-series also provided symbolic reflections of 'the structures of the values and relationships beneath the surface' of American
events in the 1970s. Indeed, the seventies marked an explosion of
socially significant televised drama and comedy, certainly confound-
ing Daniel Bell's assessment of a grievous, 'radical disjunction'
between culture and society. One of the greatest debates surrounding
1970s television broadcasting, however, is the extent to which the
decade's early reputation for challenging, even subversive, programming can withstand scrutiny.

When key examples are put under the microscope, important questions are raised about the potential of network television to act as an
oppositional force to dominant trends and ideologies. One might
easily dismiss such conventionally characteristic 'seventies' shows as
Charlie's Angels, in which big hair vied with big breasts to maintain the
sexual objectification of women on the prime-time screen – as though
the entire second wave of feminism had been stopped in its tracks
along with the Equal Rights Amendment. With the major Hollywood
film studios supplying the majority of network programmes by the
mid-decade, it is not surprising that the interests of corporate sponsors
would be entrenched and that there would be little taste for challenging or alienating large cross sections of the American viewing public.
William Keough adds to this consideration 'the whimsical nature of

Nielsen ratings' and the fact that 'since television goes directly into the home, that most sacred of all American institutions, censorship is also a sensitive issue'.[3] It is useful to explore this issue through a study of *M*A*S*H*, one of the decade's most popular and critically debated programmes.

*M*A*S*H* (1972–83)

In terms of the ratings game, few television shows in the 1970s enjoyed the popular success of *M*A*S*H*, adapted from Robert Altman's unflinchingly bloody film (1970) based on the 1968 novel by surgeon H. Richard Hornberger (pseudonym Richard Hooker). The series, which ran from 1972 to 1983, is conventionally seen as a thinly disguised commentary on the Vietnam War, although it is actually set during the Korean War of 1950–3. During the first three years of the series, which coincided with nightly news broadcasts of burning villages in Vietnam and footage of body bags and flag-draped coffins being off-loaded at Stateside airports, there was little question as to what the fictional tropics of *M*A*S*H* were meant to represent.

Darrell Hamamoto suggests that 'the denial of the war in Vietnam in combination with intense domestic discord became part of the psychopathology of everyday life in the United States' and that 'the fictional wars played out in military situation comedies internalized the turmoil of the times and relieved the resultant anxiety through the use of humor'.[4] In spite of its satiric potential, however, the network version of *M*A*S*H* marks, for many observers, one of the most chilling descents from challenging critique to safe entertainment in the history of film-to-television adaptation. As David Marc argues, the cynical, war-scarred, misogynistic doctors of Altman's 4877th Mobile Army Surgical Hospital unit, Hawkeye Pierce (Donald Sutherland) and Trapper John (Elliott Gould),

> had brought hedonistic American college-boy summer camp pranksterism into the misery of the Korean peninsula during the early 1950s with gratifying results. By maintaining their adolescence in the midst of the relentless firestorm, they managed to keep an American spirit of rebellious independence alive in such an unlikely setting. Whitmanian reverences for fellow feeling, intoxication, and orgasm were revealed as ample to the task of personal survival against the mindless, steely thud of bureaucracy, blood, shrapnel, and death.[5]

Steve Neale and Frank Krutnik likewise point out the great satiric potential of both the film's and the television spin-off's setting and characterisations:

> M.A.S.H. . . . uses the democratic and humanitarian values in whose name the war in Korea (and of course, by analogy, Vietnam) is being fought, as a set of self-professed norms against which to measure the undemocratic and inhumane practices both of the American military and governmental establishments, in particular, and of war itself, in general.[6]

Critics are divided, however, over the television show's potential to match the satirical onslaught of Altman's film. Marc suggests a degree of promise when he asks rhetorically: 'War? Death? Amputation? Ambiguous attitudes toward the US Army, the United States of America and legal authority itself? No one had yet attempted a sitcom that evoked the moods and messages of e. e. cummings's *The Enormous Room* or Ernest Hemingway's *A Farewell to Arms*.'[7] Yet, as John Ozersky implies, *M*A*S*H* was not as revolutionary as its defenders have claimed. 'The "war comedy" ', he writes, 'had been in much evidence in the previous decade, from the POW-camp mirth of *Hogan's Heroes* to the zaniness of *McHale's Navy*. *M*A*S*H* took the genre a step further, giving these high jinks a moral validity. Hawkeye Pierce was to become Sergeant Bilko with a halo.'[8] The timing of the show's introduction also had an impact upon its critical potential: 'Nor by this time could much harm come to one's career from such a project, at least politically. [Producer Larry Gelbart recalled:] "It was chic to be antiwar. You couldn't offend anybody." '[9] All the same, Marc reminds us to put even the mildest television subversion in the context of the political climate that had preceded it over a period of two decades or more:

> Despite the obviousness of the show's politically-loaded obsessions, it is difficult to get most of the people involved in *M.A.S.H.* to discuss the show's political content – or even the possibility that it had any. The hesitation of television producers to speak frankly on such issues points to a legacy of McCarthyism that continues to cast a shadow over American popular culture.[10]

Thus it was that the darker, grittier characters of Hawkeye and Trapper John in Altman's film were transformed on television into the cuddly, affable pranksters played by Alan Alda and Wayne Rogers (later replaced by the equally wholesome Mike Farrell). Ozersky observes:

> What started out as a vaguely black-humored lark became one of the most self-important shows ever. Over the course of the first two years, *M.A.S.H.* changed its emphasis from the playboy doctor theme ('Doctor, I thought you wanted to study Gray's Anatomy, not mine!') to more sober, self-conscious portrayals of men and women under difficult circumstances ('All I know is what they taught me at Command School. There are certain rules about a war. Rule Number One is that young men die, and Rule Number Two is that doctors can't change Rule Number One.')[11]

As Keough laments, the 'laundering of language and imagery' on a weekly basis 'managed not only to sanitize the operating room (all shots from the waist up), but to reduce the horrors of war to clever one-liners and atrocious puns – e.g., Hawkeye smirking, "If I touch that gun I'll just trigger an argument." '[12] Lee Siegel, however, puts such 'laundering' in context: 'Television in the 1960s and 1970s became less violent as the Vietnam War became more of an absurdist slaughterhouse.'[13] Moreover, even in its 'laundered' context, the show's 'developmental tendencies', as Neale and Krutnik call them, by which 'the characters' "moral growth" [became evident] across the run of the series', enabled the airing of the odd oppositional critique to emerge with some force.[14] Thus could Hawkeye propose in the midst of a firestorm (although broadcast three years after America's withdrawal from Vietnam): 'I just don't know why they're shooting at us. All we want to bring them is democracy and white bread, to transplant the American Dream – freedom, achievement, hyperacidity. Affluence, flatulence, technology, tension. The inalienable right to stab your boss in the back'.[15]

It perhaps takes a Marxist reading to ask the most crucial questions about the oppositional potential of any American network television show, even one that is frequently celebrated for its critical daring. As Mike Budd and Clay Steinman argue:

All these responses have been part of the process of *dematerialization*, displacing the show from its material existence into an idealized realm of celebration. If the show has been one of the most commercially successful programs in American television, it has also been seen as somehow different, unusual, better – 'quality' television rather than just another producer of quantitative ratings and capital, something that everyone, producers and consumers alike, could be proud of. How could it be both? How could capital be so mystified?[16]

These questions will appear immediately relevant in the context of other examples of 1970s television in which the contemporary reputation for a cutting edge, upon mature reflection, is compromised by the fealty of the networks to their corporate sponsors.

Figure 2.1 The cast of *M*A*S*H* ('Welcome to Korea', 1975). Wisconsin Center for Film and Theater Research.

Comedy and Criticism

Keough argues that one show in particular – *Saturday Night Live* (*SNL*), which premiered in 1975 and is still running – is a useful illustration of 'some of the forces driving for more incisive comedy and the equally strong forces at work to restrain or defeat it'.[17] On the one hand, *SNL* was known from the start for its edginess; it was indeed live, which enabled not only an immediacy between the cast and the viewers (both in-studio and at home) but also last-minute engagement with the political and social topics of the minute, no matter how disturbing. As *SNL*'s senior writer, Michael O'Donoghue, claimed: 'Our comedy reflects a violent, desperate time . . . The world is ready to nuke itself out – [safe 1960s sitcoms like] Dick Van Dyke and Donna Reed just don't cut it any more.'[18] For much of its comic inspiration, *SNL* drew on a British predecessor, the groundbreaking *Monty Python's Flying Circus*, whose anarchic sketches (anarchic in terms of their form and their rupture of presentational conventions) inspired *SNL*'s major players: O'Donoghue, the producer, Lorne Michaels, and the show's comedic stable during the 1970s, John Belushi, Dan Ackroyd, Chevy Chase, Jane Curtin and Gilda Radner. The sequential format of *SNL*, coupled with the embedded risk of its live broadcast, did take the show into sometimes challenging territory (at least in the context of mainstream television culture), much in the same way as *The Smothers Brothers Comedy Hour* had done in the previous decade. Moreover, the satirical strategies, in retrospect, appear to have had some significant contemporary impact. As Yanek Mieczkowsi suggests, Chevy Chase's caricatures of Gerald Ford as an incompetent buffoon – always tripping and bumping his head – 'indelibly marred Ford's image'.[19] Also in retrospect, however, critics have questioned *SNL*'s subversive credentials. Miller argues:

> The 'live' factor of *Saturday Night Live* gave the show an unpredictable and seemingly uncensored edge. [But] entertainment elements that seemed radical in 1975 seemed less and less so as the decade progressed. If Reagan was a much less memorable target of the program than Gerald Ford, it should be remembered that at times Reagan seemed more cutting-edge than *Saturday Night Live*. The program itself seemed less anti-establishment as its humor became more baselessly disjunctive and devoid of Republican targets, trends that were solidified when a new cast retooled the program in 1980.[20]

A programme's setting is obviously relevant to its content. Thus, the battlefield-hospital setting of *M*A*S*H* inevitably had an impact upon its topical material: even in the absence of blood and body parts there were traumatic overtones. Likewise, the implied nightclub stage of the *SNL* set, before a live audience, carried connotations of incisive comedic pioneers such as Lenny Bruce and Mort Sahl. By contrast, the televised American home and hearth had always reflected, even at its most troubling, a series of domestic struggles to be resolved between a patient dad, a wise mom and – for the most part – wholesome, dutiful children (as in the 1950s and 60s classics *Leave It to Beaver*, *My Three Sons* and *The Donna Reed Show*). For this reason, one of the most popular sitcoms of the 1970s, Norman Lear's *All in the Family*, deserves attention for its conflicting departures from, and homage to, such domestic precedents. Adapted from the British series, *Till Death Us Do Part*, *All in the Family* rarely moved beyond the environs of a blue-collar family's sitting room and kitchen. Few shows in the 1970s were so successful in presenting the American family and the home front as a domestic battleground, contrapuntal to the turmoil on the military battlefields across the Pacific. Like *M*A*S*H*, *All in the Family* represented what David Marc, in a chapter title, calls 'the Sitcom at Literate Peak'.[21] Like *M*A*S*H*, too, it had to walk a tightrope between subversion and evasion, critique and 'harmless entertainment', for as Peter N. Carroll notes, 'it commanded the top advertising dollar in the industry – $128,000 for one minute'.[22] At the height of its success, *All in the Family* found itself in the *Guinness Book of World Records* as the most widely viewed television show to date.

All in the Family (1971–9)

Originally commissioned to film a pilot for the ABC network (which subsequently backed away from the project), producer Norman Lear encountered cold feet all around. His initial choice for the lead role, the veteran actor Mickey Rooney, refused, saying: 'If you go on the air with that, they're going to kill you dead in the streets.'[23] The project was taken up by a very nervous CBS network, as Ozersky describes:

> Finally, at 9.30 p.m. on the evening of 12 January 1971, just before the show was to air, a disembodied voice informed viewers, in the solemn tones usually reserved for tests of the Emergency Broadcast System: 'The

program you are about to see is *All in the Family*. It seeks to throw a humorous spotlight on our frailties, prejudices and concerns. By making them the source of laughter, we hope to show – in a mature fashion – just how absurd they are.'[24]

In place of Mickey Rooney, *All in the Family* starred Carroll O'Connor as the irascible, highly bigoted blue-collar reactionary, Archie Bunker; Jean Stapleton as his apparently slow-witted wife, Edith; Rob Reiner as his left-leaning Polish-American son-in-law, Mike (habitually called 'Meathead' by Archie), and Archie's golden girl of a daughter, Gloria (Sally Struthers). Lear's idea – largely successful – was to contain in this one family the major cross-generational and cross-gender tensions arising from the most crucial issues facing American society: race, feminism, sexuality, United States militarism, labour and the state of the economy. Thus, within the nominally comforting frame of the American family, the individuals could snap, snarl and challenge one another over a host of positions, prompting a weekly crisis that would normally be resolved at the end of each instalment. As James B. Gilbert summarises it:

Each week Archie Bunker denounced some minority or liberal cause. In each episode, he lost (temporarily) in a struggle of values with his instinctively liberal wife. Yet the following week he returned to test new prejudices. Like the enormously popular daytime soap operas, *All in the Family* exposed the deepest problems of society, but never hoped to ameliorate them.[25]

All in the Family's critical potential lay not only in its engagement with a range of contemporary domestic issues that *M*A*S*H* was in no position to touch, but also through its mildly envelope-pushing use of language. To Archie Bunker, gays were 'fruits', 'pansies' and 'fags'; his son-in-law was not only a 'meathead' but a 'dumb Polack'; Jews were 'hebes', African Americans were 'spades' and Puerto Ricans were 'spics'. As Gerard Jones notes:

Network, producers, and advertisers braced themselves for protests from the Bible Belt, from the self-appointed guardians of good taste, from conservatives offended at being ridiculed. But the only serious protests came instead from old-line liberals. Laura Z. Hobson, author of the anti-anti-Semitic *Gentleman's Agreement*, took the show to task in the *New York Times* for making racism acceptable by placing it within an affectionately humorous context. She thought the scripts were particularly dishonest in playing at racial epithets without going all the way: *Hebe* and *jungle bunny* were quaint, almost funny; *kike* and *nigger* never passed Archie's lips.[26]

Indeed, as Thomas Alan Holmes observes, Alf Garnett, 'Archie Bunker's bigoted prototype in *Till Death Us Do Part*, could freely use even more derogatory racial slurs than American television would permit.'[27] The programme's strategy of engagement and evasion is encapsulated, for instance, in an episode in which the Bunker family is improbably visited by the actor and singer, Sammy Davis Jr, playing himself:

ARCHIE Now, if you look at me, do you figure me for the prejudiced kind?

DAVIS You? *Prejudiced*? Look, if you were *prejudiced*, Archie, when I came into your house, you would have called me a coon or a nigger. But you didn't say that. I heard you clear as a bell: right straight out, you said 'colored'.[28]

Archie is, of course, impervious to Davis's irony, just as he is unaware that his black neighbour, George Jefferson – who parries Archie's bigoted insinuations with dry, sardonic wit – is the 'more successful American' of the two.[29] As Ozersky argues: 'That Archie *never* learns his lesson is the source of his great iconic power. He was the Sisyphus of the hard hats, constantly attempting to roll Meathead, Gloria, Edith, Norman Lear, his neighbors, the scriptwriters, and the political climate of the 1960s generally back up the hill of vanished time.'[30]

The show's critical potential, as was the case with *M*A*S*H*, was often compromised by a problematic reception. As Carroll observes:

Whether Archie was legitimizing racism or betraying its idiocy . . . became a moot issue because of the passive nature of the television audience. The content of the programming, researchers discovered, seldom altered spectator opinion. Rather, through a process called 'selective perception', viewers found reinforcement for their personal preconceptions. With 40 million people watching the show each week, *All in the Family* apparently offered something for everyone.[31]

Hence the dismay of the liberal actor, Carroll O'Connor, at being frequently slapped on the back and congratulated in public by American bigots for appearing to champion their prejudices.

Nonetheless, *All in the Family* did what few other situation comedies of the decade set out to achieve: it forced American viewers to confront the very issues that network television comedy in general sought to avoid. For this reason, it may be 'emblematic', as Stephen Paul Miller says, that

in the mid-seventies, *All in the Family* was replaced as the number one television programme, a position it had occupied throughout most of the early seventies, by *Happy Days*. A critical nostalgia for a pre-sixties [signified by the *All in the Family* theme song, 'Those Were the Days'] gave way to the fantasy of one.[32]

Sitcoms and Race

In spite of Archie Bunker's explicit appeal to nostalgia as a critical stance, *All in the Family* did generate considerable creative energy, not least in its spin-off, *The Jeffersons* (1975–85). This series focused on George Jefferson and his wife Louise, who achieve an upward mobility never offered to (or actively sought by) Archie – at least, not until

Figure 2.2 Sammy Davis Jr and Carroll O' Connor in *All in the Family* (1972).
© Bettmann/CORBIS.

Archie's transformation from blue-collar wage-slave to proud owner of a local bar for a subsequent series called *Archie Bunker's Place* (1979–83). As *The Jeffersons'* theme song chants in a gospel-like frenzy, George and Louise (and implicitly any black American family) can 'move on up' to a de luxe high-rise in a middle-class neighbourhood – this at a time when gentrification policies in American cities had already resulted in an underclass of displaced, usually non-white families unable to afford the new house prices and increased property taxes in their own neighbourhoods.[33] In escaping from Archie Bunker's white, blue-collar taunts, both class and race based, the Jeffersons appear to be escaping from American racism itself, a feat not so easily matched beyond the frame of the small screen.

The same might be said of the decade's other programme openly adapted from a British serial, *Sanford and Son* (1972–7), based on the format of *Steptoe and Son*. Driven, like its British predecessor, by the dynamics of generational conflict, *Sanford and Son* replaced the white cockney ne'er-do-wells with a black junk dealer (played by comedian Redd Foxx) and his son (Demond Wilson). While, on the meta-level,

Sanford and Son (like *The Jeffersons*) signalled an advance in terms of its foregrounding of black actors and characters, it shied away from critical engagement with race, if anything reinforcing stereotypical comedic images of black men as lazy, shiftless and lecherous (in Fred Sanford's case, feebly offset by the exasperation of his strait-laced, straight man of a son). In spite of such lapses, however, as Fiske argues, 'the fact that racial minorities are treated more favourably in the symbolic world of television than in society may indicate that the liberal desire to integrate them socially is ahead of the social fact, and that television is playing an active role in this ongoing social change'.[34]

Television historian Marc Weingarten suggests that, in terms of programming and casting, there was significant irony in the fact that 'sticking to a middle-of-the-road game plan in the 1970s also meant sticking with mostly white performers', although 'more black people were watching television in the mid-1970s than whites'.[35] But black-dominated shows such as *The Jeffersons* and *Sanford and Son* may well have been playing more to white viewers than to black ones, perhaps confirming Hamamoto's perception of such situation comedies as the products of 'nervous laughter' emanating from a (largely white) 'liberal democratic ideology'.[36] After all, as Weingarten observes:

> In 1974, TV ratings company A. C. Nielsen published a study that determined more black viewers viewed TV during off-peak hours, and that one of the highest-rated shows among blacks in major cities like Washington and Cleveland was *Soul Train*, the syndicated dance show that imported urban street style to suburban America.[37]

A revealing example caricaturing liberal white neurosis and 'nervous laughter' (as well as some of the decade's most popular soap operas) was Norman Lear's third major series, *Mary Hartman, Mary Hartman*, which propelled white middle-class depression and psycho-babble to the top of the bicentennial year's viewing ratings. As though acting in concert with the Marin County crazies in Cyra McFadden's *The Serial*, Mary Hartman (played by Louise Lasser) tapped into most of the Me-centred white movements of the decade, from Arica to Zen.

Like Lear's previous programmes, *Mary Hartman, Mary Hartman* brought to the fore the problematics of the network television serial as a vehicle for social criticism. Arguably, the most dramatic moments on American television in the 1970s did not occur within relatively long-running serials but rather in extended mini-series drawing on historical fact and fiction. A twelve-part adaptation of James Michener's sweeping

Western chronicle, *Centennial* (1974), ran with great popularity in 1978–9; Taylor Caldwell's *Captains and the Kings* (1972) was broadcast as a series in 1976; and two titles from John Jakes's 'Kent Family Chronicles' or 'Bicentennial Series' (1974–9) set in the Colonial and Revolutionary period were adapted for television: *The Bastard* (1978) and *The Rebels* (1979). Broadly speaking, these adaptations were all bound up in the historical passions coalescing in the nation's bicentennial fever. Importantly, however, two special broadcasts addressed not the official history of the Founding Fathers – white men all – but rather the oral histories (as first transmitted through literature) of black Americans, fictional and historical.

African America, the TV Movie and the Mini-series

In 1974, CBS broadcast the 'TV movie', *The Autobiography of Miss Jane Pittman*, based on Ernest J. Gaines's 1971 novel of the same name. Played by Cicely Tyson, the eponymous main character, born into slavery, celebrates her one-hundred-and-tenth birthday in 1962 Louisiana and is interviewed by a northern journalist. 'How far back do you want to go?' she challenges him. 'To the end of the war? I can do that.' Thus, largely through flashbacks going back to the Civil War, Jane Pittman is in a position to make trenchant connections between Emancipation, Reconstruction, the post-Reconstruction racial backlash and the civil rights movement of the 1960s. Graphic lynchings and other murders, the exploitation of black sharecroppers and the crusade for black education in the South all form a series of episodes culminating in the aged Jane Pittman's final defiant gesture (in an obvious reference to Rosa Parks): drinking from a 'White Only' water fountain in the face of bull-necked Southern sheriffs.[38] With its direct appeal to the mystique of oral history, *The Autobiography of Miss Jane Pittman* belies the fact that it is based on a fictional work. As Gaines recalled:

> I've read several reviews in which critics have called Miss Jane a real person. A representative of *Newsweek* asked me to send the editors of the magazine a picture of Miss Jane Pittman to be used with a review of the novel . . . One lady accused me of using a tape recorder, then calling the interview a novel after I had cut out all the inconsequential material.[39]

Clearly the public passion for oral history had turned this fictional work and the film based upon it into signal expressions of the bicentennial decade.

On the other side of the bicentennial, in 1977, the ABC network aired what must by any accounts be the major television event of the decade, the mini-series, *Roots*, which, as Bruce J. Schulman notes, drew what was at that time 'the largest audience in television history. More than half the population of the United States, 130 million Americans, watched at least some part of the eight-night miniseries.'[40] Based on Alex Haley's best-selling history of his own family, *Roots* takes the viewer back through the generations to the tale of Haley's ancestor, Kunte Kinte, captured in the Gambia in 1750 and transported to an American plantation. As Carroll observes, the television broadcast of *Roots* not only increased the sales of Haley's book by 'sixty-seven thousand copies in one day, over nine hundred thousand in a single month', but it also 'revealed a burgeoning enthusiasm for American history that had been building since the beginning of the decade':

> Stimulated first by the commercialization of nostalgia – reruns, trivia contests, fifties fads – then by the politically mandated Bicentennial, which fostered over sixty-four thousand community projects and activities, Americans eagerly celebrated the national past as mass entertainment ... Such passions disturbed academic historians, who were concerned not only with declining classroom enrolments, but also with what they considered the trivialization of the past.[41]

It is true, as Carroll notes, that the *Roots* phenomenon proved a convenient hook upon which corporations could hang their wares; he points to the Continental Trailways coach advertisement, 'TAKE OUR ROUTES TO YOUR ROOTS', and Pan American Airlines' 'Two Heritage' marketing strategy, with its commercials proclaiming: 'All of us come from somewhere else.'[42] It would be wrong, however, to deny the impact of *Roots* on African American consciousness in the 1970s.[43]

As examples like *The Autobiography of Miss Jane Pittman* and *Roots* indicate, there is – and remains – great dramatic potential in fictionalised renderings of American history. But if the 1970s showed anything, there was equally dramatic potential in the broadcast of current events which, as they unfolded, secured their place in history. In this regard, the televised Watergate hearings of 1973–4 proved to be one of the decade's greatest unmissable daytime television events, a subject of rapidly unfolding drama and farce.

That Watergate Show

The Watergate hearings certainly had their stars, some of whom went on to build lucrative careers in commercial endorsement, such as the chairman of the Senate Watergate Committee, North Carolina Senator Sam Ervin, who, after the hearings, could be seen on television adverts as a 'plain old country lawyer' hawking credit cards and other products. The Watergate planners, burglars and cover-up operatives – Gordon Liddy, Attorney General John Mitchell, Nixon aides Bob Haldeman, John Erlichman and Chuck Colson – were the villains of the season; the President's Special Counsel, John Dean, was the key dramatic witness, turning state's evidence, while his radiant, blonde wife, Maureen, attracted frequent camera time for her glamour and her poise. While Vice President Spiro Agnew made a public show of ridiculing the Watergate hearings as a beauty pageant or a cheap courtroom drama with less substance than a *Perry Mason* episode, no televised public proceedings had so captured the attention of the nation since Senator Joseph McCarthy was brought down before the cameras in the Army–McCarthy hearings of 1954. As Carroll reasons:

> Television news lacked the investigatory capacity of the press. But in broadcasting plain two-dimensional symbols, the cameras crystallized a political style that communicated more information about the procedures and policies of government than all the arcane, devious vocabulary of the witnesses . . . In all the hours of testimony, the multitude of events and names and transactions became hopelessly entangled in charges and countercharges, admissions and denials. All these convulsions of government translated through television into a raucous carnival of political corruption.[44]

While the implicit chief defendant, President Nixon, never appeared at the hearings (and, in fact, did all he could to make himself invisible in relation to them), he, too, seized on the power of television for the two most salient and dramatic events of the whole scandal. On 19 April 1974, he secured the major network airwaves to reaffirm his innocence, to declare that he had 'nothing to hide' and to release 1,000-plus pages of highly edited transcripts of his Oval Office tape recordings (instead of the tapes themselves, which the Senate committee had subpoenaed). The tapes, with their infamous eighteen-minute gap, eventually proved to be the smoking gun that firmly linked Nixon to the Watergate cover-up and the obstruction of justice. This ultimately led to his other most dramatic command of the airwaves when, on 8 August 1974, he proclaimed that he had 'never been a quitter' before announcing that the following day at the stroke of noon he would quit the presidency.

In spite of the predominantly turgid testimony of details and legal minutiae, the public appetite for the more dramatic moments of the Watergate proceedings seemed to validate Daniel Bell's rueful mid-decade observation that 'contemporary culture' had become 'a visual culture rather than a print culture', with sobering implications for the understanding of current affairs:

> There are real consequences for the coherence of a culture in the relative weights of print and the visual in the formation of knowledge. The print media allow for self-pacing and dialogue in comprehending an argument or in reflecting on an image. Print not only emphasizes the cognitive and the symbolic but is also, most importantly, the necessary mode for conceptual thought. The visual media – I mean here film and television – impose their pace on the viewer and, in emphasizing images rather than words, invite not conceptualization but dramatization.[45]

Hence the memorable tendency of the cameras to cut to reaction shots in the midst of the Watergate proceedings – to Maureen Dean in hopes of catching a departure from her usual stoicism, to the rising eyebrows and comically jiggling jowls of Sam Ervin and to the uncomfortable Nixon aides as they gulped, sweated and shifted from buttock to buttock in their chairs.

None of this is to say that television totally eclipsed the print media in the unfolding of the Watergate scandal; after all, the scandal itself had begun with one of the greatest coups of the print media, the publication in the *New York Times* of what came to be known as the *Pentagon Papers*, the top-secret documents smuggled out of the Defense Department by Daniel Ellsberg, proving that the United States Government had consistently perjured itself before the public throughout the Vietnam War. It was the publication of the *Pentagon Papers* in regular instalments beginning on 13 June 1971 that first prompted the Watergate burglars to break into the offices of Ellsberg's psychiatrist, as well as the Democratic National Committee headquarters, in their search for damaging information. It was two journalists for the *Washington Post*, Bob Woodward and Carl Bernstein, whose investigative reporting uncovered the trail which led from the burglary to the Oval Office, and which in turn led to the televised hearings. It might also be argued that it was the *Doonesbury* cartoons

of Garry Trudeau that helped to tip the balance of public opinion
against Nixon, John Mitchell and other guilty parties. But, just as the
signal moment of the Army–McCarthy hearings in 1954 had been
Joseph Welch's magisterial excoriation of McCarthy before the television cameras ('Have you no sense of decency, sir?') so, too, in the
Watergate hearings it was dramatically apparent that the tide had
turned against Nixon the moment the prominent Republican senator
Howard Baker demanded, 'What did the president know and when
did he know it?'[46]

Television ultimately played an incalculable part in the downfall of
Richard Nixon, surely an example of poetic justice for those in the
broadcast news media honoured with a prominent position on the
White House 'Enemies List', such as Marvin Kalb and Daniel Schorr
from CBS and Lem Tucker and Sander Vanocur from NBC. There was
also a dramatic irony in Nixon's defeat at the hands of the broadcast
media, given his own attempts to manipulate them or stifle them
throughout his presidency. Having suffered bitterly before the
cameras in his disastrous debates against the highly televisual John F.
Kennedy in 1960, Nixon had clearly learned the importance of make-
up and hairdressing by the time of his historic visit to Beijing in
February 1972, timing his arrival 'to coincide with prime-time television viewing in the United States'.[47] Nixon the globetrotting statesman
had used the television cameras to compete with anti-war protesters on
the streets of American cities and with political opponents vying for
the presidency during his 1972 re-election campaign. When he had
not been able to use the cameras to his advantage, he tried effectively
to shut them down, for instance during his imposition of a news
embargo in the wake of his illegal bombing campaign in Laos in
February 1971.

Watergate has often been described in terms borrowed from the
theatre – 'farce', 'burlesque' or, as Nixon himself described it in the
'smoking gun' tape of 23 June 1972, 'a comedy of errors'.[48] If, indeed,
the Watergate hearings reflect a blurring of the boundary between the
public stage and the small screen, a similar blurring is evident in the
relationship between the public stage and the dramatic stage. In this,
the theatre of the 1970s demands scrutiny as a reflection of the dramatic events unfolding on the political and social stages as well as
within the psyches of individual Americans. The decade's drama is particularly important for its relatively uninhibited expression in contrast
to the corporate and political muzzling that silenced so much in 1970s
television.

1970s Drama: 'An Unspecified Locality'

The theatre of the 1970s stylised the turmoil of individual psyche, street and family to produce some of the most vibrant, assertive and disturbing dramatic productions of any American decade. These productions stand in stark contrast not only to contemporary television, but also to the elaborate, glittering musicals that evoke recollections of Broadway in the 1970s, such as George Furth and Stephen Sondheim's *Company* (1970), Marvin Hamlisch and colleagues' *A Chorus Line* (1975) and Charlie Smalls and William F. Brown's reworking of *The Wizard of Oz* as a hip African American fantasy, *The Wiz* (1975). It was on the smaller, darker dramatic stages where the great individual and social battles of the 1970s – sexuality, gender, ethnicity, politics – were exposed and examined through a visceral burst of theatrical experimentation.

As Christopher Bigsby observes, there is a tendency for the decade's plays to situate themselves in ' "an unspecified locality" – that well-known pull-in for so many playwrights of the 1970s'.[49] This may well be an indication of the extent to which the major concerns of 1970s playwrights were inwardly rather than externally focused, more fixed on personal identity than on public history. Susan Harris Smith notes the call from the journalist, James Reston, in the immediate aftermath of the American withdrawal from Saigon, for 'a non-realistic dramatization of the effects of the Vietnam War':

'The modern playwright becomes more important than the historian, for in no other war of our history was the private word more important than the public pronouncements.' . . . Because Vietnam vets are tortured by internal conflicts that the voices of soothing denial threaten to drown out, the internal conflicts 'are the stuff of the stage . . . Its tools are beyond those of the historian and the journalist, for the stage is at home with the interior of things.'[50]

This is not to say that external, public conflict was not at all a concern of 1970s playwrights. On the contrary, David Krasner interprets the drama of the decade, particularly the latter half, as a collective 'expression of rage . . . growing out of the social conditions'.[51] For this reason it is curious to read Marcia Segal's revue of Bill T. Jones's AIDS-defying dance performance of 1994, *Still/Here*, in which she identifies 'a sort of 1970s positivism, an almost poignant faith that supportive friends and self-awareness can help even those who are imperilled to live bravely'.[52] It is a curious claim because 1970s drama dwelt as much upon social exclusion, isolation and exhaustion as upon solidarity and faith. Yet, it is true that even the most troubling social depictions were wrought through the momentous creative energy and vision that characterised the work of the decade's great experimental companies such as Chicago's Steppenwolf Theatre company, founded by Gary Sinese, Jeff Perry and Terry Kinney in 1974, the Asian American Theater Workshop, established by the playwright Frank Chin and his colleagues in San Francisco in 1973 and the Negro Ensemble Company of New York, founded in 1967 and by the mid-seventies the major forum for African American theatre.

Given the turmoil of militant identity marking in the 1970s, it is not surprising that the decade's most visceral theatre should provide a markedly energetic contrast to the diminished characterisations by American dramatists who, though still writing in the 1970s, seemed to be uttering the last gasps of a closing era, for instance Tennessee Williams and Arthur Miller. Susan Abbotson singles out the 'seamy group of derelicts' peopling Williams's *Small Craft Warnings* (1972) and 'the spiritually and physically dying' characters in his *Vieux Carré* (1977) as indications of an exhausted approach to American life.[53] As Bigsby argues, the early years of the decade seemed to pit Williams against the changing tides of representation, with the 'overt sexuality' of *Small Craft Warnings* 'designed to underscore the pathos of the characters', in contrast with the use of sexuality 'as a symbol of freedom and communality' by the decade's younger playwrights.[54] Similarly, Bigsby detects a certain evasiveness in Arthur Miller's engagement with America in the 1970s: 'Miller never wrote a play about Vietnam or the America so at odds with itself in the 1970s, unless it be *The Archbishop's Ceiling* which could perhaps be regarded as a response to the confusions and ambiguities of Watergate transposed to an East European setting.'[55]

With some justification, Krasner sees as the decade's 'representative play' David Mamet's *American Buffalo* (1975).[56] The Chicago-based playwright in fact produced a series of plays in the decade engaging with miscommunication, aspiration and failure in American life, profoundly evoking the darkness beneath the bicentennial glitter through characters who alternate between fever-pitched rage and whimpering despair. Rather than focusing on a single play, it is most useful to explore Mamet's seventies plays as an internally related body of work.

David Mamet

There is a strain of Mamet criticism arguing that the playwright was react-ing against the arrival of a host of negative tendencies in the aftermath of the 1960s, the great 'urgencies' of which decade 'seemed to have been put to one side', marking a general 'move from the public to the private realm'.[57] This implicit identification of the seventies as 'the Me Decade' has particularly centred, in Mamet criticism, upon sex:

> The 'Swinging Sixties' had come and gone and, in their place, was a cynical, rather detached society that plundered the most negative aspects of the pre-vious decade's sexual revolution, emphasising promiscuity and irresponsi-bility to the detriment of emotional sanity . . . Such an emphasis upon the nonemotional aspects of sexuality was bound, sooner or later, to result in a deleterious blunting of the nation's consciousness.[58]

While much of Mamet's writing might, indeed, seem to validate the worst assessments of the seventies by the likes of Daniel Bell, Christopher Lasch and Tom Wolfe (among others), his plays engage with a national malaise grounded further back in history. As the 'Soapbox Speaker' from the play *The Water Engine* (1977) muses, ostensibly in the 1930s but, for the theatre audience, in the immediate afterglow of the bicentennial hype:

> What happened to this nation? Or did it ever exist? . . . [D]id it exist with its freedoms and slogans . . . the buntings, the gold-headed standards, the songs. With Equality, Liberty . . . In the West they plow under wheat. Where is America? I say it does not exist. And I say that it never existed. It was all but a myth. A great dream of avarice . . . The dream of a Gentleman Farmer.[59]

America's 'malevolent destiny as the New World', as the Soapbox Speaker calls it (313), is driven by a variety of factors, at the forefront of which is venal, naked commercialism. Mamet's engagement with this cor-ruption is not restricted to his 1970s plays; indeed, it is at the centre of what is arguably his most renowned play alongside *Oleanna* (1993), *Glengarry Glen Ross* (1984). In the 1970s, however, he attacked commercial corrup-tion both in *The Water Engine*, in which an inventor is murdered for his patent of a hydrogen-fuelled engine, and in his mid-decade masterpiece, *American Buffalo* (1975), in which two junk-dealing thieves lapse into a per-verse (if plausible) reading of the Declaration of Independence:

TEACH You know what is free enterprise?
DON No. What?
TEACH The freedom . . .
DON . . . yeah?
TEACH Of the *Individual* . . .
DON . . . yeah?
TEACH To Embark on Any Fucking Course that he sees fit.
DON Uh-huh . . .

TEACH In order to secure his honest chance to make a profit. Am I so out
  of line on this?
DON No.
TEACH Does this make me a Commie?
DON No.
TEACH The country's founded on this, Don. You know this. (220–1)

If Mamet is to be believed, such observations and renderings are not
meant to spur on a social reformation. 'It's not the dramatist's job to bring
about social change,' he argued. 'The purpose of art is not to change but
to delight. I don't think its purpose is to enlighten us. I don't think it's to
change us. I don't think it's to teach us.'[60] Many critics – and not only feminists – would raise an eyebrow at the 'delight' that might be obtained from
the crude and misogynist dialogue with which Mamet invests such characters as Bernie in *Sexual Perversity in Chicago* (1974), whose true colours
show when his chat-up lines in a bar are rebuffed:

> So just who the fuck do you think you are, God's gift to Women? I mean
> where do you fucking get off with this shit. You don't want to get come on to,
> go enrol in a convent. You think I don't have better things to do? I don't have
> better ways to spend my off hours than to listen to some nowhere cunt try
> out cute bits on me? I mean why don't you just clean your fucking act up,
> Missy. You're living in a city in 1976. (56–7)

Carla McDonough notes that the highly stylised misogyny in Mamet's plays
grows out of a profound identity crisis among American males linked to the
very social and economic structures which the playwright says he is not in
the business of challenging:

> Although many of his men-at-work plays have been read as critique and
> exposure of the dirty side of business, of the failure of the American dream,
> and of the cutthroat nature of capitalism, all of these issues ultimately explore
> certain expectations about manhood. More than anything else, characters
> such as Teach, Edmund [in *Edmund* (1982)] and Levine [in *Glengarry Glen
> Ross*] are concerned with their identities as men. They are driven by a sense
> of powerlessness for which they seek to overcompensate, and they labor
> under a need to establish their identities in the face of real or imagined chal-
> lenges to their manhood.[61]

Thus, to some degree, Mamet's woman-haters are reflections of a particular period in American history, as they find themselves stranded, in
McDonough's words, 'in a patriarchy that is under revision'.[62]
  However, critics also suggest that Mamet is concerned with predica-
ments that transcend the immediately topical or historical: the existential
absurdity and disconnection that preoccupy his contemporaries and predecessors such as Pinter, Beckett and Ionesco. Hence the reflections of
the two park-bench bookends in *Duck Variations* (1971):

> GEORGE . . . The battle between the two is as old as time. The ducks
>   propagating, the Herons eating them. The Herons multiplying and

losing great numbers to exhaustion in the never-ending chase of the duck. Each keeping the other in check, down through history, until a bond of unspoken friendship and respect unites them, even in the embrace of death.

EMIL So why do they continue to fight?

GEORGE Survival of the fittest. The never-ending struggle between heredity and environment. The urge to combat. Old as the oceans. Instilled in us all: Who can say to what purpose? (11)

Such expressions of transcendental absurdity are located across the span of Mamet's seventies plays – in *American Buffalo*:

TEACH *picks up the dead-pig sticker and starts trashing the junkshop.*
The Whole Entire World.
There Is No Law.
There Is No Right And Wrong.
The World Is Lies.
There Is No Friendship.
Every Fucking Thing.
Pause.
Every God-forsaken Thing.
DON Calm down, Walt.
TEACH We all live like the cavemen. (253–4)

– and in *Sexual Perversity in Chicago*:

Bernard's apartment. Bernard is seated in front of the television at three in the morning.
TV When you wish upon a star, makes no difference who you are. If, on the other hand, you apply for a personal loan, all sorts of circumstantial evidence is required. I wonder if any mathematician has done serious research on the efficacy [*sic*] of prayer. For example: you're walking down the street thinking 'God, if I don't get laid tonight, I don't know *what* all!' (A common form of prayer) And all of a sudden, WHAM! [*Pause.*] Perhaps you'd get laid, or perhaps you get hit by a cab, or perhaps you meet the man or woman of your persuasion. But the prayer is uttered – yes it is – solely as a lamentation, and with no real belief in its causal properties. (59)

As Anne Dean notes, Mamet's characters 'occasionally glimpse the possibility of something other than the tawdry lives they endure, but these momentary revelations have no chance of taking root in the febrile atmosphere in which they exist'.[63] One of the greatest barriers to their health and psychic development is their subjugation to language, something which also transcends the particulars of their decade. As Johan Callens observes, Mamet's characters 'try to use language to contain and control their experiences but . . . they are more often the products of language than its confident users'.[64] This predicament is most immediately demonstrated in *Sexual Perversity in Chicago* in which language is both implicitly and explicitly the subject of discourse between men and women. In that play, the dialogue between Danny and Deborah is initially confident in its presentation of human mastery over language:

DANNY I love you.
DEBORAH Does it frighten you to say that?
DANNY Yes.
DEBORAH It's only words. I don't think you should be frightened by words. (74)

Yet within a few moments onstage, language reveals itself in all its terrifying potential to block communication and to sow discord between individuals and genders:

DANNY Cunt.
DEBORAH That's very good. 'Cunt', good. Get it out. Let it all out.
DANNY You cunt.
DEBORAH We've established that.
DANNY I try.
DEBORAH You try and try. You are misunderstood and depressed.
DANNY And you're no help.
DEBORAH No, I'm a hindrance. You're trying to understand women and I'm confusing you with information. 'Cunt' won't do it. 'Fuck' won't do it. No more magic. What are you *feeling*. Tell me what you're *feeling*. Jerk. (88)

As Toby Silverman Zinman argues, 'language – especially the language of value, of what is worthwhile – fails' Mamet's characters.[65] This crisis, identified and explored so trenchantly by Mamet in the 1970s, was taken to its extreme two decades later in *Oleanna*, in which – for the first time – miscommunication between the sexes gives way to outright physical violence, with troubling reactions. Marc Silverstein describes a common audience response to the beating of a female student by her male professor in the play:

Never before has Mamet allowed the verbal aggression his male characters direct toward women express itself in terms of brutal physical violence, and never before has his audience (both men *and* women) shown itself so ready to embrace this misogyny. The beating is often accompanied by applause, cheers, and quite audible exclamations of encouragement to the professor.[66]

Oleanna reflects the extremity of the linguistic stonewall identified by McDonough with respect to Mamet's earlier plays: 'The possibilities, the positions available to Mamet's male characters are as reductive as their language.'[67] Perhaps this is why only the faintest glimmer of hope is offered in the rendering of the character who is arguably the most resilient, articulate and confident of Mamet's 1970s characters, the Cleaning Woman of *Squirrels* (1974):

ART [*pause*] You know, sometimes I feel that you exceed the prescribed bounds of your operation.

> CLEANING WOMAN Well, you could be right.
> ART I feel I *am* right.
> CLEANING WOMAN Well, can I tell you something?
> ART Yes, please do.
> CLEANING WOMAN Nothing is more important than that. [*EXITS.*] (123)

> Mamet's 1970s plays are among the most disturbing and challenging by any American dramatist, inaugurating what Bigsby calls 'a career that would astonish in both its range and depth'.[68] As other examples from the period show, similar careers were being forged in the drama of the same decade.

Other Dramatic Emergenc(i)es

Other male playwrights of the seventies shared with Mamet the dramatic territory on which, in Luther S. Leudtke's words, 'the fragmentation, the alienation, the pure atomic activity of the society' was played out.[69] Engaging forcefully with questions of mythic potency – particularly but not exclusively concerning the American West – Sam Shepard tapped into a variety of cultural sources, from westerns to rock and roll, to explore the dynamics of the American family, the predations of the economy and the enduring trap of violence. Plays such as *Cowboy Mouth* (1971), which he co-wrote with the punk song-writer Patti Smith, *Tooth of Crime* (1972), *Suicide in B Flat* (1976) and his two major works of the decade – *Curse of the Starving Class* and the Pulitzer Prize-winning *Buried Child* (both 1978) – place Shepard on a par with Mamet in terms of dramatic importance.

John Guare's plays – *House of Blue Leaves* (1970), *Rich and Famous* (1976), *Landscape of the Body* (1977) and *Bosoms and Neglect* (1979) – experiment with issues of urban American life and racial and generational conflict that would later feed into the playwright's best-known work, *Six Degrees of Separation* (1990). Militarism, male crises, drugs, sex, violence, isolation and rootlessness inform the work of Vietnam veteran David Rabe in such plays as *Sticks and Bones* (1971), *The Basic Training of Pavlo Hummel* (1971), *In the Boom Boom Boom* (1974) and *Streamers* (1976). From the Midwest came Lanford Wilson, with a series of plays often based on the centrifugal and centripetal dynamics of the family – *Lemon Sky* (1970), *Serenading Louie* (1970), *Hot L Baltimore* (1973) and *The Mound Builders* (1975) – as well as the first two plays of his great Talley family trilogy, *Fifth of July* (1978) and *Talley's Folly* (1979), the latter of which won the Pulitzer Prize. The decade also saw the comic and dramatic consolidation of the plays of Terrence McNally, known not only for his explorations of heterosexuality but also as one of the first playwrights to engage with the identity crises and victories of gay men in pre-and post-AIDS America. For this reason, *The Ritz* (1974), a comedy set in a gay bathouse, stands out as McNally's most important play of the 1970s.

In spite of the overwhelming focus on such alpha males as Mamet and Shepard in studies of 1970s drama, the vibrant fellowship of women playwrights must be considered as a corollary to the feminist activism in American society at large. In 1972, six women dramatists – Adrienne Kennedy, Rochelle Owens, Megan Terry, Julie Bovasso, Maria Irene Fornes and Rosalyn Drexler – formed the Women's Theater Council with the professed aim of challenging the male dominance of the dramatic stage.[70] Southern playwright Marsha Norman made her mark in 1977 with *Getting Out*, portraying the struggles of Arlene, a young woman newly released from prison, while fellow Southerner Beth Henley wrote *Crimes of the Heart* (1978), a Gothic tragicomedy of three Mississippi sisters, and another Pulitzer winner. Perhaps the decade's greatest dramatic expression of female solidarity was Ntozake Shange's 'choreopoem', *for colored girls who have considered suicide/when the rainbow is enuf* (1975). Shange drew on the political nexus of sisterhood and black consciousness in a highly experimental fusion of poetry, music, dance and stagecraft:

> *lady in brown*
> i'm outside chicago
> *lady in yellow*
> i'm outside detroit
> *lady in purple*
> i'm outside houston
> *lady in red*
> i'm outside baltimore
> *lady in green*
> i'm outside san francisco
> *lady in blue*
> i'm outside manhattan
> *lady in orange*
> i'm outside st. louis
> *lady in brown*
> & this is for colored girls who have considered suicide
> but moved to the ends of their own rainbows.[71]

Shange's affirmative work feeds into the broader assertions of African American theatre which, like feminist theatre, offered a dramatic parallel to political and social activism at large. Erroll Hill and James Hatch have noted the emerging importance of 'ritual theatre' in 1970s African American drama, initially in universities where 'black studies' had an impact upon theatre departments to encourage 'evocations of Mother Africa through costumes and drums'.[72] Militant playwrights such as Amiri Baraka, Ed Bullins and Larry Neal, central figures of the Black Arts Movement of the 1960s and 1970s, fiercely politicised both the page and the stage. The Black Cultural Nationalist hold on Baraka's work, so prominent in such early plays as *Dutchman* and *The Slave* (both 1964), relaxed in the 1970s as Baraka turned to the class-struggle focus of Third-World Marxism–Leninism; hence such give-away titles as *The Motion of History* (1975) and *What Was the Relationship of the Lone Ranger to the Means of Production?* (1976). Bullins, briefly the cultural director of the Black Panthers in San Francisco, had already enjoyed an established theatrical reputation in the 1960s with *Clara's Old Man* (1965), *A Son, Come Home* (1968) and *The Electronic Nigger* (1968). His militant 1970s plays, collected together under the highly significant titles, *Four Dynamite Plays* (1971) and *The Theme Is Blackness* (1972), include such important examples as *The Duplex* (1970) and *It Bees Dat Way* (1970). Neal who, with Baraka, had founded the Black Arts Repertory Theatre/School in Harlem, was best known for his criticism and poetry; but he produced one major play in the 1970s, *The Glorious Monster in the Bell of the Horn* (1976) which, as Mae Henderson notes, establishes Neal's 'Black Aesthetic' through the conjoining of 'Western and non-Western mythology, legends, and folklore to shape an Afro-American cosmology and perspective'.[73]

The efforts and energy of Shange, Baraka, Bullins and Neal, resulting in more or less high-profile work, were matched by what Samuel Hay calls 'a new form of revolutionary theatre', namely the 'poetry shows' of Southern urban troupes like the BLKARTSOUTH Poets and the Sudan Poets of Houston, whose drama–poetry–music–dance productions such as *The Turn of the Century: A Set for Our Rising* (1971) were picked up later in the decade by other black performance collectives including the Last Poets of New York and the Chicago-based Organization of Black American Culture.[74] Other emerging black dramatists included Joseph Walker (*The River Niger*, 1972), Philip Hayes Dean (*The Sty of the Blind Pig*, 1971), Leslie Lee (*The First Breeze of Summer*, 1975) and Paul Carter Harrison (*The Great MacDaddy*, 1974).

The explosion of African American theatre in the seventies, as Susan Harris Smith observes, was part of a larger 'resurgence in ethnic theatre in the United States . . . owing in large measure to the dominance of cultural pluralism over the melting pot'.[75] In this context, the work of Frank Chin, Janis Chan and Jeffery Chin, all founders of the Asian American Theater Workshop in San Francisco, are milestones in American dramatic history. Misha Berson cites Frank Chin's *Chickencoop Chinaman* (1972) as 'the first major play by an Asian American author', providing the 'real jumpstart' for a flowering of talent that, by the end of the decade, would include the premier work of David Henry Hwang, *FOB* (1979).[76] From the depths of Sing Sing Prison, Puerto Rican inmate Miguel Piñero wrote a play, *Short Eyes* (1972), for the prisoner's drama workshop; it catapulted him to fame when it appeared on Broadway in 1974 and won the prestigious Obie award as that year's best play. Piñero, like the BLKARTSOUTH Poets, tapped into the decade's revolutionary currents in performance poetry, co-founding the Nuyorican Poets Café as a platform for poets and actors creatively exploring Puerto Rican life in New York. The same year in which Piñero wrote *Short Eyes*, the Kiowa playwright Hanay Geiogamah led the formation of the American Indian Theater Ensemble Company (soon renamed the Native American Theater Ensemble), the country's first all-Native American repertory company. Geiogamah's first play, *Body Indian* (1972), is a bitter indictment of the same trajectory of historical injustices that, beyond the dramatic stage, had led to the formation of the American Indian Movement whose activists that year seized the headquarters of the Bureau of Indian Affairs in Washington DC, and who would go on the following year to occupy Wounded Knee in South Dakota's Pine Ridge Indian Reservation.

Thus, in the aggregate, American drama amply reflected the struggles of creative expression in the post-sixties crucible of political turmoil, anti-militarism, feminism and ethnic assertion. Relatively free from corporate and political control, dramatists were able to venture into territory that was frequently off limits to writers and producers working in network television. Similar struggles were being played out with equal contention elsewhere in the cultural arena, not least film and visual culture, the subjects of the next chapter.

Chapter 3

Film and Visual Culture

In the middle of the decade, Daniel Bell reviewed what he perceived as the sad degeneration of artistic representation. Art, he said, had strayed away from pre-twentieth-century '*mimesis*, or the interpretation of reality through imitation' which, he believed, had formerly enabled 'contemplation' and 'judgment' through 'aesthetic distance . . . to establish the necessary time and space to absorb [an object] and judge it'.[1] Now, in the 'post-industrial age', such measured, thoughtful processing was no longer possible; the developed world's culture was by now a 'mass culture' which was bound by 'the glaring fact that it is a visual culture'.[2] A visual culture, to Bell, appeared to be long in immediate impact and short on meaningful content. Unlike print, he reasoned, visual culture becomes 'rapidly depleted in the cultural sense', a depletion most readily evident in cinema,

> which, in its use of montage, goes further than any other contemporary art in the direction of 'regulating' emotion, by selecting the images, the angles of vision, the length of a single scene, and the 'synapse' of composition. This central aspect of modernity – the organization of social and aesthetic responses in terms of novelty, sensation, simultaneity, and impact – finds its major expression in the visual arts.[3]

Novelty, sensation, simultaneity, impact – these are Bell's key descriptors for the 'depleting' functions of cinema, the reigning art form of 'the world of hedonism . . . a world of make-believe in which one lives for expectations, for what will come rather than what is. And it must come without effort':

> Movies are many things – a window on the world, a set of ready-made daydreams, fantasy and projection, escapism and omnipotence – and

their emotional power is enormous. It is as a window on the world that
the movies have served, in the first instance, to transform the culture.[4]

Bell's revulsion at what he saw as the crassness of cinematic expression
was due, in part, to trends that pre-dated the 1970s but which had coalesced impressively during the decade: new technological discoveries
and the grand projects resulting from them; visual experimentations on
a mega-scale; the arrival of entrepreneurial film directors and the new,
corporate-driven concept of the 'blockbuster'.

  Bell's blanket rejection of cinema en bloc, however, obscures the
importance of cinematic developments in the 1970s which permit a
very different assessment. As David A. Cook argues, the situation of
1970s films was more complex and should rightly be viewed with more
ambivalence than Bell was prepared to give:

> Somewhere between the dumbing down of American corporate culture
> that produced the cynical young tycoons of the 'New Hollywood' and
> the remarkable aesthetic revival that produced the *auteur* directors of the
> 'Hollywood Renaissance' . . . lies a cinema of great expectations and lost
> illusions that mirrored what the historian Peter N. Carroll has called the
> 'tragedy and promise of America in the 1970s'.[5]

Cook's rather neat distinction between the intellectual and artistic corruption of the 'New Hollywood' and the integrity of the 'Hollywood
Renaissance' is somewhat misleading, as it implies a neater division of
the cinematic field than may actually have been the case.

'New Hollywood' v. 'The Hollywood Renaissance'

As Cook argues, what has come to be called the 'Hollywood
Renaissance', the auteur-driven output of films between 1967 and
1975, reflected

> a rare moment in American cinema; one that captured our society at a
> time when it literally seemed to be coming apart, but it was irretrievably
> lost to the era of the consensus-building 'super-grosser' or 'megahit' –
> the big-budget, mass- and cross-marketed blockbuster whose potential
> to drive corporate profits made it the Holy Grail of conglomerate man-
> agers and financiers.[6]

By such reasoning, the decade's least corporate-tainted auteurs would
be the likes of Bob Rafelson (*Five Easy Pieces*, 1970), Mike Nichols

(*Carnal Knowledge*, 1971), Sam Peckinpah (*Straw Dogs*, 1971), Stanley Kubrick (*A Clockwork Orange*, 1971; *Barry Lyndon*, 1975), Francis Ford Coppola (*The Godfather*, 1972; *The Conversation*, 1974; *Apocalypse Now*, 1979), Martin Scorsese (*Mean Streets*, 1973; *Taxi Driver*, 1976), Roman Polanski (*Chinatown*, 1974), Sidney Lumet (*Network*, 1976), Robert Altman (*McCabe and Mrs Miller*, 1971; *Nashville*, 1975; *Three Women*, 1977), Terence Malick (*Days of Heaven*, 1977) and Michael Cimino (*The Deer Hunter*, 1978). Perhaps in an unfair contrast – given Steven Spielberg's later works such as *Schindler's List* (1994) and *Saving Private Ryan* (1999) – the 'cynical young tycoons of the "New Hollywood"' would be a list of blockbuster directors headed by Spielberg and George Lucas, the latter of whom steered the *Star Wars* empire firmly into the present century.

Film historian Geoff King is more circumspect, however, proposing that there must be at least two versions of the 'New Hollywood', one version actually incorporating the art cinema of the 'Hollywood Renaissance' while a second version, in agreement with Cook, defines 'New Hollywood' as the territory of 'blockbusters and corporate Hollywood'.[7] A further complication with such ironclad categories (and their attendant associations) is where to place certain auteurs such as Coppola, whose unimpeachable *The Godfather*, as Cook admits, became 'the decade's first true blockbuster, which revived the flagging industry and briefly became the highest-grossing film in history'.[8]

It is thus more useful, rather than to think in terms of 'Hollywood Renaissance' versus 'New Hollywood', to turn to the output of the directors themselves. Speaking of his *Five Easy Pieces*, which championed the rebelliousness of American youth and inaugurated the decade's auteur-driven cinema, director Bob Rafelson explained: 'It became *permission*-time. Permission was granted in the '70s to behave [and] make work that, in fact, was something you were thinking about doing in the '60s, but nobody gave you permission to do . . . I'm talking about cultural permission.'[9] The 'cultural permission' conveyed by the 1970s enabled Robert Altman to begin his seventies work not only with *M*A*S*H* but also with an anti-western that targeted both American capitalism and the nobility of the mythic West associated with such earlier classics as *Stagecoach* (John Ford, 1939) and *Shane* (George Stevens, 1953). Altman's *McCabe and Mrs Miller* (1970), which ends with the protagonist (played by Warren Beatty) unheroically bleeding to death in a snowbank and his paramour (played by Julie Christie) succumbing to opium addiction, shared the foundations of other myth-debunking westerns such as Arthur Penn's

Little Big Man (1970), Ralph Nelson's *Soldier Blue* (1970) and Altman's own *Buffalo Bill and the Indians* (1976). It also paved the way for some of the decade's most significant anti-western critiques, among them Edward Sherrin's *Valdez is Coming* (1971), Tom Laughlin's *Billy Jack* (1971), Robert Aldrich's *Ulzana's Raid* (1972), Philip Kaufman's *The Great Northfield, Minnesota Raid* (1972) and Sam Peckinpah's *Pat Garrett and Billy the Kid* (1973).

The political zeitgeist certainly contributed to the 'cultural permission' assumed by Rafelson and his auteur colleagues. Thus, Altman's political satire, *Nashville* (1975) – which the director called his 'metaphor for America'[10] – fed into the national engagement with surveillance, dirty tricks and official corruption explored not only by the Watergate investigators but also by Coppola in *The Conversation* (1974), by Roman Polanski in *Chinatown* (1974) and by Alan J. Pakula in his fact-based Watergate thriller, *All the President's Men* (1976). All these films provided a disturbing counterpoint to the patriotic self-congratulation of the bicentennial fever.

The auteur deserving particular attention for his contrapuntal engagement with bicentennial America is Martin Scorsese. The documentary grittiness with which Scorsese had portrayed dysfunctional victims of urban capitalism in *Mean Streets* (1973) was honed to arresting perfection in his bicentennial-year critique, *Taxi Driver*, in which a murderously psychotic protagonist achieves heroic celebrity status on the streets of New York.

Taxi Driver (1976)

On 30 March 1981, a young would-be assassin, John Hinckley Jr, shot and wounded President Ronald Reagan and three other people. In advance of the shootings, he had bombarded the actress, Jodie Foster, with love letters claiming that only some visible affection from her could prevent Reagan's assassination. At his trial, Hinckley claimed to have seen *Taxi Driver* fifteen times; the film features Foster as a twelve-year-old prostitute and an attempted political assassination plays a pivotal part. After being shown the film, the jury acquitted Hinckley on the grounds of insanity. To the New York *Daily News* film critic, Marilyn Beck, the Hinckley case demonstrated that Martin Scorsese had made a truly 'dangerous' and 'irresponsible film'.[11]

Scorsese's 'documentary of the mind', as the film's cinematographer, Michael Chapman, called it, grew initially out of the desperate experiences of the scriptwriter, Paul Schrader, who had undergone a near-breakdown during an intense period of isolation living rough in New York.[12] Schrader's fascination with firearms, combined with his concurrent reading of Jean-Paul Sartre's existential novel of 1938, *La Nausée* (*Nausea*) and the published diaries of Governor George Wallace's would-be assassin, Arthur Bremer, inspired a creative idea. As he recalled, 'I realized that I hadn't spoken to anyone for several weeks, just living in this isolated environment. And the metaphor of the taxicab occurred to me – as a metaphor for loneliness, a certain kind of male drifting loneliness.'[13] The result was the story of Travis Bickle (played by Robert DeNiro), taxi driver and psychopath with a twisted mission to eliminate the urban corruption he perceives all around him.

Critics have seen *Taxi Driver* as a 'street western' or an 'urban western' in which, like John Ford's classic, *The Searchers* (1956), the protagonist has 'an impulse to rescue – to "return home" – a woman who does not want to be saved'.[14] In *Taxi Driver*, the object of Bickle's unwanted rescue attempt is the child prostitute, Iris, played by Foster. As Leighton Grist argues, Bickle acts upon the reactionary premise of most urban westerns: it is 'the weakness of the law (in all its senses) that is the cause of social breakdown; a perspective that evokes that of the Nixonian Right. Either protagonists are frustrated by "liberal" legal niceties or the law is "too soft" and ineffectual.'[15] Grist thus associates *Taxi Driver* with such other urban westerns and vigilante films (see below) as Don Siegel's *Coogan's Bluff* (1968) and *Dirty Harry* (1971), Phil Karlson's *Walking Tall* (1973) and Michael Winner's *Death Wish* (1974).

While Scorsese himself acknowledges his debt to Ford's *The Searchers*, he views *Taxi Driver* less as an urban western than as 'a horror film . . . New York Gothic', which he describes as 'a cross between a Gothic horror and the New York *Daily News*'.[16] Travis Bickle's obsession with urban putrefaction and pollution – in Robin Wood's words, his sense of New York as 'the Excremental City'[17] – is a reflection of Scorsese's own perception of his native New York at its most disturbing:

> There is something about the summertime in New York that is extraordinary. We shot the film during a very hot summer and there's an atmosphere at night that's like a seeping kind of virus . . . That's almost what it's like: a strange disease creeps along the streets of the city.[18]

Updating Edgar Allan Poe's depictions of the city as a site of madness and horror, Schrader explained: '[The city] is where you go to be crazy . . . You can only do true loneliness in a crowded atmosphere.'[19] As Emanuel Levy asserts, DeNiro's Travis Bickle was to loom 'prominently . . . as an embodiment of Scorsese's vision of urban society's neuroses'.[20]

Scorsese set out to formalise these 'neuroses' in a number of ways. He engaged composer Bernard Herrmann to provide a musical score as eerie and threatening as those he had written for Orson Welles's *Citizen Kane* (1941) and two of Alfred Hitchcock's classics, *Vertigo* (1958) and *Psycho* (1960); but in this case the sinister score was overlain with mockingly romantic tones of New York jazz saxophone. In terms of cinematography,

Grist points out that in combining 'an expressive use of colour and the systematic deployment of non-classical camerawork and editing (slow-motion, jump-cuts, intra-scene dissolves)', Scorsese managed to depict New York as a hellish site 'refracted through Travis's reflected subjectivity'.[21] Thus, in a telling moment of dialogue – when Iris asks Travis, 'Didn't you ever try looking in your own eyeballs in the mirror?'[22] – she is implying that Travis needs to see what the audience is continually forced to see: the vision of a psychopath fixated on his own subjectivity and imprisoned in his own narcissism. As Richard Maltby argues, 'Subjectivity is a logical condition of narcissism, and the more widespread use of subjective shots is a natural enough phenomenon of an increasingly self-conscious and self-referential cinema', of which, he notes, *Taxi Driver* is an example par excellence.[23] Through the point of view imposed by Travis's sole perspective, the film subjects the major characters and the audience to what Lesley Stern calls a 'ritualised psychosis'.[24]

Scorsese is clear about his deliberate intent to impose this psychotic experience on the viewer:

> I don't think there is any difference between fantasy and reality in the way these should be approached in a film. Of course, if you live that way you are clinically insane. But I can ignore the boundary on film. In *Taxi Driver*, Travis Bickle lives it out, he goes right to the edge and explodes.[25]

Stern's sense of the film's 'extremely tenuous' boundary line between 'containment and explosion' is palpable in much of Bickle's voice-over narration.[26] 'Twelve hours of work and I still can't sleep,' he drones. 'Days go on and on. They don't end.' This unstable boundary is also reflected in the tensions of Bickle's contradictory nature, exacerbated by his isolation, as Schrader makes clear:

> Self-imposed loneliness – that is a syndrome of behaviour that reinforces itself. And the touchstones of that behaviour [in Bickle] are all kinds of contradictory impulses: Puritanism and pornography, 'I've gotta get healthy' while popping pills at the same time . . . So he can reinforce his own doomed condition.[27]

Bickle's obsession with urban corruption and filth is self-driven, as Scorsese explains: 'Bickle chooses to drive his taxi anywhere in the city, even the worst places, because it feeds his hate.'[28] The build-up towards the film's climactic massacre is thus reflected in the increasing belligerence of Bickle's voice-overs:

> Each time I return the cab to the garage I have to clean the come off the back seat. Some nights I clean off the blood.

Later:

> All the animals come out at night. Whores, skunks, pussies, buggers, queens, fairies, dopers, junkies – sick, venal. Someday a real rain'll come and wash this scum off the street.

Still later:

> Listen, you fuckers, you screwheads. Here is a man who would not take it anymore, who would not let – here is a man who would not take it anymore, a man who stood up against the scum, the cunts, the dogs, the filth, the shit. Here is someone who stood up.

As Schrader points out, it is part of Bickle's obsessive-compulsive make-up to fixate on the pure, the virginal, just as he fixates upon the corrupt. His first view of Betsy, the blonde campaign worker (played by Cybill Shepherd), invites this observation by Bickle: 'She was wearing a white dress. She appeared like an angel, out of this filthy mess . . . She is alone . . . They. Cannot. Touch. Her.' Yet, caught in a spiral of denial and attraction, 'desiring what he consciously rejects',[29] Bickle subjects Betsy to a porno film on their first date precisely because, as Schrader notes, 'he wants to sully her'.[30] Rebuffed by the outraged Betsy, Bickle turns on her: 'You're in a hell and you're gonna die in a hell. Like the rest of them. You're like the rest of them.'

Following Betsy's rejection and Bickle's attempted assassination of the presidential candidate for whom she campaigns, Bickle transfers his obsession to another subject, setting out to save the child prostitute, Iris, from her pimp, Sport (played by Harvey Keitel). As Maltby argues, in spite of Bickle's often inexplicable projections, the audience – and the camera – are at his mercy. Not only does the camera concede 'authority' to Bickle, but 'the inconsistency of his behaviour permeates the entire film: the audience are subject to and victim of random and unexplained incident.'[31] Bickle's domination of the narrative point of view means, as Grist notes, that the audience has no choice but to 'share both his perceptual *and* ideological space', becoming imprisoned in what Maltby describes as 'the psychopathic text'.[32]

This audience/protagonist identification is highly significant in terms of the climactic vigilante massacre in which Bickle kills Sport and two of his associates in order to 'save' Iris. He is subsequently hailed as a hero in the media, fulsomely thanked by Iris's parents, ultimately integrated with his work colleagues and, it is implied, finally desired by Betsy, whose rejection had triggered his psychotic vengeance in the first place. This denouement implicates the audience as much as the wider society it depicts with such distortion. 'The audience face the absence of a normalizing perspective,' Maltby argues, 'a perspective other than Bickle's which could ratify or place his in context, at the same time that they are forced to identify him (and identify with him) as both heroic and demonstrably psychopathic.'[33]

Bickle's psychosis is also connected implicitly to a wider national delusion, if not a national psychosis. He is a Vietnam veteran, and as Scorsese explains:

> It was crucial to Travis Bickle's character that he had experienced life and death around him every second he was in South-East Asia. That way it becomes more heightened when he comes back; the image of the street at night reflected in the dirty gutter becomes more threatening.[34]

Moreover, this twisted Vietnam vet does not hail from just anywhere; nor is he from New York. DeNiro explained that it was 'important' for him to perfect Bickle's Midwestern accent in order to fix his place of origin.[35] Thus, the ironic reference to the corrupted American Dream of *The Great Gatsby* is inescapable. As Fitzgerald's Midwestern narrator, Nick Carraway, says, the East – implicitly New York – always has for him 'a quality of distortion'; he shares with Gatsby and all the major characters of the book (also Midwesterners) 'some deficiency in common which made us subtly unadaptable to Eastern life'.[36] It is a grim irony, indeed, that Travis Bickle's ultimate adaptation to the highly distorted streets of New York, and his integration into urban life and community as a hero (something Gatsby never achieved), should have been enabled by such a bloody act of psychotic butchery.

Scorsese's New York, like that of William Friedkin's drug-bust exposé, *The French Connection* (1971), is a microcosm of urban American vice, waywardness and soured dreams. In the face of such representations it is perhaps unsurprising that another important auteur and New York native, Woody Allen, would have attempted to close the decade with what amounts to a love letter to New York in black and white, *Manhattan* (1979). Yet, undercutting the luscious cinematography of well-heeled neighbourhoods and the majestic soundtrack of George Gershwin's *Rhapsody in Blue* is a nostalgia for another city, one that cannot have produced *Mean Streets*'s gangsters and small-time mafiosi, *The French Connection*'s murderous policemen and drug pushers, or *Taxi Driver*'s psychopathic vigilantes, pimps and johns. Indeed, in the film's opening monologue, the main protagonist, the writer Isaac Davis (played by Allen) appears highly aware of Scorsese and Freidkin's renderings of his beloved city. One of the many narrative openings that Isaac rejects for his work-in-progress is: 'Chapter One. "He adored New York City, although to him it was a metaphor for the decay of contemporary culture. How hard it was to exist in a society desensitized by drugs, loud music, television, crime, garbage—" Too angry. I don't wanna be angry.'[37]

Arguably, with its Allen-copyrighted obsessions with faddish psychology and sexual embarrassment, *Manhattan* demonstrates a considerable social disengagement in comparison with the films of the other directors who drove the decade's auteur cinema. In any event, all their efforts, as Cook argues, proved to be 'an aberration' in the history of American film: 'The Reagan years would provide a "mid-course correction" and set the American cinema sailing toward the turn of the century, when the blockbuster calculus would reach new levels of fiscal absurdity.'[38]

Blockbusters

To some extent the flourishing of independent-minded auteur directors in the first half of the decade had been enabled by the near disintegration of the Hollywood studio system. Bruce J. Schulman neatly summarises a breathtaking change in the Hollywood landscape:

> Not surprisingly, as American cinema enjoyed this outpouring of caustic, critical attacks on traditional sources of authority, the film empire struck back. If half the story of Seventies cinema concerned the independent directors and their dark, personal visions, the other half featured a new Hollywood corporate order struggling to assert itself amid the ruin of the studio system. International megaconglomerates absorbed the film companies: Transamerica Corporation took over United Artists; MCA engulfed Universal Pictures; Gulf & Western absorbed Paramount; and the Kinney Corporation, known as the King of Parking Lots, bought Warner Brothers. [39]

Leading the way of the blockbuster onslaught was a stable of disaster films riding on the back of special-effects technology that had come into its own with the appearance of George Seaton's *Airport* (1970). With the formula for the disaster blockbuster firmly established – a potential or actual disaster confronted by a cast of recognisable character types played by recognisable stars, each with their own personal subplots (broken marriages, love affairs, alcoholism) – the special effects were piled on: the wide-screen panoramas afforded by 70-mm film; the stereophonic rumblings of 'Sensurround' (to enhance the experience of earthquakes) and ever more realistic renderings of fire, flood and technological or natural catastrophe.

In the wake of *Airport* came *The Poseidon Adventure* (Ronald Neame, 1972), *Towering Inferno* (John Guillerman and Irwin Winkler, 1974) and *Earthquake* (Mark Robson, 1974), all of which reflected the domination of the industry by marketing and distribution executives most concerned with repeating the successes of what had become a low-risk, high-yield formula: technological innovation driving the content. In corporate terms, the success of the three main blockbuster genres of the decade – the disaster film, the horror film (for example *Jaws*, 1975; *The Exorcist*, 1973; *Amityville Horror*, 1979) and the science-fiction film (*Star Wars*, 1977; *Close Encounters of the Third Kind*, 1977) – relied as much upon demographic-focused strategies as on special-effects enhancement.

Cook encapsulates 'the blockbuster mentality' in the industry's great powerhouse of the decade (and arguably afterwards), 'the Spielberg–Lucas juggernaut' that extended well beyond the cinema screen into the arena of 'ancillary merchandising':

> Soundtrack albums and novelizations had brought income to the studios since the fifties, but the idea of product tie-ins was born simultaneously with the need to create mass market consciousness for blockbusters like *Jaws* . . . The profitability of merchandising was certified indisputably by *Star Wars* (George Lucas, 1977), whose spin-off toys, posters, T-shirts, clothing, candy, watches, and other products grossed more money by the end of the decade (reportedly $1 billion) than the film took in at the box office.[40]

Stephen Paul Miller goes so far as to name *Jaws* 'perhaps the central American film of the seventies' because of its implication that, whatever the predatory shark might stand for, it 'can overtake all facets of society'.[41] On the industrial level, certainly, the shark 'Jaws' might refer to the onslaught of saturation booking and mass-marketing hype with which Spielberg and Universal Studios thrust the film into the midst of the American consciousness. As Howard Sounes observes by way of an understatement, 'the hype for *Jaws* was immoderate. "None of man's fantasies of evil can compare with the reality of *Jaws*", boasted the trailers. "See it – *before* you go swimming".'[42] The box-office record-breaking film, based on Peter Benchley's 1974 novel about a small seaside town terrorised by a killer shark, was, to Carroll, both highly relevant to bicentennial America and, paradoxically, a momentous distraction:

> Americans became preoccupied with scenes of disaster. In an imaginary community named Amity on the eve of the July Fourth weekend, the invasion of nameless calamity served as a perfect metaphor for America under Ford. 'The town is dying,' wrote Peter Benchley in *Jaws*. 'People are out of work. Stores that were going to open aren't. People aren't renting houses, let alone buying them. And every day we keep the beaches closed, we drive another nail into our coffin.' For the nation's birthday, the town leaders decide to open the beaches. There is joy in the air – until the killer shark returns . . . 'Such movies', observed novelist Gore Vidal, 'distract people from the thoughts of robbery and deceit to which they are subjected daily by oil companies, politicians, and banks.'[43]

While *Jaws* laid the foundations for many of the characteristics associated with the Hollywood blockbuster (special effects, saturation booking, demographic targeting, pre-release marketing build-up and, in particular, product franchising), the decade's signal endeavour in this regard is indisputably George Lucas's *Star Wars*. As Maltby notes, if any misfortune was associated with this film, it was simply 'not having the children's toys in the stores in time for Christmas'[44]. Otherwise, Lucas succeeded in building an entire industry based on his idea of a Manichaean universe in which a corrupt galactic empire is defeated by a resurgent republicanism and where virtuous underdogs in semi-medieval dress and rust-bucket starfighters, guided by a quasi-religious 'Force', defeat the power-crazed technocrats who have gone over to 'the Dark Side'. The fantasy is unashamedly faithful to recognisable stereotypes: Luke Skywalker, the young idealistic farmboy-turned-war hero (Mark Hammill); Leia, the beautiful princess he rescues (Carrie Fisher); Han Solo, the cynical, Bogartesque sidekick (Harrison Ford); and the two samurai-like masters fighting respectively for pure Good and pure Evil, Obi-Wan Kenobe (Alec Guinness) and Darth Vader (voiced by James Earl Jones). *Star Wars* is perhaps most important for its influence in the succeeding decades, spawning six sequels and prequels and infiltrating political discourse if not policy itself.

Star Wars (1977)

Star Wars is a pastiche built ironically on an epic scale – ironic in that it is a special-effects-driven sci-fi fantasy that sets out to undermine all notions of technological advancement. In semi-feudal settings reminiscent of the North African desert where much of it is filmed, bizarre creatures in medieval rags point rusty, outlandish weapons at the heroes, who fly around in broken-down, shabby vehicles and spaceships (such as Han Solo's *Millenium Falcon*) cobbled together out of bits of junk. As David Wyatt observes, 'If we come to *Star Wars* for the "special effects", we come, the movie seems to imply, for the garbage.'[45] Just as much of the film's technology appears to have been scavenged from any number of intergalactic dumpsters (except for the state-of-the-art death technology always in the service of 'the Dark Side'), the film itself relies on the scavenging of various forms and genres, drawing on such diverse influences as *Flash Gordon*, swashbucklers, B westerns, samurai films, fairy tales and comic books. Although the film is set in an indistinguishable time and place (as the prologue proclaims, 'a long time ago in a galaxy far, far away'), it is nonetheless, for Fredric Jameson, 'a nostalgia film' harking back to specific cultural experiences: Saturday afternoon shoot-em-ups, science-fiction serials and other cosy, familiar televisual and cinematic experiences in which the body count piles up bloodlessly, moral complexities are smoothed over and goodness triumphs over evil. Jameson argues:

> *Star Wars*, far from being a pointless satire of such now dead forms, satis-fies a deep (might I even say repressed?) longing to experience them again: it is a complex object in which on some first level children and adolescents can take the adventures straight, while the adult public is able to gratify a deeper and more properly nostalgic desire to return to that older period and to live its strange old aesthetic artefacts through once again.[46]

Indeed, as Sounes observes, the film's main characters – Luke, Leia and Solo – 'behave as children in what is essentially a Saturday morning tele-vision serial brought to the big screen' (at one point prompting Harrison Ford to complain to Lucas during the filming, 'You can type this shit, but you can't *say* it').[47] Blithely dealing out hackneyed lines like 'I've got a bad feeling about this' and ponderous, quasi-biblical benedictions ('The Force will be with you always'), *Star Wars* situates the viewer in an easily digestible universe far removed, on the face of it, from contemporary concerns.[48]

But the darker temporal undercurrents of *Star Wars* have been noted by many critics including Miller, who identifies in the film the seventies' pre-occupations with surveillance and espionage. 'Like Watergate,' he argues, '*Star Wars* involves a struggle for tapes' and it also reflects a desire to undo the fatal damage of Vietnam: 'After the Vietnam War, a credible war can only occur in the outer space of a distant future or past . . . However, there is an ideological need for such a fantastic war, to repair Vietnam's rip in enabling Cold War perceptions.'[49]

This function of *Star Wars* virtually to erase the past may well amount to what Wyatt calls 'the movie's repression of history' (he notes that Lucas pointedly instructed the scriptwriter to make 'no references to time').[50] Perhaps more significantly, *Star Wars* and its initial popularity also reflect wider, equally magical erasures in the consciousness of the body politic, in particular, the erasure of painful associations with the beleaguered one-term president, Jimmy Carter, who had tried to warn the country of its tech-nical, military and political limitations. If, indeed, such an erasure did prepare the way for the embracing of Ronald Reagan's 'morning again in America', there was more to the new morning's herald than what Cook calls 'the boyish charm and facile optimism of a Saturday matinee idol', through which Reagan could be 'the perfect political simulacrum of blockbuster heroes like Luke Skywalker and Indiana Jones'.[51] For this new herald not only capitalised on a 'repression of history' but he also symbolically returned to a pre-Vietnam past, taking significant cues from this apparently simple film. As Miller notes:

> *Star Wars* helps renew Cold War commitments to a binary opposition between good and evil. The film provides the Reagan administration with the

tropes of the 'Evil Empire' for the Soviet Union and the 'Star Wars' nuclear shield for the Strategic Defense Initiative [SDI].[52]

The SDI was first proposed in 1983. It was only long after Reagan's departure from office – in Episode 3: *Revenge of the Sith* (2005) – that Obi Wan Kenobe could declare of his evil adversaries, 'Only a Sith thinks in absolutes,' in a pointed attempt to distance *Star Wars* from the rigid 'binary opposition' of Cold War mentality.[53]

Reagan's use of rhetoric drawn from *Star Wars* is important for one other reason: it opens up an interrogation into the slippery nature of filmic irony. In spite of the playful scepticism with which Reagan's critics drew upon *Star Wars* to ridicule the SDI initiative, there was something very serious in his appropriation of the cartoon or comic-book phrase, 'the Evil Empire', for a statement on the direction of United States foreign policy, as though the departments of Defense and State could be guided by the ethics of a Saturday afternoon sci-fi adventure. It is difficult to say whether, in applying the rhetoric of *Star Wars* to the realm of realpolitik, the Reagan administration was implicitly affirming or denying the fundamental aesthetic and driving force of the film: its irony. As Wyatt notices, through the filter of irony, any degree of unthinkable devastation might be tolerated:

> *Star Wars* begins, for all its epic intimations, as a massive retreat from time into a fantasy of space. Space permits the illusion of detachment and distance: As [the *Star Wars* robot] See-Threepio [*sic*] says about the receding imperial starship: 'That's funny, the damage doesn't look as bad from out here.'
>
>   The Death Star wipes out a planet the way *Star Wars* blocks out the past . . . We care about loss in epics; in irony, there is nothing to lose.[54]

Thus, Reagan's transformation of the ironic rhetoric and vision of *Star Wars* into a serious mode of political discourse constitutes a number of possibilities. First, it may have been a bold attempt to instigate a great cultural reversal, to stop the malaise of postmodern irony in its tracks and, from the standpoint of the victorious and optimistic Radical Right in the 1980s, send it back to the hated 1970s where it came from. Secondly, it may have been an admission that even that hated decade's signal tropes could prove useful at the dawn of the neoconservative 'morning' ushered in by Reagan. Thirdly, the Reaganite appropriation of *Star Wars* may have signalled a more complex possibility, the combination of acceptance and denial indicative of the ironic double-bind. While Cook closes down all options in arguing that 'an aesthetic of serious representation had become virtually impossible' by the time of Reagan's arrival,[55] Schulman identifies 'a kind of double identity' as 'the most obvious marker of the Seventies sensibility – its signature in literature, film, music, politics, advertising', which enabled the decade's actors to produce 'works that were a parody of something – a biting, knowing satire – and simultaneously the very thing itself'.[56] Thus, to the extent that Reagan *could* apply the unbelievable rhetoric of *Star Wars* to the real political stage, he might then have brought

the 'obvious marker of the Seventies sensibility' – 'a kind of double identity' – into the political discourse of the 1980s. Within a few years, the
Soviet 'Evil Empire' had almost miraculously become, under 'perestroika',
a partner with whom the West could do business and the SDI was
scrapped. Thus, even at his most alarming, Reagan well may have been
another actor operating under the dual code of irony, both serious and
playful – very much like the actors portraying Luke Skywalker, Princess
Leia and Han Solo.

Other Genres: Ghouls, Vigilantes, Palookas and Gangsters

As *Star Wars*'s ironic play with dysfunctional technology indicates, the
1970s blockbusters employed state-of-the-art special effects in order
to interrogate and undercut precisely the equation of technology with
Utopia. In the 1970s, the science-fiction genre dovetailed significantly
into horror, with such films as Joseph Sargent's *Colossus: The Forbin
Project* (1970), Robert Wise's *The Andromeda Strain* (1971), Boris
Sagal's *The Omega Man* (1971), Michael Crichton's *Westworld* (1973)
and Donald Cammell's *The Demon Seed* (1977) ultimately pitting
information technology and nuclear or biomedical technology against
the survival of the human race itself. In some films, the fearsome associations between technology and horror might only be implicit, as in
the social satire *The Stepford Wives* (Bryan Forbes, 1975) in which the
perfect robotic wife reflects more on the stalling of feminist initiatives
than on monstrous technology. But the horror of the machine, as in
Michael Anderson's *Logan's Run* (1976), in which a nasty, brutish and
short life is lived and terminated according to the demands of a super-
computer, and the horror of the biological monster encountered
through the machine, as in Crichton's *Coma* (1978) and Ridley Scott's
Alien (1979), are main currents running through the decade's most
technologically advanced Hollywood productions. Benign depictions
of machines, such as the extraterrestrial 'mother ship' in Spielberg's
Close Encounters of the Third Kind (1977), are the exception; otherwise, even a modest chainsaw can become an instrument of profound
technological horror, as in Tobe Hooper's *The Texas Chainsaw
Massacre* (1974).

Other social preoccupations in the 1970s generated their own particular film genres and subgenres. In addition to the technophobia so
often driving the horror film, the dark side of New Age spirituality –
the occult – spurred on the popularity of such films as Richard
Donner's *The Omen* (1976) and the highest-grossing horror film yet

Figure 3.1 Mark Hammill as Luke Skywalker in *Star Wars* (1977). Wisconsin Center for Film and Theater Research.

made, William Friedkin's *The Exorcist* (1973). Films like these situated horrific potential in the cosy bosom of the American nuclear family, a perversion reflected beyond the screen in the lingering recollection of Charles Manson's murderous 'family', whose trial for the Tate–LaBianca killings began in June 1970. A series of small-town Gothic and slasher films, in particular Wes Craven's *The Hills Have Eyes* (1977) and John Carpenter's *Halloween* (1978), also contributed to making the 1970s what Robin Wood calls 'the Golden Age of the American horror film', precisely for the decade's success in producing 'films more gruesome, more violent, more disgusting, and perhaps more confused, than ever before in history'.[57]

Elsewhere, public apprehension of urban crime and a lack of faith in official law enforcement (contributing to the proliferation of private gun ownership) was reflected in the vigilante subgenre exemplified by Don Siegel's *Dirty Harry* and Michael Winner's *Death Wish*. What Cook refers to as the 'paranoid conspiracy film' – underwritten not only by Watergate but also by the general sense of an overly surveillant culture controlled by elite interests – was exemplified by such films as David Miller's treatment of the JFK assassination, *Executive Action* (1973), Alan J. Pakula's *The Parallax View* (1974), Coppola's *The Conversation* (1974), Pakula's *All the President's Men* (1976), Sidney Lumet's *Network* (1976) and James Bridges's *The China Syndrome* (1979).[58]

In concert with the lone vigilantes battling across the screen against corrupt officials or corporate villains were the individual heroes of the developing martial arts genre, gracefully spearheaded by Bruce Lee in *Enter the Dragon* (Robert Clouse, 1973) and – less gracefully – its all-American counterpart, the boxing epic revived by Sylvester Stallone in John G. Avildsen's *Rocky* (1976), itself an updating of Robert Wise's inspirational homage to Rocky Graziano, *Somebody Up There Likes Me* (1956). Stallone's Rocky is not merely a working-class underdog punching above his weight in the arena of individual success; he is both 'ethnic' and white. Carroll situates the film in the context of the superstar professionalism and hype surrounding the decade's greatest champion, Muhammad Ali, still riding high from his victory against George Foreman in the 1974 'Rumble in the Jungle':

> But in March 1975, an eighth-ranked palooka named Chuck Wepner, a.k.a. 'the Bayonne bleeder', scored a surprising knockdown and almost went the distance against the champion. Inspired by the near upset, filmwriter Sylvester Stallone transformed a streetwise ethnic named

Rocky Balboa ('the Italian Stallion') into a contender against Ali look-alike Apollo Creed . . . As the white ethnic underdog staggered through fifteen rounds of punishment, movie audiences erupted in frenzied cheers for what critic Andrew Sarris called 'the most romanticized Great White Hope in screen history'.[59]

Rocky is thus instructive for the fine line it walks between the assertion of white identity vis-à-vis blackness in particular and what Schulman identifies as a more general 'ethnic revival among white Americans . . . Irish and Italians, Eastern European Jews and Eastern Orthodox Slavs, Poles, Greeks, and French Canadians'.[60]

The rags-to-riches success of Rocky Balboa through *Rocky* and its sequels can usefully be viewed in contrast to Scorsese's *Raging Bull* (1980) whose main character, boxer Jake LaMotta (Robert DeNiro), follows a much more troubling, for the most part downward, trajectory than *Rocky*. Because of its upward trajectory, Stallone's film also offers a revealing contrast to the decade's greatest exploration of white ethnicity, Coppola's *The Godfather* (1972) and its first sequel, *The Godfather, Part II* (1974). As Schulman argues, *The Godfather* films marked 'a new kind of immigrant saga', a tale of 'failed assimilation, of deassimilation, of the lingering, inescapable imprint of the ethnic heritage . . . the new immigrant counternarrative of the ethnic revival'.[61] Coppola's brutal and lyrical saga of the Mafia boss, Don Vito Corleone (played by Marlon Brando) and his children presents the Italian American family, in Vera Dika's words, as 'a lost unit of love and protection in 1970s American society'.[62]

Coppola and his associates double coded this particular Italian American family by presenting it as both honourable and corrupt, in a sense reflecting the degradation of values at the national level. As writer–director Robert Towne recalled:

> In the seventies, we felt families were disintegrating, and our national family, led by the [Nixon] family in the White House, was full of back-stabbing . . . Here [in the Corleones] was this role model of a family who stuck together, who'd die for one another . . . It was really kind of reactionary in that sense – a perverse expression of a desirable and lost cultural tradition.[63]

Peter Biskind observes that 'Coppola compared Michael Corleone [played by Al Pacino] to Nixon; he began as an idealist, distancing himself from the Family, and ended up by embracing and replicating its values.'[64] Thus, the *Godfather* saga, with its focus on this one complex ethnic family, is hardly a celebration either of ethnic pluralism or of 'family values'. As Dika persuasively argues, the films should collectively

> be seen as a significant fantasy, one that embodies the wish for an all-white militant group, one that exists to the exclusion of all other races and ethnic Americans. (Again, the wish here is for a time when organized crime could be controlled by one ethnic group, and is dramatized in the film by the active exclusion of African Americans, Puerto Ricans, and other ethnic groups in an antiseptic dream of racial and ethnic purity.)[65]

A further consideration of 1970s film reveals that a similar pattern of 'fantasy' and 'exclusion' was operating for another ethnic group as well, resulting in one of the signal genres of the decade.

Blaxploitation

Ethnicity and crime combined in the 1970s to produce the 'blaxploitation film', with over two hundred titles released between 1971 and 1975. As a distinctly African American film genre, blaxploitation *appears* to have absorbed the dynamics of a counter-cultural race protest movement, creating a fertile arena for the growth of a visual black culture and propelling to the public consciousness the work of black actors, producers, directors and musicians. Such positive assessments are frequently challenged, however. Cook, for one, argues that 'most 1970s black action films were created by whites' who reinforced 'negative themes of crime and drugs in the inner city'.[66]

Another common objection to the blaxploitation genre is its problematic treatment of the relationship between race and gender. Carroll's dismissal focuses on this drawback, implicitly condemning the black auteurs who proved the exception to the rule of white domination of the genre:

> A series of highly successful Hollywood 'blaxploitation' films – *Sweet Sweetback's Baadasssss Song* [Melvin Van Peebles, 1971], *Shaft* [Gordon Parks Sr, 1971], and *Superfly* [Gordon Parks Jr, 1972] – all of which were extremely popular among black audiences – celebrated the black pimp as folk hero, outsmarting the white establishment, while portraying black women as whores.[67]

Conversely, Jennifer Devere Brody argues that these early blaxploitation films 'inverted value systems, making black beautiful':

> Whiteness is not normative. Indeed, one of the functions of the blaxploitation film is to render 'whitey' bad (but never *baaaaad!*). To a certain extent, this representation subverts hegemonic representations of whiteness. Here it may be instructive to remember that blaxploitation films were marketed for and seen by predominantly black urban audiences. These films were meant to rupture the idea that 'white is right' . . . [68]

Moreover, Brody observes, in spite of the perceived male bias in the early blaxploitation films in particular, 'several of the "original" blaxploitation films starred black women'.[69] It is thus significant that Quentin Tarantino's 1997 homage to the genre, *Jackie Brown*, not only stars Pam Grier, the original star of such 1970s female-led blaxploitation films as *Coffey* (Jack Hill, 1973) and *Foxy Brown* (Jack Hill, 1974), but it also serves to link the blaxploitation film explicitly to the snowballing of black feminism in the 1970s, as represented by such initiatives as the National Black Feminist Organization, formed in 1973, and the 'black lesbian feminist' Combahee River Collective, formed in 1974. Brody situates these initiatives against the release of the two other main female-driven blaxploitation films starring Tamara Dobson, *Cleopatra Jones* (Jack Starrett, 1973) and *Cleopatra Jones and the Casino of Gold* (Charles Bail, 1975).[70]

A reassessment of the male-driven blaxploitation films, like that offered by Brody for the female-driven films, also allows for a broader, more socially reflective reading than that offered in the blanket dismissals of the genre, not only by critics such as Carroll but also by a number of contemporary civic and industry organisations such as the Black Artists Alliance of Hollywood, the Coalition Against Blaxploitation and the National Association for the Advancement of Colored People (NAACP), whose Hollywood branch official, Junius Griffin, condemned the 'so-called black movies that glorify black males as pimps, dope pushers, gangsters, and super males'.[71] As Charles Kronengold argues, a review of even the most masculinist films of the genre, such as *Shaft*, reveals an injection of political significance into the *film noir* conventions adopted by blaxploitation:

> *Shaft* follows the classic noirs in making money a crucial part of the texture, partly because it serves as a mode of evaluation and helps to place emphasis on questions of value . . .

> Viewers will likely sense . . . the definite political weight that attaches
> to the depictions of African Americans receiving equal pay for equal
> work. The strong presence of money serves thereby to establish the pos-
> sibility of an anti-racist critique . . .[72]

Moreover, in Kronengold's reading, style, another of the genre's fixa-
tions, carries as much political weight as does money. In *Shaft*, for
instance, the protagonist's relentless attention to his appearance, to his
sartorial style – down to the smallest scuff mark on his shoes – is an
element of his labour in the pursuit of economic gain:

> Why so much concern for appearance? Black action films suggest
> that the performance of everyday acts with style has political conse-
> quences . . . If the characters act all tired, with no style, they will fail.
> Political speculation requires that some kind of aesthetic integrity be put
> up as collateral.[73]

Looking back at the 1970s, the politicisation of style appears to be
significant in the readings of many cultural texts. If style in the blaxploitation film is indeed political, an assertion of labour where other,
more conventional, opportunities are denied black men and women, a
similar interpretation might be placed on John Badham's disco film,
Saturday Night Fever (1977), in which the sartorial and dance styles of
the working-class protagonists are also invested with inordinate effort
as means of self-assertion in the face of limited opportunities for
upward mobility. As critics of the disco culture have noted, similar
modes of stylistic assertion were to be found off-screen on the disco
floors themselves. But style as a mode of cultural engagement is crucial
in one further cinematic arena, the Vietnam film, not so much in terms
of visual or sartorial style, but rather *narrative* style. In this sense, style
becomes both a mode of engagement and evasion.

Vietnam: The Movie

It is striking how few films explicitly about the Vietnam War – the
decade's great 'wound', to repeat David Wyatt – were produced in the
1970s. There was an immense degree of *implicit* engagement, to be
sure; and as Wyatt argues, much of that engagement was on the level
of style: 'Vietnam found itself, in the writing of it, caught in a style
match between what could be called innocent and informed
accounts.'[74] To the extent that style determines a narrative strategy,

styles of implicit engagement characterised some of the decade's most salient films about Vietnam – films which, on the face of it, are about wholly other subjects. Miller explores the implications of this, arguing that such films as *Patton* (Franklin J. Schaffner, 1970) and *Deliverance* (John Boorman, 1972), 'in which Vietnam is not an overt subject but which involve Vietnam in an actively critical fashion, are our most authentic Vietnam War films, in the sense that they approach the war as a living presence'.[75] The war was indeed a 'living presence' to virtually all American film audiences in the first half of the decade. Carroll's eloquent description of this 'presence' and the knowledge it brought to Americans' daily experience deserves quotation in full:

> While public attention focused on political assassinations and related questions of domestic violence, the ultimate issues of mass death quietly drifted across the Pacific Ocean into the jungles of Vietnam. There, a Strangelovian assortment of technological inventions devastated the countryside, while Pentagonese wrapped the atrocities in the neutral language of free fire zones, protective reactions, and body counts. Such destruction, thanks to American electronics, then recrossed the Pacific and slipped into the nation's living rooms, where civilians also could experience a powerful death encounter in the form of self-immolating Buddhist monks and napalmed children, amid the crack of automatic fire and buzzing helicopters on the national news.[76]

With film-going audiences so attuned, filmmakers could rely on the power of implicit critiques embedded in the form of their productions, especially during the first half of the decade when Hollywood studios generally avoided explicit engagement with the war. Wyatt makes clear the centrality of style, of approach, in this context, as directors of the most 'informed' renderings seized on a voice that could invest any scenario with (to repeat Carroll's phrase) the 'living presence' of Vietnam: 'The informed account that was to prevail in Vietnam stories was Conrad's, the voice that can say "this also has been one of the dark places of the earth".'[77] Through this implication, other scenarios – besides Coppola's *Apocalypse Now* (1979), which is solidly based on Joseph Conrad's *Heart of Darkness* – contribute to the Vietnam narrative by way of allegory or association. As Michael Anderegg explains:

> Hollywood's failure to participate imaginatively in America's war against Vietnam has been often noted: only one wartime film, John

Wayne's *Green Berets* (1968), took as its primary subject the combat in Southeast Asia. Other films of the period use the war as background or premise for characters and situations located within some other, non-Vietnam context. We can find, as well, films that allude to the war obliquely or indirectly; indeed, some would say that a Vietnam allegory underlies virtually every significant American film released from the mid-sixties to the mid-seventies, from *Bonnie and Clyde* (1967) and *Night of the Living Dead* (1968) to *Ulzana's Raid* (1972) and *Taxi Driver* (1976).[78]

One might add to this list such films as Ralph Nelson's *Soldier Blue* (1970) which draws on the My Lai massacre for its depiction of American atrocities against the Cheyenne, and Arthur Penn's *Little Big Man* (1970), which compounds the genocidal violence against the Sioux with depictions of American generals and policy-makers as deadly buffoons. Such 'Vietnam Westerns', as the subgenre has been called,[79] serve to challenge 'the ascendancy of officially sanctioned violence as a response to political confrontations'.[80] By the time the American withdrawal from Vietnam could enable Hollywood to engage explicitly with the war in critical retrospect – particularly in the decade's three major Vietnam films, *Coming Home* (Hal Ashby, 1978), *The Deer Hunter* (Michael Cimino, 1978) and *Apocalypse Now* – American film-goers had already considerably processed the voice of Conrad's *Heart of Darkness*. It had spoken to them not only through the 'Vietnam Westerns' but also through war films in pre-Vietnam settings, such as *Tora! Tora! Tora!* (Richard Fleischer et al., 1970), *Catch-22* (Mike Nichols, 1970) and Altman's *M*A*S*H*. It had spoken, too, in domestic films set in American jungles, whether the rural jungle of Boorman's *Deliverance* or the urban jungle of Scorsese's *Taxi Driver*.

In conclusion, the most engaged and engaging films of the 1970s must certainly confound Daniel Bell's assessment of a visual culture as necessarily depleted or fixated on sensation at the expense of thought and reflection. Bell's concerns about the depletion of culture, however, appear to have extended beyond cinema to all forms of visual representation.

Visual Culture beyond Cinema

Bell's main objection to contemporary visual culture is by now familiar: 'the break-up of aesthetic distance', meaning that 'one has lost control over the experience – the ability to step back and conduct one's "dialogue" with the art'.[81] With visual art in general, as with cinema, the problem is one of insufficient encouragement for thought, judgement and contemplation:

> Thus, one discerns the intentions of modern painting: on the syntactical level, to break up ordered space; in its aesthetic, to bridge the distance between object and spectator, to 'thrust' itself on the viewer and establish itself immediately by impact. One does not interpret the scene; instead, one feels it as a sensation and is caught up by that emotion.[82]

Bell's tendency to make totalising judgements should also be familiar. He discusses modern painting as though it were a monolithic entity – as though the 1970s did not host (in J. David Hoeveler's words) 'a bewildering variety of styles' and genres, including

> conceptual art, pattern and decoration, photo-Realism, light-and-space art, minimalism, narrative art, neo-expressionism, sound art, body art, 'bad' painting, crafts-as-art, feminist art, fashion art, high-tech art, media art, new image, performance art, systematic abstraction, abstract illusionism, figurative expression, homoerotic art, environmental art, and post-pop art.[83]

Bell's concerns with the breakdown, or 'break-up', of representation were to some extent matched by official nervousness during the early and mid-decade, when, as Schulman observes, the Nixon administration shifted the bulk of Federal arts funding 'from elite, avant-garde forms of artistic expression to more popular and populist forms: representational painting, commemorative sculptures, folklore, folk art, folk music'.[84]

To the extent that critics sensed the arrival of postmodernism as the defining spirit of 1970s art, it received considerably bad contemporary press – from the Left, where it was perceived as 'the triumph of a contented middle America, complacent and smug', signifying 'the dissolution of the radical will', and from the Right, where it 'registered the collapse of bourgeois culture, the triumph of an indiscriminate pleasure principle, the democratization of all distinction and standards, the reign of permissiveness'.[85] Hoeveler perceives the common critical objection from both sides of the political spectrum over the commodification of art. Seventies artists, it was feared, had

> abandoned their segregation from the dominant commercial world and entered into the cash nexus that threatened to define all human relations

under late capitalism. Postmodernism seemed to be indiscriminately accepting, tolerant, and playful rather than challenging; passive rather than engaged, at home in the world rather than in contest with it.[86]

Bell, for one, reserved his greatest contempt for pop art, which he called 'the appropriate cultural style' for the new 'hedonistic age' (but which could in fact be traced back to as early as the 1920s in the works of Stuart Davis, Charles Demuth and Gerald Murphy, among other American artists):

> Pop art . . . reflects the aesthetics of plenty. The iconography of pop art comes from the everyday world: household objects, images from the movies and the mass media (comic strips and billboards), food (hamburgers and Coca-Cola bottles), and clothing. The point about pop is that there is no tension in the painting – only parody.[87]

At the time of writing, Bell had no recourse to Linda Hutcheon's theory of parody, which focuses on the tensions of parodic expression, 'a double process of installing and ironizing' by which whatever is being parodied is simultaneously being reaffirmed.[88] Thus, 'parody is doubly coded in political terms: it both legitimizes and subverts that which it parodies'.[89] Hutcheon's theory would in fact challenge not only Bell's but also Hoeveler's equation of pop art with the simple affirmation of 'American consumer capitalism': as Hoeveler argues, 'Even if one concedes to pop art a posture of parody towards its subjects – the Campbell's soup cans and Brillo pads and the other iconography of the supermarket, the kitchenware and electronic devices – pop art effected a normalizing relation with the social values encoded in it.'[90]

Hutcheon warns, however, that while postmodern parody 'may indeed be complicitous [sic] with the values it inscribes as well as subverts . . . the subversion is still there':

> It is rather like saying something whilst at the same time putting inverted commas around what is being said . . . Postmodernism's distinctive character lies in this kind of wholesale 'nudging' commitment to doubleness, or duplicity. In many ways it is an even-handed process because postmodernism ultimately manages to install and reinforce as much as undermine and subvert the conventions and presuppositions it appears to challenge.[91]

Thus, in opposition to Hoeveler's charge against pop art – its 'normalizing relation with the social values encoded in it' – Hutcheon would argue that 'the postmodern's initial concern is to de-naturalize some of the dominant features of our way of life; to point out that those entities that we unthinkingly experience as "natural" (they might even include capitalism, patriarchy, liberal humanism) are in fact "cultural"; made by us, not given to us'.[92]

These theoretical arguments are helpful when engaging with the work of an American artist who is often associated with the 1970s despite of the fact that his most imaginative output appeared in the previous decade: Andy Warhol. In singling out the 'Coca-Cola bottles' and 'Campbell's Soup cans and Brillo pads' as iconic pop art images, Bell and Hoeveler both implicitly concede a dominant position to the artist who produced them. In spite of Warhol's undeniably high profile in the seventies, however, there is a great danger in allowing him to serve as an index of, or indeed a stand-in for, 1970s art, precisely because he can so readily confirm the charges of flatness, emptiness, 'cultural depletion', banality and consumerism casually and habitually levelled at the art of the 'Me Decade'. Even with the implied caveats of Hutcheon's theories of parody, which would assign to Warhol's work a greater complexity than that allowed by Bell and other critics, Warhol did much to confirm such negative assessments, primarily because of his ostentatious obsession with celebrity in the 1970s.

As Sounes observes, Warhol's 'most high profile work' throughout the seventies were his portraits of celebrities (Liza Minnelli, Mick Jagger, Michael Jackson, Brigitte Bardot and a politically neutralised Chairman Mao) and his publishing venture, *Interview* magazine. None of these efforts were designed to confound critics of the 'Me Decade':

> [In] *Interview*, the primary subject . . . was movie stars, who were *the* most exciting people in the world as far as Andy was concerned . . . In *Interview*, movie stars – later also rock singers, models, sports figures, almost anybody famous – would be interviewed at length, often by Andy or another celebrity, the conversation revolving around clothes, perfume, favourite night clubs, money and sex . . . *Interview* celebrated fame.[93]

The celebrity portraits, naturally, were the visual corollary to the magazine, with Warhol, as Miller describes him, 'the portrait artist of an age saturated with marketing strategies'.[94]

But Warhol should not be perceived as the exemplar of seventies art, as Geoff Ward appears to perceive him: 'The 1970s . . . may be read with hindsight as a period of aftermath, in which individual careers were consolidated, but where artistic individualism as a trail-blazing credo sank to the point of parody in the culture of narcissism exemplified and recorded by Andy Warhol.'[95] In reality, an enormous amount of creative energy was being applied across the visual field, challenging Warhol's purported dominance of the decade. Land art, which relies on the shaping of landscapes, and related efforts in environmental art flourished in the 1970s through such works as Robert Smithson's *Spiral Jetty* (1970), Isamu Noguchi's *Night Wind* (1970) and Walter De Maria's *The Lightning Field* (1977). In 1972 James Turrell began a monumental work that is still in progress, reshaping the landscape surrounding Roden Crater in Arizona. A wealth of sculpture in a variety of forms – architectural, environmental, minimalist, kinetic and commemorative – appeared from the hands of Alexander Calder, Louise Nevelson, Starr Kempf, Donald Judd and Dan Flavin. George Segal cast his bronze sculpture, *Abraham and Isaac*, now at Princeton University, in 1978 to commemorate the Kent State shootings, while in the same year pop-artist Roy Lichtenstein departed from the canvas to create *Lamp*, a huge painted bronze sculpture towering over a public square in St Mary's, Georgia.

Painting likewise flourished in the 1970s, in places other than Warhol's studio. Pop art was by no means dead, with Alex Katz, James Rosenquist, Wayne Thiebauld, Tom Wesselmann and Lichtenstein all producing significant works. Robert Indiana saw his painting, 'LOVE' – with its signature tilted O – enshrined on the 8 cents postage stamp, another iconic moment in seventies art. Frank Stella not only enjoyed a 1970 retrospective at the Museum of Modern Art in New York, but he also produced one of his most celebrated works, *Tuftonboro*, in 1974. The school named by art critic Clement Greenberg as 'post-painterly abstraction' in 1964 was perpetuated into the seventies by Helen Frankenthaler (*Coral Wedge* and *Spoleto*, 1972; *Cleveland Symphony Orchestra*, 1978), while the post-abstract expressionist, Robert Ryman, saw thirty-eight of his paintings exhibited at New York's Guggenheim Museum in 1972. Conceptual art, installation art and site-specific art were variously represented by Hans Haacke's *MoMA Poll* (1970) and *Shapolsky et al.* (1971) – which respectively critiqued Nelson Rockefeller's conservatism and dubious practices by corrupt real estate magnates – and by Alexander Calder's monumental project to turn a DC-8 into a huge flying canvas for Braniff Airways (1973). Gordon Matta-Clark blended together photography and architectural destruction with *Day's End* and *Conical Intersect* (1975), while the conceptual artist, Jenny Holzer, began her series of public projections of disruptive imagery with *Truisms* (1977). Away from the New York art centres, south-western and West Coast cities witnessed an explosion of Chicano wall art that portrayed, in Willie Herron's words, 'the tear of two cultures, the feeling of violence and the fear of being ripped apart by them'.[96]

One of the most exciting art forms to emerge in force in the 1970s was video art, either on its own or in conjunction with live performance art. Significant practitioners in this arena included Dan Graham, Joan Jonas (also known as 'Organic Honey'), Richard Serra, Paul McCarthy, Sherrie Levine, Cindy Sherman, Jack Goldstein and Dennis Oppenheim. Still photography had its frontiers pushed with the championing of colour by William Eggleston (*The Red Ceiling*, 1973; *14 Pictures*, 1974), Gordon Matta-Clark's architectural critique, *Window Blow-Out* (1974), Robert Morris's sadomasochistic poster artwork and Robert Mapplethorpe's homoerotic images and Polaroid portraits of punk artists such as Patti Smith, which reflected a depth and a low-tech grittiness that seemed, if anything, deliberately anti-market. The 1970s were also highly rewarding for the photojournalists winning the annual Pulitzer Prize. Two of these photographers provided iconic images of the decade: Huynh Cong (Nick) Ut, with his harrowing photo of Kim Phuc and other napalmed children fleeing from their burning Vietnamese village (1973), and Stanley Forman with 'The Soiling of Old Glory' (1976), capturing an angry white man using the American flag as a lance to attack an African American lawyer, Ted Landsmark, amid the backlash against school bussing in Boston.

The decade also brought to national and international attention the work of a photographer who, in fact, only managed to witness its first two years. In 1971, Diane Arbus, younger sister of the future American Poet Laureate, Howard Nemerov, committed suicide. The following year, the Museum of Modern Art hosted a retrospective of her work, at which time the cultural critic, Leslie Fiedler, proposed that Arbus's photographs appeared to be 'an attempt to solve a riddle', indicating a depth and complexity that stood in direct opposition to the postmodern surfaces of Andy Warhol.[97]

Diane Arbus

In 1963, forty-year-old Diane Arbus submitted an application for a Guggenheim Fellowship, proposing a photographic series on 'American Rites, Manners and Customs'. She would photograph, she said, 'the considerable ceremonies of our present', to be gathered and preserved 'like somebody's grandmother putting up preserves, because they will have been so beautiful':

> There are the Ceremonies of Celebration (the Pageants, the Festivals, the Feasts, the Conventions) and the Ceremonies of Competition (Contests, Games, Sports), the Ceremonies of Buying and Selling, of Gambling, of the Law and the Show; the Ceremonies of Fame in which the Winners Win and the Lucky are Chosen or Family Ceremonies or Gatherings (the Schools, the Clubs, the Meetings).

In addition, there were:

> the ceremonial places (The Beauty Parlor, The Funeral Parlor or, simply the Parlor) and Ceremonial Costumes (what Waitresses wear, or Wrestlers), Ceremonies of the Rich like the Dog Show, and of the Middle Class, like the Bridge Game. Or, for example: the Dancing Lesson, the Graduation, the Testimonial Dinner, the Seance, the Gymnasium and the Picnic. And perhaps the Waiting room, the Factory, the Masquerade, the Rehearsal, the Initiation, the Hotel Lobby and Birthday Party. The etcetera [sic].[98]

These 'rites', 'manners' and 'customs', and the places where they unfolded, were, Arbus argued, 'our symptoms and our monuments'. Her desire was 'to save them, for what is ceremonious and curious and commonplace will be legendary', and she vowed: 'I will go wherever I can to find them.'[99]

Arbus was true to her word, leaving by way of a legacy a catalogue of images evoking what Sandra S. Phillips calls 'the ritualistic aspect of everyday life . . . the folkloric in photography'.[100] As opposed to Warhol's increasing focus on contemporary celebrity and surface flash, Arbus drew her inspiration from the deep mythological sources reflected in numerous works with which she was familiar: Robert Graves's *The Greek Myths*, *The White Goddess* and his translation of Lucius Apuleius's *The Golden Ass*; James Stephens's *The Crock of Gold*; James Frazer's monumental *The Golden Bough*; Joseph Campbell's *The Hero with a Thousand Faces*; J. R. R. Tolkein's *The Hobbit* and Ovid's *Metamorphosis*. With such a grounding, as Phillips observes, 'Arbus was attuned to the ancient, folkloric, or talismanic aspects of contemporary life', tracing with her camera 'a continuity with an ancient past, to reveal a mythological richness in the unexalted present'.[101]

A failure to appreciate Arbus's rationale for bringing ancient and mythological delineations into her contemporary images has led many to condemn her as a voyeur preying on social outcasts, deviants and what she herself quite problematically called 'freaks'. A cursory overview of her image titles between 1956 and 1970 might at first glance lend credence to this charge: 'Fire Eater at a carnival', 'Female impersonator's dressing room', 'The Human Pincushion', 'Dominatrix with a kneeling client', 'Mexican dwarf in his hotel room', 'Transvestite showing cleavage', 'Tattooed man at carnival', 'Seated man in bra and stockings', 'A Jewish giant at home with his parents in the Bronx, NY'. A letter to a friend gives further indication of what most captured Arbus's imagination and sympathy:

> Friday night . . . I went into a Child's – I mean the restaurant . . . and at a near table there was a couple and the woman was an incredible spastic, very plain and pale and middleaged like lillian gish [sic], like an out of order mechanical doll. She was eating her custard when I came in and dancing while she was eating it, seven motions for every once the spoon got to her mouth. The man was very tall and thin, graceful fatherly agile cheerful, affable, talkative, when they got up he held her coat for her to dance into and her face didn't ever change, she looked terribly plain and dazzled, like someone seeing visions, and after she got into her coat he bent over like a tree and kissed her.[102]

As Fiedler argues, Arbus is clearly not focusing on 'freaks' simply to present 'our last taboo in the guise of entertainment'; on the contrary, he quotes her by way of explaining her rationale:

> 'There's a quality of legend about freaks. Like a person in a fairy tale who stops you and demands that you answer a riddle. Most people go through life dreading they'll have a traumatic experience. Freaks were born with their traumas. They've already passed their test in life. They're aristocrats.'[103]

Many will no doubt hear echoes of Arbus in the songs of Tom Waits, who has been similarly attuned, as Cath Carroll notes, to the anonymous, the non-celebrities, 'the great minority of losers and down-and-outs, melancholics and hookers . . . the true outsiders of current society – scary neighbors and the so-called freaks of circus and carnival'.[104] To Phillips, Arbus's work is, rather than an exercise in cheap voyeurism, an attempt to illuminate American 'subcultures and the rituals of self-contained miniature societies', whether they be 'dwarves, street people, costumed women' or 'Masons, baton twirling clubs, female impersonators, gangs, prisons, old age homes, singles clubs, families [and] nudists'.[105] Consequently, as Elisabeth Sussman and Doon Arbus argue, 'Each subculture she begins to explore turns out to be, not only a territory unto itself, but a key to deciphering the rules of another, apparently unconnected, subculture so that the world, as she puts it, *seems . . . not so much small as done with mirrors*'.[106]

Advocates of Arbus's photography have taken pains to emphasise the non-exploitative nature of her relationship with her subjects. Phillips maintains that, 'in a manner unique among her contemporaries, Arbus rendered the interaction between [photographer and subject] as a self-conscious and collaborative meeting'.[107] Allan Arbus, Diane's former husband, recalled: 'Her subjects moved her deeply and she treated them very nearly reverently. She was captivated by their self-images and the discrepancy between their view of themselves and the world's perception of them.'[108]

Members of one subculture appear to have been exempt from Arbus's sympathy, however – the very subculture over which Warhol so publicly and obsessively fawned: celebrities. As Sounes notes, Arbus 'was not averse to photographing celebrities, but [she] wanted to subvert rather than celebrate their fame'.[109] Hence her relatively unflattering portraits of the presidential candidate, Eugene McCarthy, the Argentine writer, Jorge Luis Borges and, especially, the feminist icon, Germaine Greer, all of whom appear tired and dishevelled, somewhat soiled and seedy. Greer's recollection of her portrait sitting betrays a particularly bitter power struggle between the photographer and her subject:

> I was staying at the Chelsea Hotel in a seedy room. Diane arrived and immediately asked me to lie down on my bed . . . Then all of a sudden she knelt on the bed and hung over me with this wide-angle lens staring me in the face and began click-clicking away.
>
> It developed into a sort of duel between us, because I *resisted* being photographed like that – close-up with all my pores and lines showing . . . but because she was a woman I didn't tell her to fuck off. If she'd been a man, I'd have kicked her in the balls.
>
> It was tyranny. Really tyranny. Diane Arbus ended up straddling me – this frail little person kneeling, keening over my face. I felt completely terrorized by the blasted lens. It was a helluva struggle. Finally I decided, 'Damn it, you're not going to do this to me, lady. I'm not going to be photographed like one of your grotesque freaks!'[110]

Implicitly acknowledging her own bitterly manipulative intent when dealing with celebrity subjects, Arbus confided to a friend that Greer 'was fun and is terrific looking but I managed to make [her look] otherwise'.[111]

It is possible that there was a political intent, unconscious or not, in Arbus's determination to deflate the pretensions of celebrity and to subvert the surface allure of glamour. Curator John Szarkowski places Arbus's late photographs in the context of the Vietnam War and all that it revealed on the home front:

> For most Americans the meaning of the Vietnam War was not political, or military, or even ethical, but psychological. It brought us to a sudden, unambiguous knowledge of moral frailty and failure. The photographs that best memorialize the shock of that new knowledge were perhaps made halfway around the world, by Diane Arbus.[112]

Arbus's *oeuvre* thus stands – if read in that direction – as a powerful critique of American narcissism, yet one more example to challenge the presumed zeitgeist of the 'Me Decade'.

Figure 3.2 Diane Arbus teaching at the Rhode Island School of Design (1970).
© Stephen A. Frank.

Whether represented in film or static visual art, as this chapter has demonstrated, seventies culture was hardly 'depleted' (as Bell and others so short sightedly maintained). On the contrary, seventies culture gave rise to a plethora of styles, genres and fusions across the spectrum from 'high' to 'low' art. The dynamic fecundity that characterised film and visual culture also reached into other areas demanding a renewed scrutiny. Among the most important and influential of these cultural areas was a host of popular music genres and the styles associated with them, the subjects of the next chapter.

Chapter 4

Popular Music and Style

On 30 August 1970, Jimi Hendrix played his last concert, an ill-rehearsed, half-hearted set before an irritable crowd at the Isle of Wight Festival in England. Footage of the concert shows the audience calling for the Hendrix of Woodstock, the pyrotechnic wizard of the Stratocaster, playing the guitar with his teeth and kicking the stuffing out of sacred cows like the 'Star Spangled Banner'. Hendrix virtually ignores them except for the odd sardonic utterance as he wrestles with a temperamental sound system and the demands of a backward-looking audience. After two hours of false starts, technical glitches and flashes of musical brilliance, Hendrix leaves the stage muttering.[1]

Three weeks later, Hendrix was dead at the age of twenty-seven from an overdose of barbiturates mixed with alcohol. He was followed a month later by another Woodstock legend, Janis Joplin, also dead at twenty-seven from a heroin overdose. A third twenty-seven-year-old, Jim Morrison of the Doors, would be dead within a year. On the last day of 1970, Paul McCartney formally dissolved the Beatles through a court order: if ever an era had ended, pundits argued, it was that day. The following year, Don McLean released 'American Pie', his elegy for the lost rock and rollers, Buddy Holly, Richie Valens and J. P. 'the Big Bopper' Richardson, all killed in a plane crash in 1959. If that February day twelve years earlier was indeed 'the day the music died' (as McLean sings), the elegiac mood of 'American Pie' nonetheless reflected as much upon the seventies as upon the fifties. As Peter N. Carroll suggests, the musical zeitgeist of the early seventies implied that 'the only hopeful vision of the American future seemed to exist in the past'.[2]

With the commencement of the 1970s, iconic figures of the 'Woodstock Nation' (as Abbie Hoffman called the 1960s counter-culture) certainly appeared to be looking backwards. On the 1971

album, *Déjà Vu*, Crosby, Stills, Nash and Young (CSNY) sing Joni
Mitchell's 'Woodstock' like old soldiers recalling the glory days of past
battles, even though the concert had been staged only two years
before. Howard Sounes implicitly dismisses the first half of the
decade's music as a process of winding down, seeing 1975 as the watershed after which

> the old fashioned got junked, and in rushed the new-fashioned, like a
> line of cocaine: blockbuster movies, disco, punk. The first five years of
> the seventies were, in many ways, an extension of the sixties, particularly
> in films and rock music. It was metaphorically, and often literally, the age
> of marijuana: of mellow, hophead introspection.[3]

Similarly, Carroll argues that in the early seventies, the music industry and its consumers 'embraced the introspective songs of James
Taylor, John Denver, and Carole King' as though such acoustic
singer–songwriters were preparing the ground for the wholesale
occupancy of the Me Generation.[4] As if to confirm this critique, Bob
Dylan – to many the major voice of the sixties protest movement –
ushered in the decade with his highly evasive *Self Portrait* (1970). Of
the album itself, a perplexed Greil Marcus wrote in *Rolling Stone*,
'What is this shit?'[5] Of the album's deliberate place as the death
knell to Dylan's reputation as the spokesman of the sixties counter-
culture, the singer argued: 'I was representing all these things that I
didn't know anything about . . . It was all storm-the-embassy kind of
stuff – Abbie Hoffman in the streets – and they sorta figured me
as the kingpin of all that. I said, "Wait a minute, I'm just a musi-
cian." '[6]

It would be disingenuous, however, to allow such examples to characterise American popular music in the first half of the 1970s. Rather,
the early years of the decade were a period of gathering force as the cultural landscape shifted and adjusted to a variety of developments,
social, political and technological. Far from validating Daniel Bell's
claim of a culture cut off from the society that produces and consumes
it, American popular music ushered in the decade with a fierce
regional, political and cultural battle variously pitting North against
South, progressivism against conservatism and, at times, musical styles
against one another. As is often the case with internecine warfare,
members on opposing sides also found themselves locked together in
a mutual embrace. Country music in the 1970s is highly indicative of
these tensions.

Flush Times in the Country

As Bruce J. Schulman has argued, 'after 1970, the great American cen-
trifuge spun freely', distributing into the southern Sunbelt growing
power blocs based on 'votes, dollars and songs'.[7] The power bases –
condominium communities in Florida, army bases in the South-West
and the expanding aerospace and defence industries sweeping the land
from Los Angeles to Atlanta – boosted the southern population
twofold in relation to the rest of the country. The musical soundtrack
to this regional expansion was steeped in 'a populist, conservative
political philosophy' that marked a resurgence of reactionary southern
pride:

> Country lyrics continued to champion poor whites, frequently plotting
> the working stiff's revenge against welfare chiselers, taxes, and the boss
> man, taking pride in a hardscrabble, marginal, rural way of life. A
> cascade of songs explicitly celebrated the virtues of 'rednecks' and 'hill-
> billies', transforming these terms of derogation into badges of honor.
> Johnny Russell's 'Red Necks, White Sox, and Blue Ribbon Beer' led the
> wave in 1973, followed by Jerry Jeff Walker's 'Redneck Mother' and
> Vernon Oxford's 'Redneck! (The Redneck National Anthem)'.[8]

Country music's resurgence was due, in part, to an internecine war.
On one side stood the forces of cheesy commercialism, best exemplified in the 1973 closing of downtown Nashville's Ryman Auditorium,
which had hosted WSM radio's Grand Ole Opry since 1943, and the
removal of the Opry to its current location, the glitzy theme park
known as 'Opryland'. Opposed to such cultural vandalism were the
likes of the singer–songwriter, John Hartford, who spearheaded a
campaign to preserve the Ryman, and Willie Nelson and Waylon
Jennings who, by 1975, had made Austin, Texas the capital of 'Outlaw
Country' music, the alternative genre contemptuous of all that the
'Nashville Sound' and 'Countrypolitan' music had become.[9] While
Outlaw Country would lay important groundwork for the emergence of such 'New Country' figures as Gram Parsons, Ricky Skaggs,
Nanci Griffith and Steve Earle – all of whom have helped to shake off
the wider genre's politically reactionary associations – in the mid-sev-
enties the automatic equation between country music and 'redneck'
ideology was a common, if misinformed, assumption.

In the 1970s, the enormously popular songs of Merle Haggard did
nothing to prevent such an assumption, as Schulman argues:

Without overt racial messages, they expressed subtle antiblack or anti-city sentiments, usually directed against welfare and government programs. 'There's folks who never work and they got plenty', Merle Haggard complained in 'Big City'. In another song . . . Haggard asked over and over again, 'Are the Good Times Really Over?' He longed for former and better days before welfare when 'a man could still work and still would', before 'microwave ovens, when a girl could still cook and still would'.[10]

In 1969, Haggard wrote that year's most popular conservative hit, 'Okie from Muskogee', an up-front swipe at the dope smokers and flag burners who presumably characterised the counter-culture. 'Okie from Muskogee' was followed in 1970 by Haggard's anti-antiwar-protester song, 'The Fightin' Side of Me'. As Haggard, an ex-convict, would later explain to radio host, Bob Edwards:

> I knew what it was like to lose my freedom, and I was getting really mad at these protestors. They didn't know anything more about the war in Vietnam than I did. I thought how my dad, who was from Oklahoma, would have felt. I felt I knew how those boys fighting in Vietnam felt.[11]

Gordon Friesen, radical editor of New York's *Broadside* folk music magazine, condemned Haggard for his '[John] Birch-type songs against war dissenters'.[12] At the same time, however, music critics Jens Lund and R. Serge Denisoff argued that the relationship between the youth counter-culture and country music was more complex than merely adversarial. Writing in 1971, when Haggard was actually enjoying a following among college students, they pointed out that his popularity was due to more than an ironic adoption by the mocking counter-culture; it was also due to the early country/folk traditions out of which his music, like that of CSNY, grew. Both 'Okie from Muskogee' and 'The Fightin' Side of Me', they noted, 'received extensive underground airplay. Arlo Guthrie and Phil Ochs use "Okie from Muskogee" in their concert performances. . . The "folk freaks", as they are now called, sing many of Haggard's songs.'[13]

Another mutual antagonism in 1970–1 between Neil Young and the Lynyrd Skynyrd band indicates that vicious domestic battle-lines were being redrawn along previously war-torn territory, the Mason–Dixon Line. Young, a transplanted Canadian, chose to do battle in the 1970s, as he had done at the close of the 1960s, against the conservative values that he associated with the American South. With

Woodstock barely a year behind him, and co-terminous with the release of CSNY's *Déjà Vu*, Young turned to two provocative American subjects in quick succession. In 1970, responding to the news of the Kent State shootings, he penned and released a single, 'Ohio', condemning the 'tin soldiers' of the Ohio National Guard and Richard Nixon personally for the loss of four student lives (on the B side was Stephen Stills's anti-war anthem, 'Find the Cost of Freedom'). Popular radio stations across the United States refused to give the song air time, while Haggard's 'Okie from Muskogee' and 'The Fightin' Side of Me' continued its circulation on both the popular and underground airwaves. While Young's 'Ohio' provoked no response from overt patriots like Haggard, its successor, 'Southern Man' (1970), sparked one of the decade's greatest musical conflicts. As Barbara Ching recounts, the vicious battle ensued when Young released his scathing attack on 'the steamy, swampy South of antebellum white privilege', replete with images of lynchings, burning crosses and white women's lust for black men.[14] 'Southern Man' brought in rebuttal Lynyrd Skynyrd's 'Sweet Home Alabama' (1974), a song that not only excoriated Neil Young by name, but which also revived the century-old Southern charge of Northern hypocrisy and political corruption. The segregationist crimes of Alabama governor George Wallace, the song argues, were no worse than the political crimes of Nixon and Watergate. To Jim Cullen, 'Sweet Home Alabama' marks 'one of the most vivid examples of a lingering Confederate mythology in Southern culture'.[15]

To a large degree, the Southern musical resurgence was a cultural reflection of the Southern political resurgence marked by the prominence of a new generation of post-segregation Southern governors such as Georgia's Jimmy Carter, positioning himself for a run at the White House in 1976. A host of cultural and stylistic developments added to the new country chic that grew in step with Southern political clout, as Schulman describes:

> Country music and southern rock, cowboy boots and pork rinds, even Pentecostal churches and the Confederate flag appeared throughout the nation. In 1973, the Country Music Association held its annual convention in Manhattan, and Mayor John Lindsay declared Country Music Day in New York City. 'There's a swing over to the simple, the clean, to the healthy,' a Yankee convert to the Nashville sound enthused. 'Country music celebrates the goodness in America, faith in America, patriotism.'[16]

Country singers such as Ray Stevens ('Everything Is Beautiful') and Norman Greenbaum ('Spirit in the Sky') tapped into the wider evangelical fervour that marked not only the development of a subgenre of confessional Christian music, but also the growing political support for self-proclaimed 'born again' Christians such as Jimmy Carter. The evangelical Christian inflections of country music were, of course, nothing new; devotional hymns were staples of the repertoire going back to the 1920s, when the Carter Family began recording. But what was new in the seventies was the gathering corporate efficiency and smoothness of the Christian country music industry which, by the end of the decade, had paved the way for the emergence of Amy Grant and other denizens of 'Christian Contemporary Music'. Even Bob Dylan was not immune to the born-again spirit, closing the decade with the wholesale embracing of a 'lifestyle relationship' with Christ and the release of his Christian-themed album, *Slow Train Coming* (1979).[17]

Corporate efficiency and smoothness were not only the preserve of godly music, however. As the following case study shows, the decade witnessed the incorporation of a highly stylised decadence, both lyrical and behavioural, on an unparalleled scale in the music industry. It was spearheaded by the band whose music, in Gary Herman's words, 'is the very culmination of California rock'.[18]

The Eagles

In 1976, the Recording Industry Association of America introduced a new award category, the platinum record, for an album selling over a million copies. This award was conferred for the first time upon the Eagles' *Their Greatest Hits, 1971–1975*, acknowledging the position of what is arguably the most commercially successful American band to date. Four California-based musicians – Glenn Frey, Bernie Leadon, Randy Meisner and Don Henley – had formed the band in 1971 to back the singer Linda Ronstadt on tour. Although the Eagles were to see some personnel changes through the years (the departure of Leadon and Meisner; the addition of Don Felder and Joe Walsh), one constant remained. To quote record producer Elliot Roberts, 'The Eagles were *made* to sell a million records. . . They wrote to be huge.'[19] The release of their best-selling album, *Hotel California*, in the bicentennial year, marked the zenith of a trajectory that had begun on the heels of the Los Angeles folk boom of the 1960s, bringing the band to the height of rock-star wealth and (so the album's imagery would suggest) decadence. As Michael Walker describes it, despite the groupies and affairs, wine-and-cocaine nights, private Learjets and trashed hotel rooms, 'tucked away in their collective limo of the soul was the memory of starting out young, broke, and ideal-istic – although, as Henley pointed out, "it's hard to be an underdog when you're selling 12 million records".'[20]

To chart the distance the band had travelled before they fell apart in 1980 under the pressures of apparently limitless wealth and temptation (they reunited in 1994), one might begin with the small stage of the Troubadour folk club, the centre of the Los Angeles folk scene in the 1960s, corre-sponding roughly with Gerde's Folk City in Greenwich Village, New York, where Bob Dylan, Joan Baez, Ramblin' Jack Elliott and Dave Van Ronk were spearheading the East Coast folk music revival. As Glenn Frey wrote in his song, 'The Sad Café', the Troubadour 'seemed like a holy place' from the retrospective vantage point of the seventies.[21] The 'Folk Movement', in *Crawdaddy* journalist Peter Knobler's words, had been 'perhaps the first of [the sixties'] generation's Capitalised causes to merge politics and culture.'[22] Projecting itself as a forum for purity and authenticity as opposed to crass commercial culture, folk music 'fostered a sense of beleaguered community. A particular attraction to youthful malcontents was the sense of "us" (liberal, left-leaning pacifists) against "them" (Republicans and bland, middle-class materialists).'[23] The Troubadour was central to this movement and community, 'indispensable', in Walker's words, 'in bringing together the first wave of L.A. folkies', while in the next decade 'it became the stage, salon and saloon for the singing–songwriting young men and women flocking to Laurel Canyon. If the canyon was where everyone in the L.A. music scene lived either in fact or spirit, the Troubadour was where they played.'[24]

The 'spirit' of Laurel Canyon in the seventies was captured by Graham Nash of CSNY, who recalled:

> It was very much like maybe Vienna was at the turn of the century or Paris in the '30s, where something happens and you don't know what it is and it's catching fire and there's more music coming out and more people making music and more people discovering each other and discovering the fact that love is better than hate and peace is better than war and really trying to emphasize those kinds of things that we all truly believed in.[25]

The LA folk scene, however, could not survive the onslaught of musical as well as commercial forces. While the actual birth date of 'folk rock' is much in dispute, it is clear that folk-based, or vernacular, American music under-went a remarkable transformation at the turn of the decade, much of it California based. As John Einarson explains:

> In the late sixties, a small faction of young, long-haired musicians sought to inject some country music into their rock & roll. They worked in Southern California, but their roots represented a broad spectrum of the North American experience. From a variety of personal perspectives and motiva-tions, these musicians either played country with a rock & roll attitude, or added a country feel to rock, or folk, or bluegrass.[26]

Thus, by the mid-1970s, Laurel Canyon-based singer–songwriters such as Jackson Browne, solo interpreters such as Linda Ronstadt, and bands such as CSNY and America helped to consolidate the laid-back 'L.A. Sound' by bringing folk, country and soft rock into mutual conversation. A slightly harder edge and up-tempo reference back to bluegrass and Western swing was provided by such musicians as the Byrds and the Flying Burrito Brothers – in particular, the legendary, short-lived guitarist Gram Parsons, who was a member of both. All of these musical forces and influences led directly to the Eagles.

But for Parsons, what came to be known as 'country rock' (the hybrid for which he is most often given credit for establishing) was nothing more than a 'plastic dry-fuck'.[27] He reserved his greatest contempt for the Eagles, whom Eliot Roberts called 'a bridge between avant-garde and commercial'.[28] Early signature singles such as the Jackson Browne–Glenn Frey co-penning, 'Take It Easy' and Jack Tempchin's 'Peaceful Easy Feeling' soon defined both the Eagles' sound and, it appeared, the loose and mellow Southern Californian dream itself (a highly ironical fact since none of the Eagles hailed from California). It was not merely the hijacking of the Golden State as an identity marker, however, that caused the hostility of some of the first reviews upon the release of the debut album, *Eagles*, in 1972. Robert Christgau, writing in the *Village Voice*, admitted the band's undeniable professionalism (he called them 'the tightest and most accomplished rock band to emerge since Neil Young's Crazy Horse'); but their music left him, as he said, 'feeling alienated from the things I used to love':

It's no accident . . . that the Eagles' hip country music excises precisely what is deepest and most gripping about country music – its adult working-class pain, its paradoxically rigid ethics – and leaves bluegrass-sounding good feelin' . . . The music, the lyrics, the distribution machine are all suave and synthetic. Brilliant stuff – but false.[29]

The Eagles' next two albums, *Desperado* (1973) and *On the Border* (1974), consolidated the band's visual and musical iconography: western-themed artwork and photography on the album covers and the gunfighter imagery in such songs as 'Doolin Dalton' and 'Desperado'. As Henley recalls,

the outlaw metaphor was probably a little bullshit . . . We were in L.A. staying up all night, smoking dope, living the California life, and I suppose we thought it was as radical as cowboys in the old West'.[30]

The mid-decade, however, signalled a change. Again, Henley recalls:

Society and music were becoming more urbanized and hard-edged . . . Around 1976, when we made *Hotel California*, most traces of country had gone. With the addition of Joe Walsh and Don Felder to the group, we pretty much left the country influence behind. Disco and punk had come, and we wanted to rock.[31]

What *Hotel California* signals, beyond technical proficiency and smooth musicianship, is – as the title track in particular indicates – an implicit desire to travel back to a pre-stadium-rock innocence, the days of singer–songwriters on the small, lone stage. The imagery of desperation, panic and imprisonment amid the fountains of champagne, medieval gluttony, sexual deviants and lines of cocaine on the mirror dominate much of the album. Titles such as 'Life in the Fast Lane', 'Wasted Time' and 'Victim of Love' are also indicative of the California dream gone horribly wrong. The music industry itself, where pills are dropped as frequently as names, is as much a target of critique as the celebrity-and-profit-fuelled society at large. Walker quotes two of the band members on 'Hotel California's unsparing allegories about the soul-sucking wages of Los Angeles in the 1970s':

> 'There was a time during 1976, 1977, when the record business went crazy,' Glenn Frey later recalled. 'That was when Hotel California came out, and Saturday Night Fever and [Fleetwood Mac's] Rumours. That was the music business at its decadent zenith . . . I seem to remember the wine was the best and the drugs were good and the women were beautiful and, man, we seemed to have an endless amount of energy.' Said Henley: 'Those kinds of record sales were unprecedented. I guess everybody thought it was going to continue like that.'[32]

The fact that it could not 'continue like that', as the increasingly embittered Eagles began to leave their concerts in separate limousines, did not signal the demise of corporate-backed music or rock-star celebrity. Elsewhere in the musical galaxy of the seventies, new stars were being born and promoted with intense determination and skill.

The Future of Rock and Roll: From Dylan to Springsteen

Bob Dylan may have signalled his abdication from public responsibility at the beginning of the decade with his comments surrounding the release of *Self-Portrait*, and he may have implied a retreat into evangelism at the end of the decade with his release of *Slow Train Coming*, but it would be a mistake to see him as any less than a central figure in American rock music throughout the 1970s. With *Blood on the Tracks* (1975) and *Desire* (1976) each reaching the top of the US charts upon their release, Dylan was clearly enjoying the peak of his success at mid-decade. Moreover, if ever there were a sign that the counter-cultural, crusading spirit of Dylan's 1960s had not been wholly extinguished with the new decade, it would be the Rolling Thunder Review, the musical campaign of 1975 organised by Dylan to draw attention to the plight of the wrongfully imprisoned middleweight boxer, Rubin 'Hurricane' Carter. Convicted of two New Jersey murders under highly dubious and racially charged circumstances, Carter became a cause célèbre for Dylan and colleagues such as Joan Baez, Allen Ginsberg, Roger McGuinn and T-Bone Burnett.

Dylan engaged the playwright Sam Shepard to chronicle the travel-
ling revue which, both in its explicit political mission and in its musical
ethos, appeared to Shepard as an immediate contrast to the glitter of
disco and the self-absorbed nihilism of punk and New Wave that had
emerged with such force by mid-decade. Despite the magnitude of his
reputation, Dylan and his coterie were keeping the flame of grass-roots
protest alive, as Shepard surmised: 'All of us working together for the
same purpose – to try to live in constant movement on the road for six
weeks, traveling by land, putting on music, filming this music in the
surroundings of broken American history in small New England
towns in the dead of winter.'[33] The contrast between Dylan and his
competition could not have been be more pronounced than when
Shepard reviewed the increasingly popular New Wave band, The
Tubes, performing in Boston in the midst of the Rolling Thunder tour:

> We're admitted to the monster show. 'White Punks on Dope.' It's like
> walking into a crypt festival. TV sets flashing all over the place, violent
> distorted feedback that sounds like a cow stepping on her afterbirth and
> not knowing what hit her. An eight-foot transvestite in stilted platform
> heels, silver skin-tight jumpsuit, teased blond hair, and the drummer
> behind slashing away at his kit as though he was caught in his own mos-
> quito netting. If this is supposed to be satire, I don't get it. If it's not, then
> somebody's in bad shape.[34]

At this moment of the tour, the transition from the sixties to the
seventies appears to be complete in Shepard's eyes:

> Strange thoughts are going through me. 'What are all these kids doing
> watching this shit when they could be hearing good music? What do
> they care about good music? What do they care about a bunch of West
> Village folk singers from the sixties? . . . Is this that generation stuff that
> you hear about all the time? What's going on anyway? Am I a part of the
> old folks now? Is Dylan? Is Dylan unheard of in certain circles? Like
> Frank Sinatra? Bing Crosby? Is this time flying? Is this time flying right
> past us on all sides?'[35]

While Shepard could sense that, in his brief encounter with New
Wave, there was a growing cadre of new musicians apparently unconnected with Dylan and the activism of the sixties, one other musical
figure was emerging who would raise immediate associations not only
with Dylan but with his legacy into the twenty-first century. The
influential film and music critic Jon Landau wrote in Boston's *Real*

Paper of 22 May 1974, in the same city in which Shepard was to perceive the grievous end of sixties musical idealism: 'Last Thursday, at the Harvard Square theatre, I saw my rock 'n' roll past flash before my eyes. And I saw something else: I saw rock and roll future and its name is Bruce Springsteen . . . like a cross between Chuck Berry, early Bob Dylan, and Marlon Brando.'[36] Destined to become America's greatest stadium rocker of the 1980s, Springsteen in the 1970s was already walking a tightrope between, on the one hand, his desire for autonomy and working-class authenticity and, on the other hand, the dynamics of corporate hype.

Bruce Springsteen

Springsteen had emerged at the front of an electric band from the New Jersey shore, honing his delivery through live performances in small venues and barrooms. By the time Landau heard him he had produced two albums, *Greetings from Asbury Park, N.J.* (1973) and *The Wild, the Innocent, and the E Street Shuffle* (1973). Towards the end of 1975, with the release of *Born to Run* and wall-to-wall radio airplay, the CBS corporate machine made sure that readers of all the music magazines would know through full-page advertisements that 1976 would be 'the year of Bruce Springsteen'.[37] Music critics immediately began locating and speculating on the eclecticism of Springsteen's influences – from Woody Guthrie through Dylan, Elvis Presley, Phil Spector, Chuck Berry, Roy Orbison, Van Morrison, The Band, James Brown, Sam and Dave – and indicating his heavy debt to American popular music history. As David Wyatt has noted, Springsteen's music in the seventies appeared to mark 'the passage from the adolescent to the adult world', giving the impression of trying 'to outrun time' itself:

> He builds up a song through three basic devices: images of distance and longing, plots and melodies suddenly broken off, a driving beat that overtakes the careful articulations of the lyrics and leaves the singer hoarse in his attempt to control its motion. His style thus enables him to translate an immediate social problem – the loss of economic mobility – into a music expressive of the enduring human fear that love cannot survive the sheer momentum of time.[38]

Springsteen's overt social engagement – his focus on the plight of the American working class in the midst of recession, on the closing down of American options – clearly leads him to an increasingly bleak perspective throughout the decade, with *Darkness on the Edge of Town* (1978) marking the dying days of adolescent and post-adolescent glory. The album's tenor is also linked to particular events in Springsteen's life and times: his own bitter feud and prolonged lawsuit with his manager, Mike Appel, the death of Elvis Presley in 1977 and his deepening relationship with Landau, who was to succeed Appel as his manager. As Springsteen's biographer, Dave Marsh, recalls, the post-mortem revelations of Presley's sad dissolution and his exploitation at the hands of his ruthless manager, 'Colonel' Tom Parker, provoked a troubling parallel:

> Bruce identified with Elvis's career, the way it seemed totally in the artist's control at one moment, and careening without guidance the next. 'He was an artist, and he wanted to be an artist,' Bruce said soon after Presley died, which also summed up Bruce's feelings about himself. But he wasn't about to allow himself to be caught up in anyone's expectations, as Elvis had done. 'Mike Appel thought he'd be Colonel Parker and I'd be Elvis,' Springsteen would later say. 'Only he wasn't the Colonel, and I wasn't Elvis.'[39]

Thus, as Marsh concludes, 'the lessons of hype, the lawsuit, the failures of his idol, Elvis, and the natural maturity that came with simply being twenty-eight worked a transformation in Springsteen and his music', a transformation towards a more brooding, less celebratory ethos than that which had marked the road-running energy of his first three albums.[40]

Bryan K. Garman points to other important developments that fed into the making of *Darkness on the Edge of Town*:

> In the late 1970s he began to listen to Jimmie Rodgers, Johnny Cash, Hank Williams, and the performers on the standard collection of American folk music, *The Folkways Anthology*. As Springsteen continued to write about working-class lives, he found that for inspiration he went 'back further all the time. Back into Hank Williams, back into Jimmie Rodgers. Because the human thing in those records is just beautiful and awesome.'[41]

Under Landau's influence, Springsteen also became acquainted with the gritty, dark Westerns of the Italian director, Sergio Leone, the films of John Ford and, through Ford's cinematic treatments, the writings of John Steinbeck. As Garman claims, these influences, in the light of Springsteen's 'austere working-class upbringing' and his bitter lessons at the hands of corporate power brokers, fed into a rich musical–literary–cinematic nexus: '*Darkness* claims its cultural roots in John Steinbeck's *The Grapes of Wrath* as well as John Ford's film based on the novel.'[42]

Steinbeck's great Dust Bowl epic presents numerous examples of American workers at the mercy of ruthless corporate agents and distant bureaucracies. *Darkness on the Edge of Town* indicates that Springsteen – like Steinbeck and the Dust Bowl balladeer, Woody Guthrie (whose music Springsteen would increasingly champion in the 1980s and afterwards) – was becoming involved in what Michael Denning calls 'the laboring of American culture' and the expansion of 'a proletarian public sphere'.[43] As Marsh argues,

> for all the cars, the violence and the searching, the dominant image of *Darkness on the Edge of Town* is labor. There are lines about working in 'Badlands', 'Adam Raised a Cain', 'Racing in the Streets', 'The Promised

Land', 'Factory,' and 'Prove It All Night' and in three of the other four songs, there are references to wealth or the lack of it.[44]

And, in an echo of Steinbeck, 'a vague, disembodied "they" creeps into songs like "Something in the Night", "Prove It All Night" and "Streets of Fire" to deny people their most full-blooded possibilities'.[45]

Jim Cullen points to the change with which Springsteen employs one of the iconic images that had stood out so powerfully in *Born to Run*: the freedom of the road:

> On no album . . . are automobiles more important than *Darkness on the Edge of Town*. With one (significant) exception, every song at least mentions cars and/or driving. And more than on any other album, cars are intimately bound up in questions of work and play.
>
> Tellingly, those who have given up – the men of 'Factory' – walk. Sung from the point of view of a son sadly observing his father, 'Factory' describes men who have lost the will to make a break.[46]

Thus, *Darkness on the Edge of Town* powerfully reflects the diminished expectations of Jimmy Carter's America, beleaguered by oil embargos, five-mile petrol queues, defaults on loans, repossessions and stagflation. Springsteen himself explained the shift marked by *Darkness* in a 1984 interview in *Rolling Stone*:

> I was always concerned with gettin' a group of characters and followin' them through their lives a little bit. And so, on *Born to Run*, *Darkness on the Edge of Town* and *The River*, I tried to hook things up. I guess in *Born to Run* there's that searchin' thing. . . That searchin', and faith, and the idea of hope. And then on *Darkness*, it was kind of like a collision that happens between this guy and the real world. He ends up very alone and real stripped down.[47]

Again, in the *New Musical Express*, Springsteen observed:

> The characters [in *Darkness*] ain't kids . . . they're older – you been beat, you been hurt. . . They throw dirt on you all your life, and some people get buried so deep in the dirt that they'll never get out. The album's about people who will never admit that they're buried that deep.[48]

The film director, Martin Scorsese, recalled hearing Springsteen for the first time in the mid-1970s: 'There was no one else like him around at the time. The punk and New Wave explosions were happening here and in England, but that was a different kind of music – anarchic, relentlessly abrasive. Springsteen was something else – deeply romantic, even extravagantly so.'[49] Scorsese also notes, 'During the '70s, the word "epiphany" was used quite often by certain film critics – referring to those moments when everything breaks through, when the audience finds itself delivered to a new and unexpected place by the artist'; Springsteen, he argues, 'has given us many such moments'.[50] That Springsteen's 'laboring' of American music could have had such an epiphanic impact amid the economic crises of the 1970s is corroborated by an interviewee in Daniel Cavicci's study of 'music and meaning among Springsteen fans'. The reflections of this Pennsylvania woman deserve quotation in full, since they neatly place Springsteen's proletarian cultural work in the context of the 1970s as well as significant preceding decades:

> One song in particular hit me right between the eyes and caused an epiphany that changed the course of my life. That was 'Factory'.
>
> At the time (I was 18) I had just started dating my husband, an auto worker who steam cleaned and shovelled metal into a furnace all day. He'd come home so covered in grease and bits of metal that he had to roll up his pants to walk into the house. My husband (boyfriend) *hated* it there. It was hot, dirty work, and about the best he could expect, having dropped out of school (I think he lied about that to get the job). I hated watching him go there every day.
>
> My grandfather had worked at the same place since he came back from WWII. He'd never say a bad word about the place. He was a toolmaker, and as a skilled worker had it a little better. The factory had enabled him to support his family his whole life and having lived through the Depression, he didn't expect anything more.
>
> I dated my husband for four years while he worked there and 'Factory' clearly prophesied his future if he stayed there hating every minute of his job. The image invoked by the song was all too real. Anyway, when my husband (fiancé) confided that he wanted to be a cop, I decided we'd do whatever it took to get him out of that hellhole. And that's what we did. I helped him study for his GED [General Education Diploma] and get through the police academy.[51]

In the wake of *Darkness on the Edge of Town*, Springsteen's *The River* (1980) inaugurated the decade of Ronald Reagan's neoconservative ascendancy with depictions of more decidedly mature characters caught in a social and economic double bind of limited hopes and clipped wings. Springsteen recalled: 'On *The River*, there was always that thing of the guy attemptin' to come back, to find some sort of community.'[52] As that album's title song indicates, such a hope for working-class Americans remained severely challenged amid the trickle-down economics ushered in with Reagan's 'Morning in America'.

Glitter and Glam

Springsteen's eulogies to the hard-working men of small-town New Jersey reinforced, if anything, a sense both of stoic tradition and of betrayed bread-and-butter dreams among American males. Sex in Springsteen's music was epic or tragic, rarely playful and – prior to his AIDS-era anthem, 'Streets of Philadelphia' (1994) – decidedly hetero-sexual. Across the Hudson River was another world, the lower Manhattan of Andy Warhol and Lou Reed, the latter of whom had glamorised the city's transsexuals, celebrity hunters and drag artists on

Figure 4.1 Bruce Springsteen (1980). Muse/The Kobal Collection.

the album *Transformer* (1972), particularly in his gender-bending anthem, 'Walk on the Wild Side'. Sounes places Reed's music squarely in the context of 'the changing times in the USA' exemplified, in particular, by 'the recent proliferation of bisexual bath houses in the major cities, formerly gay saunas where men *and* women now had sex in bewildering permutations, defying the categories Gay or Straight, or indeed Bisexual'.[53] This social context at least partially explains the phenomenal American reception of David Bowie as the icon of glitter in the early 1970s, a figure whom Gary Herman describes as 'the single most important influence in the development of an explicit and outrageous sexualization of rock'.[54] Reed, Bowie, Alice Cooper, Iggy Pop and other glitter performers steered rock music through the turbulent waters of gender destabilisation, as Van M. Cagle argues:

> Glitter rock was the first absolutely *forthright* form of rock and roll to move queerness from subtext to text and make it unashamed, playful, and decoded for mass consumption. In the process, glitter provided gay and bisexual (rock and roll-oriented) youth with what were perhaps their first-ever role models, while suggesting to others that they might 'try on the roles' of sexual subordinates through experimenting with androgynous style.[55]

Through 'recasting situational notions of sexual/performance subversion through commercial means', the agents of glitter did much to broaden and normalise (if not neutralise) the concepts of alternative sexual norms.[56] In the sexual sphere, if not in the economic sphere, there was still considerable room for manoeuvre, or so the music and style of glitter and glam seemed to indicate. The New York Dolls, formed in 1971, are noteworthy in this regard, building on the sexual phenomenon that had been pioneered in Britain by Bowie. Katrina Irving, for one, dismisses any political significance to the stylisations of the Dolls and other sexual subversives: 'The protest of groups like the New York Dolls was one of style, an ambiguous playing with sexuality, reminiscent of the Rolling Stones at their androgynous best. Its obsession with style was merely narcissistic and had no socio-political overtones.'[57] As Leerom Medovoi observes, however, there was more than empty narcissism operating in the territory carved out by Bowie and his acolytes:

> Bowie was perhaps the first to construct (elaborate) narratives of a rebel who shocked by *confusing* genders, as in his song 'Rebel, Rebel', where he explicitly conceptualizes rock rebellion as threatening a straight world (rather than a feminine world) with one's sexual undecidability . . . This threat parallels, and arguably was mediated by, the gay liberationist struggle in the early seventies to dismantle rigid gender distinctions in favour of a more polymorphously perverse sexual order, giving at least this segment of rock music an implied political referent. The New York Dolls and the entire rock-in-drag phenomenon can be located in this trajectory.[58]

Other practitioners demonstrated the same determination to map out new landscapes in the musical culture of 1970s America,

Figure 4.2 New York Dolls (1974). © Bettmann/CORBIS.

fragmenting the audience and the popular music territory hitherto held together within the broad familial arms of rock and roll. Stadium and soft rock cut across a range of styles, from Van Halen, Alice Cooper and Kiss at the hard end to Foreigner, Journey, Boston and REO Speedwagon at the softer end. As Dave Laing argues: 'The myth (or the motif) of the unified audience or generation inspired by a new music clearly rooted in classic rock 'n' roll becomes unsustainable by the time 1970 or 1971 is reached.'[59] Central to this fragmentation were the not-so-distant musical cousins of glitter and glam: punk and New Wave.

Punk and New Wave

By the mid-decade, 'the changing times in the USA' had brought the
American music scene to a broad watershed that was marked by a sig-
nificant development across the Atlantic: the appearance of the Sex
Pistols' single 'Anarchy in the UK', which, as Sounes notes,

> was released on 26 November 1976, the week by chance that Dylan
> joined the Band on stage in San Francisco for their farewell concert,
> filmed by Martin Scorsese. As *The Last Waltz* was an adieu to the poetic
> folk-rock of the first half of the 1970s – with guest artists including Neil
> Young, Van Morrison and Joni Mitchell – 'Anarchy in the UK' ushered
> in the abrasive musical style that, along with disco, defined the second
> part of the decade.[60]

While Sounes's division of the decade so neatly into two parts might
not withstand too much scrutiny, it is fair to say that the music being
brewed in the New York Bowery club CBGB, as well as suburban
garages and small-town clubs throughout the East Coast, signalled
outright contempt for Springsteen's blue-collar Americana and the
folk-inflected sound of the Woodstock generation currently dancing
their last waltz. While the perception of the word 'punk' is confused
through its muddled transatlantic origins (it was first used as a genre
designation in Britain by the *Melody Maker* journalist Caroline Coon
who, in 1976, had borrowed the year-old title of the underground
American magazine, *Punk*), there is less confusion surrounding the
aesthetics of bands such as Television, the Ramones and the Dead
Kennedys. As Schulman explains:

> Despite common roots, American punk lacked that political edge, that
> overt class consciousness [of British punk]. Still, it borrowed much from
> the Brits and domesticated it for American consumption. First,
> American punk retained the outrageousness – the raw, unproduced
> sound, the brazen lyrics, the edgy and even offensive style . . . A group
> calling itself Dead Kennedys obviously enjoyed flouting established
> notions of good taste.[61]

In exploring the American reception of British punk and its smoother
relation, New Wave, Carroll observes the extent to which the musical
aesthetics of both genres were informed by broader subcultural
markers of dress, style and bodily carriage:

[As] reflections of English working-class youth, groups like the Sex Pistols minimized style, fashion, and lyric in a gut protest against established values. Wearing safety pins and chains, punk/new wave aficionados parodied the changing styles of haute culture and swayed to a nondance 'pogo' beat that denied the commercialization of rhythm. Musicians like Elvis Costello and Tom Robinson explicitly meshed social-protest lyrics with a style of resistance.[62]

Schulman notes that both punk and New Wave broadcast an 'anti-corporate agenda' and an 'asceticism' reflected in their championship of independent labels and small clubs; in this, 'the thin ties and suit jackets' of the Talking Heads were merely alternative markers to the 'jeans and leather jackets' of the Ramones.[63] As Cagle argues, critics and fans alike applauded bands that could appear ' "true" to their roots, especially if this meant signing with local, independent labels. By way of comparison, bands were quickly labelled "inauthentic" if they wilfully succumbed to the managerial/promotional practice of "creating" (and therefore "manipulating") an audience.'[64]

The kinship between American punk and New Wave was further cemented by their shared birthplace, CBGB:

The club opened in 1973 with that seemingly ill-fitting name. CBGB stood for Country, Blue Grass and the Blues, but the club's full name, CBGB & OMFUG, also promised 'other music for uplifting gourmandizers' for a cheap one-dollar admission fee. . . In its heyday, from 1975 to 1978, CBGB became the home turf and launching pad of such performers as the Ramones, the Dictators, Television, Patti Smith, Blondie, Tuff Darts, and Richard Hell and the Voidoids.[65]

If, to repeat Scorsese, punk and New Wave distinguished themselves through an 'anarchic, relentlessly abrasive' sound and aesthetic, another musical genre was developing to challenge the punk/New Wave dominance of the decade's music.

Disco

As Stephen Paul Miller observes, a telling moment in popular music history occurred when, in the late 1970s, 'Andy Warhol moved his primary site of social engagement from artist bars such as Max's Kansas City to the famed exclusive disco, Studio 54', which opened in April of 1977.[66] As one of the decade's most visible social barometers, Warhol understood the centrality of Studio 54 as the locus of 'a scene that all Americans could understand'.[67] The scene – and the dance music at its base – was disco, destined at one extreme to become 'hated with more intensity than any form of popular music before or since'.[68] At the other extreme, the key figures of disco – Gloria Gaynor, Donna Summer, KC and the Sunshine Band, the Bee Gees and Village People – still threaten to colonise the popular historical imagination to the extent that, for many people, theirs is the definitive soundtrack to the seventies.

The complexity of disco as a social phenomenon gives rise to a host of contradictory impressions. It was damned as shallow, narcissistic and commercial, the signal music of the 'Me Decade'. Critics of that decade would find nothing to applaud in singer Kathy Sledge's assessment: 'Disco snowballed the way it did because it got to be not just music, it got to be people's social lives. People got to be stars and shine on their own.'[69] Through disco, an average office worker could tap into the same currents (although not share the same exclusive space) as the celebrated devotees of Studio 54: Warhol; Mick and Bianca Jagger; Mikhail Baryshnikov; political figures such as Hamilton Jordan, President Carter's Chief of Staff, and Margaret Trudeau, the wife of the Canadian prime minister, all gyrating beneath 'the picture hanging over the dance floor. It showed the man in the moon grinning goofily with a coke spoon under his nose.'[70] As Carroll notes, the appeal of disco to young American workers fed a momentous corporate gold mine exploiting the periodic release from workaday drudgery and anonymity:

> In the popular hit '(I Just Can't Wait Till) Saturday', for example, singer Norma Jean described the disco scene as sufficient reward for a boring job. Promising to liberate the spirit with the chant, dance, dance, dance, the disco beat simultaneously spawned a $4-billion-a-year entertainment industry that included, besides the sale of records and tapes, disco clothing, accoutrements, clubs, cruises, skating rinks, and over two hundred dedicated radio stations. 'We're in a period of the McDonald's of music,' conceded Melba Moore, whose hit song was 'You Stepped into My Life'. 'I don't know what *good* is anymore.'[71]

Carroll, for one, has focused on disco's essentially 'conservative message of conformity, expensive dress, and self-discipline', particularly as it was reflected in the film *Saturday Night Fever* (1977), 'the most popular expression of the disco world', in which John Travolta plays a working-class Italian youth fixated on an upwardly mobile 'new life in Manhattan'.[72] The film's appeal was such that, 'in a film/music cross-marketing watershed', it became the first film to gross more from its soundtrack sales than from cinema viewings.[73] Travolta, as the king of the dance floor, 'became the decade's most distinctive masculine icon'.[74] Even in the context of such enormous popularity and obvious commercial faddism, Schulman marvels at the 'fear and loathing' prompted by disco to an unparalleled degree:

Throughout the nation's vanilla suburbs, the white noose surrounding the increasingly black and Latino central cities, white youth rallied behind the slogan, 'Disco sucks'. Clubs and concert halls sponsored 'disco sucks nights', occasionally resulting in ugly racial incidents. The antidisco frenzy reached its peak in Chicago on a hot July night in 1979. Desperate to revive sagging attendance at home games, the White Sox sponsored Disco Demolition Nite at Comiskey Park. Before a game with the Detroit Tigers, the master of ceremonies detonated a mountain of disco records piled up on the stadium floor. Thousands of white teenagers flooded onto the field; the resulting riot lasted for two hours, causing much damage, many injuries, and isolated incidents of mayhem in the surrounding black community.[75]

Yet, Schulman and Miller both identify precisely disco's provocative origins and oppositional potential towards official norms and values. Schulman points out: 'As popular music, especially youth-oriented rock and roll, became increasingly white, male, and macho in the early 1970s, alternative cultural streams fed the disco phenomenon: black pride, female sexual assertion, gay liberation'; thus, the disco beat 'signalled more than the arrival of dancing; like Woodstock, it fostered the gathering of a community'.[76] The same liberating associations that disco held for both working-class and middle-class wage earners also established its connection with such liberational moments as Stonewall. The playful irony of, say, Village People's hyper-masculinity ('Macho Man', 'YMCA', 'In the Navy') does little to disguise or negate the seriousness of what disco might signify. As Miller argues,

> The Stonewall riots concern the constitutional right to assemble in a gay bar – to assemble as a culture. Discos as we know them arise from the same impulse. Dancing on the open disco floor is a rite of coming out, metaphorically in full view of gay culture, even, paradoxically, for those who are not homosexual.[77]

The concept of liberation enables Donna Summer's 'Love to Love You Baby' (1975) and Gloria Gaynor's 'I Will Survive' (1978) to be read and heard as expressions of black women's seizing of personal and sexual control. In formal terms, thinking of 'liberation' enables disco to be perceived as a site of stylistic promiscuity rather than prescription (in spite of its rigid dance beats) in its fusion of Latin and African American musical elements. Moreover, as Schulman argues, it evades the tight categorisation upon which much of its antagonism has been founded:

> Disco, in its naïve togetherness, its sexy, 'stooped' intermingling of musical and cultural styles, challenged [both] racism and pluralism, discrimination and diversity. It obviously threatened suburban white boys who found it too feminine, too gay, too black. But its hybrid form also mocked ethnic nationalists dedicated to preserving distinct black and Latino cultural identities. The black musical establishment hated disco just as fervently as white rock-and-rollers did. African American critics labelled disco assimilationist: they dismissed it as bleached and blue-eyed funk.[78]

The promiscuity of disco reflects a broader process underlying popular music trends of the 1970s: 'Synthesizing (sometimes literally synthesizing with the aid of new electronic instruments) distinct musical styles and cultural expressions, disco artists fused black, gay, and Latin strands and found a huge, mass audience.'[79] Indeed, *fusion* preoccupies the work of musicians, musical instrument technologists and critics of music throughout the decade.

Figure 4.3 Donna Summer with Gerald and Betty Ford at Disco Dinner Benefit (1979). © Bettmann/CORBIS.

Fusion

In naming what he judged (with distinct cultural miserliness) the few 'dazzling experiments of form' in the decades since the 1930s, Daniel Bell singled out 'those efforts to fuse technology with music'.[80] In discussing the most significant technological musical development since the electrification of the guitar, Sounes observes that 'the synthesizer in particular helped define the music of the decade, in every genre from classical to funk, from the art-rock of [Pink Floyd's] *Dark Side of the Moon* (1973) to Donna Summer's 1977 disco hit 'I Feel Love'. In many ways, the synthesizer was the sound of the '70s.'[81] Bob Moog's 1964 invention – a machine 'that created electronic monotonal noises, the timber and pitch of which could be controlled by oscillators and filters, the resulting notes played on a keyboard' – created a chain of influences stretching from Walter (subsequently Wendy) Carlos's *Switched on Bach* (1968) to Bob Margouleff and Malcolm Cecil's *Zerotime* (1971) to Stevie Wonder's 'classic 1970s albums: *Music of My Mind* and *Talking Book* (both 1972), *Innervisions* (1973) and *Fulfillingness' First Finale* (1974)'.[82]

If fusion in its technological sense is a strikingly identifiable characteristic of 1970s popular music, the word itself problematises the definitions and categories of much of that music. The fusion of soul, Motown and jazz, it is true, gave rise to an identifiable genre, funk (variously assigned to the work of Stevie Wonder, Earth, Wind and Fire, The Commodores, Kool and the Gang and Parliament Funkadelic). Likewise, West Coast rock and country was fused identifiably into the country rock of the Eagles and the Grateful Dead. But a crisis of definition is obvious when (for example) the fusion of jazz and rock results in the simple appellation, 'fusion', to denote the work of Herbie Hancock, Chick Corea, Pat Methany and Weather Report as well as particular albums such as Miles Davis's *Bitches' Brew* (1970). For the question inevitably arises, if these examples can be called, simply, 'fusion', then how would one describe or categorise Joni Mitchell's jazz-based integrations with acoustic folk: *Blue* (1971), *The Hissing of Summer Lawns* (1975) and *Herjira* (1976)?

Indeed, the word *fragmentation*, rather than *fusion*, might best describe the characteristic trend of 1970s popular music. While smaller record labels were gobbled up by multinational conglomerates such as CBS and Gulf & Western, their strategists had to contend with an increasingly fragmented musical market. Style was a key indicator of such fragmentation, not only for performers but for audiences as well.

Style and Fashion

The outrageous theatrical trappings of bands like Kiss (face paint, towering platforms and tight spandex wrapped around slinky thighs) and the dripping eye make-up of Alice Cooper spilled offstage into the cauldron of 1970s fashion and style. Singer Barry White observed, 'The seventies was very glamorous – the first time I ever saw regular jeans go from $5 to $250. The consumers dressed up like they were the stars.'[83] Anne-Lise François has explored the signification of 1970s fashion, identifying complexities in that arena matching, and allied to, those of popular music: 'Whereas . . . punks wilfully call attention to themselves by their intransigent "fuck you"s to culture, adulthood, and conformity, the diffusion of loudness in seventies fashions works both to deflect and focus attention. To turn up the volume and tone it down.'[84] The catalogue of iconic 1970s fashion items indeed indicates this persistent dual coding:

> Skintight bell-bottoms, satin hot pants, velour T-shirts, three- to five-inch platforms, four- to five-inch wide ties, twenty-six inch flares, collars out to the shoulders, polyester everywhere . . . [S]eventies looks play on the simple but deeply interesting fact that clothes always perform a double function of concealing and revealing, of directing and deflecting attention.[85]

This double coding might allow some very negative connotations to emerge. Consumers of fashion, willingly or otherwise, found themselves visibly the product of boardroom construction. As Carroll observes (obviously without approval), 'designer labels, silkscreen art, T-shirts with slogans, political statements, personal messages [and] brand names' turned individual Americans into 'free-floating billboards', marking 'the most blatant invasion of American capitalism into the private sphere – the purchase not of products but of advertisements'.[86] Thus, the 'bigness in fashion' that characterises 'those seventies looks' represents 'a mainstreaming of late-sixties counter-culture: ex-hippies enter the corporate workplace with longer or bigger hair; would-be executives no longer shed business suits for blue jeans but, instead, wear suits made of denim.'[87]

Miller and Carroll have both identified aspects of increased social control and currents of repression that appeared to parallel the mainstreaming of 1970s fashion. Just as 'the seventies saw the individual desire to wear apparel with prominent consumer product logos', in the public sphere 'the inverse – the organized circulation of personalized graffiti on subway cars and other public spaces – was repressed. By the eighties, graffiti-proof cars were standard.'[88] Similarly, 'the invisibility of feminist achievement' was paralleled by 'a resurgence of traditional stereotypes' not quite erased by the extreme expressions of seventies fashion: 'the disco style celebrated spike heels, tight pants, transparent tops, and sleek dresses made of body-hugging fabrics – clothing that restored the image of women as sex objects'.[89]

At the same time, François has seen the codification of bigness in seventies fashion – 'its power to embarrass' – in an ironic counterpoint to the embarrassments and failures of American power in the decade:

the Watergate scandal; Patty Hearst's 'media stunt at the expense of the FBI'; Jimmy Carter's admission of failure in the aborted, fatal attempt to rescue the Iran hostages; the triumph of foreign-made, fuel-efficient compact cars over 'American gas-guzzlers', all of which demonstrated that 'big things were being shown up, sometimes in painfully public ways, as no longer necessarily so powerful'.[90]

Thus, in the final analysis, there may be more to 1970s fashion than a simple reflection of blind consumerism or social regression; for 'by working and reworking unobtrusiveness into conspicuousness and vice versa', 1970s fashions 'raise the heavily charged question of what it means to accept anything as ordinary'.[91] As the next chapter shows, a trend towards more and more spectacular display was begging the same question elsewhere in the public sphere.

Chapter 5

Public Space and Spectacle

In 1971, the sociologist Erving Goffman published his influential *Relations in Public*, an analysis of 'face to face action' in 'public life' that extended the field of dramaturgical sociology. Goffman had lain the groundwork for this field in his earlier, most popular, work, *The Presentation of the Self in Everyday Life* (1959).[1] In that study, Goffman had argued that all individuals, whether on or off the stage, 'perform', and that 'performance' could be defined as 'all the activity of an individual which occurs during a period marked by his continuous presence before a particular set of observers and which has some influence on the observers'.[2] Moreover, he argued, performers in life – as on the theatrical stage – always perform in a 'setting' that supplies 'the scenery and stage props for the spate of human action played out before, within, or upon it'.[3]

To some extent, there was nothing new here: Shakespeare's cliché of the 'all the world' as 'a stage' and its inhabitants as 'merely players' was already quite hackneyed by the time he put it into the mouth of Jaques in *As You Like It* (1599). William Butler Yeats had also formulated his concept of the 'second self' which attaches to all human endeavour a 'theatrical sense', a 'consciously dramatic' existence in which 'the wearing of a mask' is 'the condition of an arduous full life'.[4] By the 1970s, however, such scattered observations had coalesced into a strong body of theory exploring the place of performance on and off the theatrical stage, as Elin Diamond explains: 'Since the 1960s performance has floated free of theater precincts to describe an enormous range of cultural activity. "Performance" can refer to popular entertainments, speech acts, folklore, political demonstrations, conference behavior, rituals, medical and religious healing, and aspects of everyday life'.[5] Such phrases as 'performance discourse' and 'performativity' are now staples of social and sociological theory in which humans are viewed as 'actors' and their physical environment as a performative space. Thus, as Peggy Phelan observes:

> Architecture has of course long been considered theatrical. Buildings are said to 'stage' ideas about space and time, to dramatize a certain argument about form. Architecture also establishes a specific relation with its inhabitants (think of Foucault's Benthamite prisons), and often insists on a mimetic relation to the human body. In this insistence, architecture is performative as well as theatrical, for it actively shapes and forms the bodies that inhabit it.[6]

By a similar reasoning, architecture (among other elements of the public space) 'actively shapes and forms' the perceptions of the public (the audience) who perceive it aesthetically as well as 'inhabit it'. Architects and other contributors to the public space 'produce representations through objects and so produce a space and a subjectivity for the spectator'.[7] As Vivian Patraka argues, physical space hardly allows for complete freedom of interpretation; rather, it 'produces sites for multiple performances of interpretation which situate/produce the spectator as historical subject'.[8] Inevitably, public performance, as well as 'performances of interpretation', generate an enormous degree of friction, culturally and politically.

The American public space was in the 1970s a highly charged territory that saw the performances of 'actors' and 'interpreters' through a range of political and aesthetic battles. The 'settings' of some of these battles varied: the skyline of the American city and the sky above it; the strip and the boardroom; the steps of the Capitol and the streets leading to it; the sports arena and the town hall. The spectacles that were staged in these public settings could range from the farcical to the gladiatorial, from the inspirational to the derisory. But they were all instrumental in shaping seventies culture and its legacies.

The Sky and the Skyline

A revealing pair of events occurred during the first half of the 1970s, reflecting both the decline and the reassertion of visible symbols of American power before the world. In March of 1971, during the politically and economically beleaguered administration of Richard Nixon, the United States Senate rejected any further funding for the development of the Boeing Supersonic Transport project (SST), to the delight of two foreign rivals: the Anglo-French developers of the Concorde and the Soviet developers of the Tupolev Tu-144 – which remain the only commercial supersonic passenger planes to have flown to date.[9] To the champions of American aviation, it suddenly appeared that their glory days – which began in 1903 with the invention of the powered aeroplane – might well have ended with the maiden flight of the Boeing 747 the previous year. The question remained: was the great, lumbering American jumbo jet to be overtaken by sleekly tapered, compact machines of foreign design, reflecting in the air what had already occurred in the car industry on the ground?

If the symbols of American grandiosity were being challenged in the commercial air corridors overhead and on the nation's highways, however, the skyline of the American city was the site of a highly visible, public thrust of corporate power in the form of the rising skeletons of modernist skyscrapers. The project that most captivated the public imagination was the twin-towered World Trade Center (WTC),which, in 1972, briefly secured the title of the world's tallest building. The WTC project was as much a symbol of a domestic battle over the aesthetics of the urban American skyline as it was a statement of global economic supremacy (which is how it was ultimately viewed by its Islamist destroyers in September 2001). For the WTC not only pitted New York against the nation's 'Second City', Chicago, but it was also one of the last gasps of modernist architecture in the face of the postmodernist onslaught that was to take hold by the 1980s. In Chicago, two buildings were already clawing skyward in a bid to outdistance the WTC even before the latter was completed. In 1973, the WTC was surpassed by Chicago's Amoco Building which, in turn, was topped by the neighbouring Sears Tower in 1974.

This frantic vertical steeplechase – this jockeying for the visible dominance of modernist skyscrapers – represented an embattled aesthetic sensibility at a time when the principles of architectural modernism were being strenuously challenged. As Howard Sounes observes, well-intentioned (if not near-utopian) modernist housing projects had since the late 1940s been turning 'cities in the sky' into 'high-rise slums', ultimately implicating even the architect of the 1970s' most 'iconic' building project:

In the early 1950s, two decades before the completion of his shimmering World Trade Center towers, Minoru Yamasaki was the architect responsible for one such disaster: the notorious Pruitt–Igoe project in St Louis, Missouri, a high-rise city for 10,000 people that proved such a horrible place to live that its residents deliberately set fire to it. In 1972,

Figure 5.1 World Trade Center under construction (1971). © Bettmann/CORBIS.

the local housing department had the charred remains of the unloved complex dynamited.[10]

That the destruction of Yamasaki's Pruitt–Igoe project happened to coincide almost exactly with the celebrated completion of his World Trade Center does nothing to diminish the sense that architectural modernism was on the retreat. In a tongue-in-cheek updating of Virginia Woolf's claim that 'on or about December, 1910, human character changed',[11] the postmodern architect and historian, Charles Jencks, wrote: 'Modern [meaning 'modernist'] Architecture died in St Louis, Missouri, on July 15, 1972, at 3.32 p.m. when the infamous Pruitt–Igoe scheme, or rather several of its slab blocks, were given the final *coup de grâce* by dynamite.'[12] Indeed, the same year as the dynamiting of Pruitt–Igoe and the completion of the WTC, Jencks's colleague, the architect Robert Venturi, along with his partners Denise Scott Brown and Steven Izenour, published their manifesto, *Learning from Las Vegas*. This 'report from the desert', in J. David Hoeveler's words, 'stood as the greatest affront against modernism in the 1970s'.[13]

The appearance of this influential tract confirmed that the champions of postmodern architecture and planning had found their voice.

Learning from Las Vegas (1972)

In 1966, Venturi had famously challenged the austere dictum of the modernist architectural godfather, Mies van der Rohe, that 'Less is more'. Venturi had argued: 'Blatant simplification means bland architecture. Less is a bore.'[14] Now, by the early seventies, the collective architecture of the Las Vegas strip – its parking lots, billboards, neon signs, gaudy casinos and hotels – had only confirmed to Venturi and his partners that gleeful promiscuity, messiness, plurality and playfulness in civic design would help to turn cities into sites of joyous, collective 'intertwined activities', rather than the grim deserts of isolation and individual despair that the modernists had built.[15] Venturi and his partners' critique stemmed from a profound disenchantment with the forms, structures and ethos of modernist architecture, the 'dead ducks', as the authors called them, which had threatened to turn the American built landscape into a sterile, humourless, dead space. (162) In their 'purist' championing of austere form for form's sake, modernist architects had eschewed the lively and delightful mixing of styles that characterised pre-modernist architecture in order to produce the forbidding 'megastructures' that continued to sap the lifeblood from the American public space. 'The Italian landscape has always harmonized the vulgar and the Vitruvian,' Venturi argued; 'Naked children have never played in *our* fountains, and [modernist architect] I. M. Pei will never be happy on Route 66.' (6) Modernist architecture, to Venturi and his colleagues, was the work of both visual and political tyranny: ' "Total design" comes to mean "total control", as confident art commissioners who have learned what is right promote a deadening mediocrity by rejecting the "good" and the "bad" and the new they do not recognize, all of which, in combination and in the end, make the city.' (149–50)

The authors thus looked to the vibrancy of the haphazard, largely unplanned 'urban sprawl' for evidence of life in the American built environment, as opposed to the 'boardrooms of cultural foundations' and 'the pages of *Time* magazine', (149) from where modernism had been imposed upon a populace that deserved better. In a striking and highly damning comparative scheme, Venturi and partners pitted the 'urban sprawl' against the modernist 'megastructure', the latter of which invited both mockery and contempt for its pretentiousness:

Urban Sprawl	Megastructure
Ugly and ordinary	Heroic and original
Depends on explicit symbolism	Rejects explicit symbolism
Symbols in space	Forms in space
Image	Form
Mixed media	Pure architecture

	[. . .]	
Takes the parking lot seriously and pastiches the pedestrian		'Straight' architecture with serious but egocentric aims for the pedestrian; it irresponsibly ignores or tries to 'piazzafy' the parking lot
Disneyland		Piazzas
	[. . .]	
Popular lifestyle		'Correct' lifestyle
	[. . .]	
Process city		Instant city
	[. . .]	
Heterogeneous images		The image of the middle-class intelligentsia
The difficult image		The easy image
The difficult whole		The easy whole (118)

Hammering home their attack on the reigning modernist ethos, Venturi, Brown and Izenour called upon an array of voices – the architectural historian, Camillo Sitte:

'Modern systems! Yes, indeed! To approach everything in a strictly method-ical manner and not to waver a hair's breadth from preconceived patterns, until genius has been strangled to death and *joie de vivre* stifled by the system – that is the sign of our time'; (81)

– the poet, Wallace Stevens:

'Incessant new beginnings lead to sterility'; (87)

– and Herman Melville:

'Not innovating wilfulness but reverence for the archetype'. (87)

The authors' greatest objection to modernism was its privileging of form over symbolism, pure 'expression' over 'representation', abstraction over 'meaning', and its basic refusal to communicate:

When it cast out eclecticism, Modern architecture submerged symbolism. Instead it promoted expressionism, concentrating on the expression of archi-tectural elements themselves: on the expression of structure and function. It suggested through the image of the building, reformist–progressive social and industrial aims that it could seldom achieve in reality. By limiting itself to strident articulations of the pure architectural elements of space, structure, and program, Modern architecture's expression has become dry expres-sionism, empty and boring – and in the end irresponsible. (101–2)

In the search for an instructive alternative to the deadening plans of totalist architecture, the authors seized on the electric, shape-shifting 'communication system' of Las Vegas: (8)

> Allusion and comment, on the past or present or on our great commonplaces
> or old clichés, and inclusion of the everyday in the environment, sacred and
> profane – these are what are lacking in present-day Modern architecture. We
> can learn about them from Las Vegas, as have other artists from their own
> profane and stylistic sources. (53)

Las Vegas was a site pregnant with meaning, a site of breathtaking 'symbolic
evolution' (106) dominated by the Strip, the highway and, most importantly,
the signs, which 'through their sculptural forms or pictorial silhouettes, their
particular positions in space, their inflected shapes, and their graphic meanings . . . identify and unify the megatexture' of the entire desert city:

> They make verbal and symbolic connections through space, communicating
> a complexity of meanings through hundreds of associations in a few seconds
> from far away. Symbol dominates space. Architecture is not enough.
> Because the spatial relationships are made by symbols more than by forms,
> architecture in this landscape becomes symbol in space rather than form in
> space. Architecture defines very little: The Big Sign and the little building is
> the rule of Route 66. (13)

Las Vegas thus invited and embraced interpretation – an activity that
modernist architecture had not only resisted imperiously, but positively
discouraged:

> Evolution in Las Vegas is consistently toward more and bigger symbolism.
> The Golden Nugget casino on Fremont Street was an orthodox decorated
> shed with big signs in the 1950s – essentially Main Street commercial, ugly
> and ordinary. However, by the 1960s it was all sign; there was hardly any
> building visible. The quality of the 'electrographics' was made more strident
> to match the crasser scale and more distracting context of the new decade,
> and to keep up with the competition next door. (107)

The commitment to symbolism, interpretation and communication made
Las Vegas an enabling, rather than a disabling, site. It enabled the visitor
to adopt 'a new role: for three days one may imagine oneself a centurion
at Caesar's Palace, a ranger at the Frontier, or a jet setter at the Riviera
rather than a salesperson from Des Moines, Iowa, or an architect from
Haddonfield, New Jersey'. (53)

The communicative capacity of Las Vegas was all the more impressive,
and apt for an age dominated by the motorcar, in that it generated a plethora
of meanings at high speed from the vantage point of the highway, a fact
which plodding modernist developers had failed to take into account:

> Attention is . . . more focussed on 'moving' objects than on 'stable' ones. . .
> Speed is the determinant of focal angle, both for driver and passengers.
> Increases of speed narrow the focal angle with a resulting visual shift from
> detail to generality; attention shifts to points of decision. (74)

Las Vegas was thus a dynamic location for a new understanding of architectural meaning. It required new interpretive approaches and vocabulary

in keeping with a shift from the modern to something else: the postmodern. The authors argued that:

> The emerging order of the Strip is a complex order. It is not the easy, rigid order of the urban renewal project or the fashionable 'total design' of the megastructure. It is, on the contrary, a manifestation of an opposite direction in architectural theory. (52)

What Las Vegas most offered those with the vision to embrace it was a new way of perceiving the built environment and its social objectives:

> The Las Vegas Strip is not a chaotic sprawl but a set of activities whose pattern, as with other cities, depends on the technology of movement and communication and the economic value of the land. We term it sprawl, because it is a new pattern we have not yet understood. (76)

Consequently, 'we need new concepts and theories to handle it'. (75)

One of the most controversial arguments in *Learning from Las Vegas* was the assertion that any new architectural theory would need to accommodate the reality and admit the value of a commercial aesthetic which was, in any case, inescapable in postmodern life:

> The intensity of light on the Strip as well as the tempo of its movement is greater to accommodate the greater spaces, greater speeds, and greater impacts that our technologies permit and our sensibilities respond to. Also, the tempo of our economy encourages that changeable and disposable environmental decoration known as advertising art. (116)

Venturi, Brown and Izenour thus championed the aesthetic and communicative impact of the desert city's commercial symbolism which, they argued, reflected 'the quicker tempo of our times, if not the less eternal message of commercial rather than religious propaganda'. (106) The pressures of capitalist competition ensured that the Las Vegas Strip would continually reinvent itself with supercharged visual energy: 'A motel is a motel anywhere. But here the imagery is heated up by the need to compete in the surroundings. The artistic influence has spread, and Las Vegas motels have signs like no others. Their ardor lies somewhere between the casinos and the wedding chapels.' (35)

Ultimately, learning from Las Vegas meant learning to embrace eclecticism, 'complex combinations of media beyond the pure architectural triad of structure, form and light at the service of space'. (9) It meant turning to mixed media in 'violent juxtapositions of use and scale', (18) making 'connections among many elements, far apart and seen fast'. (9) It meant fitting into new American architecture

> double-functioning or vestigial elements, circumstantial distortions, expedient devices, eventful exceptions, exceptional diagonals, things in things, crowded or contained intricacies, linings or layerings, residual spaces, redundant spaces, ambiguities, inflections, dualities, difficult wholes ... the phenomena of both–and ... inclusion, inconsistency, compromise,

> accommodation, adaptation, superadjacency, equivalence, multiple focus, juxtaposition . . . good *and* bad space. (128)
>
> Learning from Las Vegas also meant learning from pop artists who had 'shown the value of the old cliché used in a new context to achieve a new meaning – the soup can in the art gallery – to make the common uncommon'. (72) More than anything, learning from Las Vegas meant learning 'to have fun with architecture', (53) to engage in 'moral subversion through irony and the use of a joke to get to seriousness': (161)
>
>> Irony may be the tool with which to confront and combine divergent values in architecture for a pluralist society and to accommodate the differences in values that arise between architects and clients. Social classes rarely come together, but if they can make temporary alliances in the designing and building of multivalued community architecture, a sense of paradox and some irony and wit will be needed on all sides. (161)
>
> Thus, in *Learning from Las Vegas*, Venturi, Brown and Izenour brought architecture directly into the politics of postmodernism, yet one more arena of contest and negotiation in a highly charged, turbulent decade.

The Spectacle of Public Protest

The architectural contests of the 1970s are only one indication of the extent to which the American physical spaces were sites of spectacular public agitation. Given that architecture is not merely concerned with utilitarian function but also with visibility, a critical champion of the WTC might argue, as does Sounes, that Yamasaki's twin towers were not only 'a symbol of the wealth and power of New York and the United States' but also 'a monumental work of art' to be appreciated visually, aesthetically.[16] The visual, as Daniel Bell mourned in 1976, had become 'the dominant outlook' of an overly sensory-driven 'mass society':

Mass entertainments (circuses, spectacles, theaters) have always been visual, but there are two distinct aspects of contemporary life that necessarily emphasize the visual element. First, the modern world is an urban world. Life in the great city and the way stimuli and sociability are defined provide a preponderance of occasions for people to *see*, and *want* to see (rather than read or hear) things. Second is the nature of the contemporary temper, with its hunger for action (as against contemplation), its search for novelty, and its lust for sensation. And it is the visual element in the arts which best appeases these compulsions.[17]

As had already been demonstrated in the late 1960s, visibility in the arts had begun to dovetail spectacularly with political protest. In the

Figure 5.2 Protesters in front of Capitol, Washington DC (1971). © Bettmann/CORBIS.

wake of the 1967 Monterey Pop Festival, as Bruce Schulman observes, 'the counterculture . . . relied on music as a means of communication, a communal ritual, a gathering of the tribes' that had lead directly, on the eve of the new decade, to one of the most visible, in-your-face gestures of musical protest ever seen:

> At Woodstock, Country Joe [McDonald] introduced 'Fixin' to Die' by leading the assembled mass in an obscene chant: 'Give me an F, Give me a U, Give me a C, Give me a K, What's that spell!' The F-U-C-K chant, with its deliberate attempt to shock sensibilities, by rejecting established, repressive standards of propriety, asked why Americans could find such language profane, but not the war in Vietnam . . . The obscene chant was as much a political protest as the antiwar song that followed; political protest and countercultural sensibilities went hand in hand.[18]

By 1970, with the war's body count relentlessly climbing, increased visibility became the goal of the anti-Vietnam War movement which, as Melvin Small and William Hoover note, 'was the largest and most important antiwar movement in American history'.[19] To the pro-war forces, being seen and heard likewise became an end in itself.

Vietnam: Protest and Counter-protest

Melvin Small points out that '[Antiwar] Movement activities and elite opposition in the media helped to keep the war "on the front burner" from 1965 through 1971'.[20] Rhodri Jeffreys-Jones describes the anti-war movement as 'a cumulative, repetitive series of protests running from the mid-sixties to the early seventies' and spearheaded by four major groups –'students, African Americans, women, and labor' – whose protests reached 'a distinctive crescendo at an unpredictable moment' and 'gave the politicians no respite'.[21] The most important force to galvanise the anti-war movement and, in steadily growing reaction, the pro-war movement, was television. As Nora M. Alter argues:

> The war as spectacle was consumed by the American public principally on television. For television had become the visual medium par excellence: the main supplier and conduit of films, shows, debates, and especially the nightly news reports that played a capital role in forming public opinion, having begun to supersede print journalism . . . Any assessment of the public knowledge of the Vietnam War, therefore, needs to take into account the 'image' of the war as conveyed by television. It was over that image that public opinion about the war was waged in the United States, both for and against it.[22]

Crucial to 'the filmic mediatization of the first "television war" ', as Alter describes it, was 'the often revolting, almost always disturbing nature' of the visual images that were the 'major source of the global protest movement' – images such as

> the self-immolation of a Buddhist monk; a news report by Morley Safer showing US marines burning down a *South* Vietnamese village with Zippo lighters; the shooting of prisoners of war by South Vietnamese officers; the image of a napalmed naked girl running helplessly toward the camera of an American journalist; and of course the images from Tet and My Lai.[23]

Vietnam protest and counter-protest undoubtedly fed into the broader processes of social and political spectacularisation analysed by such theorists as Murray Edelman and Guy Debord. For Edelman, 'the construction of political spectacles' is inextricably linked with the news media:

> The spectacle constituted by news reporting continuously constructs and reconstructs social problems, crises, enemies, and leaders and so creates a succession of threats and reassurances. These constructed problems and personalities furnish the content of political journalism . . . They also play a central role in winning support and opposition for political causes and policies.[24]

While Debord goes to extremes in arguing that 'the spectacle is the *leading production* of present-day society', he is right in suggesting that 'an ever-increasing mass of image-objects' marks 'the general shift from *having* to *appearing*': 'all "having" must now derive its immediate prestige and its ultimate purpose from appearance'.[25] This was certainly the case for both the anti-war and the pro-war camps, each claiming to 'have' the moral high ground in the argument over Vietnam and setting out visibly to demonstrate their possession of it through force of numbers and dramatic confrontations.

One of the first observers to engage with the anti-war movement as spectacle was Norman Mailer, himself one of the movement's most spectacular figures. His controversial and highly problematical *Armies of the Night* (1968) describes and inflates his part in a 1967 march on the Pentagon, during which he set out to get himself arrested. While Mailer's egotistical centring of himself in the narrative – in the third person, no less – makes *Armies of the Night* highly suspect as history, it is useful for its description of the protest movement's theatricality and its dependency upon the media, which continued into the 1970s. Although Mailer exaggerates the tendency of the protesters, as a group, to dress up in outlandish costume, the elements he describes were there in significant enough numbers to have contributed to the movement's visual iconography:

> The hippies were there in great number, perambulating down the hill, many dressed like the legions of Sgt. Pepper's Band, some were gotten up like Arab sheiks, or in Park Avenue doormen's greatcoats, others like Rogers and Clark of the West, Wyatt Earp, Kit Carson, Daniel Boone . . . and wild Indians

with feathers, a hippie gotten up like Batman . . . They were close to being assembled from all the intersections between history and the comic books, between legend and television, the Biblical archetypes and the movies.[26]

Most importantly, they were there to be filmed:

After fifteen minutes of pushing, eddying, compressing and decompressing from ranks, the March at last started up in a circus-full of performers, an ABC or CBS open convertible with a built-on camera platform was riding in privileged position five yards in front of them with TV executives, cameramen, and technicians hanging on, leaning out, off on their own crisis run as they crawled along in front. Two monitors kept working like cheerleaders through portable loudspeakers to dress the front rank, which kept billowing and shearing under the pulses of inertia and momentum from the ranks behind, and a troop of helicopters, maybe as many as eight or ten, went into action overhead, while ten to twenty cameramen, movie and still, walking backward, wheeling, swinging from flank to flank, danced in the hollow square.[27]

Contributing to the spectacle was the dramatic political argot adopted by the counter-cultural elements of the protest movement, highlighting the importance of the auditory as well as the visual in securing public notice. Jeffreys-Jones points to the slogans of the student and underground anti-war activists 'vowing "to return all power to the people", and furthering "Black Power, Chicano Power, Student Power, Hippy Power, G.I. Power, Worker Power, Rock Power, Theatre Power, and even white middle-class Power".'[28] As David Farber notes, 'In New York between 1967 and 1972, the Yippies, the Crazies, and the Up Against the Wall Motherfuckers, all advocated what was called "armed love":' 'In the words of the Motherfuckers: "We defy law and order with our bricks, bottles, garbage, long hair, filth, obscenity, drugs, games, guns, bikes, fire, fun and fucking." Though few in number, such zealots gave anti-war protests a negative image and provided ammunition to administration supporters struggling to discredit the movement as anti-American.'[29] Even opponents of the Nixon administration and friends of the anti-war movement could be alienated by such spectacular rhetoric. Farber cites as an example Jann Wenner, editor of *Rolling Stone*, who 'believed that politicizing the counterculture' in such a way 'would turn off most young people':

In the 11 May 1968 *Rolling Stone*, Wenner's front-page story blasted Yippie attempts to mix radical politics with a counter-culture celebration. He labelled Abbie Hoffman, Jerry Rubin, and their allies 'a self-appointed coterie of political "radicals" without a legitimate constituency', and argued that their planned protest / festival of life was 'as corrupt as the political machine it hopes to disrupt'. As he saw it, 'Rock and roll is the only way in which the vast but formless power of youth is structured.'[30]

Wenner was correct in identifying music as a rallying point for American youth, and both the anti-war and the pro-war movements had certainly collected enough musical voices to provide the soundtrack as well as the stagecraft of protest. A very partial list of musicians associated with both studio and live performance on behalf of the anti-war movement would have to include Joan Baez, Buffalo Springfield, Judy Collins, Country Joe and the Fish, Crosby, Stills, Nash and Young, Bob Dylan, Arlo Guthrie, John Hartford, Jimi Hendrix, Jefferson Airplane, Phil Ochs, Tom Paxton, Peter, Paul and Mary, John Prine, Earl Scruggs and Pete Seeger. The pro-war activists – or, at least, the anti-anti-war activists – included a host of performers singing highly indicative songs: Merle Haggard with 'The Fightin' Side of Me', 'Okie from Muskogee' and 'A Soldier's Last Letter'; Staff Sergeant Barry Sadler with 'The Ballad of the Green Berets'; Dave Dudley with 'Hello Vietnam', Pat Boone with 'Wish You Were Here, Buddy' and Stonewall Jackson with 'The Minutemen (Are Turning in Their Grave)'.[31] For the anti-war camp in particular, the recruitment of high-profile performers signed to major record labels was a double-edged sword, for what Keith Richards observed about the Rolling Stones in relation to their label, Decca, would have held true for American musicians recording on large corporate labels such as RCA (Jefferson Airplane) and Columbia (Bob Dylan, Pete Seeger):

> We found out, and it wasn't for years that we did, that all the bread we made for Decca was going into making black boxes that go into American Air Force bombers to bomb fucking North Vietnam. They took the bread we made for them and put it into the radar section of their business . . . Goddam, you find out you've helped kill God knows how many thousands of people without even knowing it.[32]

Thus, the quest for a prominent musical voice in service of the anti-war movement was in some ways a highly compromised one.

By 1970, the movement had secured an overwhelmingly visible and audible presence, thanks to the efforts of the New Mobilization Committee to End the War in Vietnam (New Mobe), which had staged spectacular 'moratorium' protests in Washington, San Francisco and other cities in the autumn of 1969. Jeffreys-Jones writes: 'Hundreds of thousands participated. One historian puts the total attendance at "millions", and another describes the combined demonstrations as "the most potent and widespread antiwar protests ever mounted in western democracy" '.[33] In addition to the moratorium, students mounted demonstrations and seized buildings on a number of campuses in early 1970, including the University of California at Berkeley, which prompted Governor Ronald Reagan to declare ominously: 'If it takes a bloodbath, let's get it over with. No more appeasement.'[34] At the same time, Vice President Spiro Agnew urged law enforcement officers to imagine the student protesters as 'wearing brown shirts or white sheets and act accordingly'.[35] With the political atmosphere already at boiling point, two closely related events in May 1970 ensured that the temperature of protest and counter-protest would rise even further. In the wake of the United States invasion of Cambodia, four protesting students at Kent State University, Ohio, were gunned down by National Guardsmen on 4 May (two more students were killed at Jackson State College, Mississippi, ten days later). At an 8 May rally at New York's City

Hall, where Mayor John Lindsay had ordered the flag to be flown at half mast in memory of the Kent State students, two hundred construction workers wearing hard hats weighed in to a crowd of a thousand student protesters, swinging 'their fists, crowbars, and metal wrenches' before swarming the City Hall and raising the flag back to full mast.[36] The hard hat quickly became an icon of reactionary, pro-war aggression (and a term of contempt among the anti-war camp). President Nixon pointedly invited the organisers of the hard-hat demonstration – all conservative union leaders – to the White House to register his thanks. Before leaving, they 'presented Nixon with a hard-hat labelled "Commander in Chief" '.[37]

Jeffreys-Jones situates this surreal episode in its broader context:

> The president systematically exploited the student-protest issue in his bid to destroy the antiwar movement and secure re-election in 1972. By the midterm elections of 1970, his strategy was well formed. He would appeal to blue-collar workers, normally a key element in Democratic support, playing on their dislike of middle-class students and on their patriotic aversion to draft dodgers. By this means, he was giving flesh to the political animal he had reinvented: the silent majority.[38]

An important element in Nixon's strategy was the seizure of the televised field. Thus, as George W. Hopkins notes, when New Mobe staged its largest single protest rally in Washington almost a year to the day after the hard-hat demonstration (3 May 1971),

> more than 7,200 people were incarcerated that day. More than 5,000 arrests followed at May Day actions during the next two days. Although the activists failed in their ultimate goal [to 'shut down' the government], controversy over the nature of the protests and the government's response (illegal dragnet arrests and preventive detention) polarised public opinion.[39]

Arguably, the main point of the mass arrests in Washington was less the execution of law than public visibility in its own right, by which the Nixon administration could be seen to be responding forcefully to the protest, especially in front of the gathered news cameras. Performative action – public drama – thus significantly marked the anti-war and pro-war discourse and strategy of the 1970s, as it did other areas involved in what numerous commentators have referred to as 'political theatre'.

Political Theatre

This phrase is not necessarily neutral, as Michael Staub reveals in his analysis of the journalism of Gail Sheehy who used the phrase in scorn for the celebrity-seeking strategies of the Black Panthers during a high-profile 1970 murder trial in Connecticut:

> For Sheehy, the Panthers really were all about style, not substance. Bobby Seale, for example, was 'Mr Publicity'. What the Panthers offered

Figure 5.3 Richard Nixon receives the gift of a hard hat following the hard-hat riot in New York City (1970). Nixon Presidential Material Project, National Archives and Records Administration.

was 'pure theatre', 'political theatre'. And it was the '*delivery* of his testimony' that got one 'actor'/defendant in the murder trial in New Haven (that 'Broadway-tryout town') the lowest possible sentence from his 'audience'/jury.[40]

Such scepticism notwithstanding, dramatic political stagings were not confined to the anti-war or Black Power movements. Native American groups responded to the 1972 presidential election with a great cross-country march on Washington DC (as had many anti-war groups) which they called 'The Trail of Broken Treaties'. The following year, in a move to take the ground from less radical tribal leaders, armed militants led by the American Indian Movement seized the highly symbolic location of Wounded Knee, South Dakota, where the Sioux had fought their last stand against the US Army in 1890. As Carroll observes, the public visibility of this ultimately doomed act, like that surrounding the inmates' seizure of the Attica prison in New York State two years earlier, had done significant political work:

'AIM won support from sympathetic public figures – *New York Times* columnist Tom Wicker, the black caucus of the House of Representatives, Angela Davis, and actor Marlon Brando – and obtained valuable publicity which prevented precipitous military intervention.'[41]

The women's movement also engaged in extensive, sustained campaigns of public performance, with its precedents extending back to the early suffrage movement. Schulman has observed the power of what he calls the 'guerrilla theatre' of the radical feminists of the 1960s, who had 'burst onto the national scene in September 1968 with dramatic protests at the Miss America Pageant in Atlantic City':

> Demonstrators crowned a live sheep Miss America and paraded her down the boardwalk to protest the ways contestants – and all women – 'were judged like animals at a county fair'. Some chained themselves to a giant Miss America puppet, mocking women's submission to conventional standards of beauty. Others hurled 'instruments of torture to women' into a 'Freedom Trash Can': high heels, girdles, bras, copies of *Ladies Home Journal* and *Cosmopolitan*, hair curlers, false eye lashes. (They had planned to burn the contents but never did.) Inside the convention hall protesters disrupted the pageant with cries of 'Women's Liberation' and 'Freedom for Women'. These inspired acts of guerrilla theatre won national attention for the emerging women's movement . . .[42]

By the 1970s, in addition to the 'Take Back the Night' rallies organised by such collectives as Women Against Violence and Pornography in Media (San Francisco) and Pittsburgh Action Against Rape, a generation of individual performance artists dedicated to feminist advancement had begun building upon the collective expression. Hoeveler explains this emergence:

> Feminism easily allied itself with performance art. It shared with the avant-garde an impatience, or often hostility, toward formalism, judging it to have no political force and no social reference. Performance artists such as Laurie Anderson, Eleanor Antin, and Carolee Schneemann gave dramatic renderings that often clearly joined their work to a message of female sexual liberation.[43]

Rebecca Schneider points out that

the 1970s was a decade art critic and historian Moira Roth has called 'The Amazing Decade' of women's art. Feminist performance art burgeoned on the West Coast around Judy Chicago and Womanhouse and in New York among women who had been either excommunicated, like Schneemann, from the Art Studs Club, or who were entering the scene with their 'consciousnesses' already raised.[44]

Stephen Paul Miller adds to this list of performance artists (or 'body artists', as they were sometimes called) such names as Yvonne Rainer, Linda Francis, Hannah Wilke, Jill Johnston and Cindy Sherman, whose art across a variety of media 'was both performative and feminist': 'Seventies feminists had little choice but to experiment with identity and notions of presence, since they inevitably pointed toward something that did not yet exist, and all manner of identity-positions were increasingly called into question as the decade progressed.'[45]

It is thus highly significant that dramatic frontier-pushing, both progressive and reactionary, should have marked the 1970s on both the collective and the individual levels. Indeed, given the decade's increased preoccupation with what Miller calls 'forefronting personalities', it is not surprising that much political debate took on the appearance of public gladiatorial battles between singular champions across a range of arenas.[46]

Gladiators

The 1970s are known for a number of particularly spectacular sporting contests. One was the 1974 'Rumble in the Jungle' fought in Zaire between Muhammad Ali, hoping to regain his World Heavyweight title, and the reigning Heavyweight Champion, George Foreman. The 'Rumble in the Jungle', which first brought the flamboyant boxing promoter, Don King, to the world's attention, was just one of many indications that the age of the celebrity sportsman had arrived. Ali – or, as Kasia Boddy fittingly describes him, 'Ali-as-Davy-Crockett' – used a pre-match press conference to inflate himself to superhuman proportions before a global audience:

Last night I had a dream. When I got to Africa, I had one hell of a rumble. I had to beat Tarzan's behind first for claiming to be King of the Jungle. I done something new for this fight. I done wrestled with an alligator. That's right. I have wrestled with an alligator. I done tussled with a whale. I done handcuffed lightning, thrown thunder in jail. That's bad!

> Only last week I murdered a rock, injured a stone, hospitalised a brick!
> I'm so mean I make medicine sick![47]

Such self-aggrandising among boxers was in keeping with traditional pre-fight conventions going as far back as Classical Greece.[48] But this was a time when (for instance) the New York Jets quarterback, 'Broadway' Joe Namath, could shave off his moustache for $10,000 in a thirty-second commercial for Schick razors.[49] Thanks to television, the 1970s witnessed a markedly increased tendency to reward inflated sports personalities with equally inflated purses. The 'Rumble in the Jungle' paid each of the contestants five million dollars regardless of the fight's outcome. As Boddy points out, a 'complicated' political–economic nexus characterised this particular global spectacle; Don King 'promoted it as a celebration of black political and economic independence: "A fight between two Blacks in a Black Nation, organized by Blacks and seen by the whole world".'[50]

The Ali–Foreman fight generated considerable cultural as well as economic output: the soul singer James Brown, the blues guitarist B. B. King, Stevie Wonder and the Fania All Stars were there to perform, while George Plimpton, Hunter S. Thompson and Norman Mailer were on hand to chronicle the events in their particular journalistic fashions. Mailer's *The Fight* (1975) gives perhaps the best indication of a process described by Miller, in which sportsmen and sportswomen were transformed into a wholly other class of celebrities: 'A sense of the personal . . . became more prominently organized within the marketplace'; hence the rise of *People* magazine and the fall of *Life*; and hence the major television networks' new strategies in sports broadcasting, with their '"up close and personal" introductory features, close-ups, and narratives about what was personally at stake for individual athletes'.[51] In Mailer's case, the object was to transform Muhammad Ali into a gladiatorial deity upon whom the average man or woman could barely survive looking with the naked eye:

> There is always a shock in seeing him again. Not *live* as in television but standing before you, looking his best. Then the World's Greatest Athlete is in danger of being our most beautiful man, and the vocabulary of Camp is doomed to appear. Women draw an *audible* breath. Men look *down*. They are reminded again of their lack of worth. If Ali never opened his mouth to quiver the jellies of public opinion, he would still inspire love and hate. For he is the Prince of Heaven – so says the silence around his body when he is luminous.[52]

The hype into which Mailer fed was also a factor in another of the decade's major sports contests which, in social terms, was far more significant than the Ali–Foreman fight because there was more at stake than the fortunes and reputations of the individual contestants. In 1970, Billie Jean King's victory in women's tennis at the Italian Open had netted her a mere $600; her male colleague, Ilie Nastase, received $3,500 for winning the same tournament. King subsequently spearheaded a campaign to ensure equal pay for women athletes, inviting derision and an ill-judged challenge from the self-proclaimed chauvinist and former World Number One tennis champion, Bobby Riggs. As Charles Maher reported in the *Los Angeles Times* after King trounced Riggs in three straight sets at the Houston Astrodome (20 September 1973), the match 'was surely the most ambitious, hyperbolic promotion conceived on this continent since Barnum bumped into Bailey', having been covered by over three hundred journalists, televised in thirty-seven countries and grossing the promoter over $1.2 million.[53] In spite of the carnivalesque promotional backdrop against which 'the Battle of the Sexes' was played – with King arriving at the match dressed as Cleopatra and Riggs showing up in a chariot drawn by bathing beauties, proclaiming before the cameras that 'women belong in the bedroom and kitchen, in that order' – *New York Times* sports correspondent Selena Roberts called it the 'necessary spectacle' that ultimately 'leveled the game'.[54] The match, as Schulman observes, dramatised far more than women's achievement in the sports arena. It also signalled 'the arrival of the women's movement as a broad cultural force'.[55] The previous year, in the editorial pages of the newly launched *Ms.* magazine, Gloria Steinem presciently described the cultural and social milieu that would so embolden Riggs and, as he thought, validate his sneering modus operandi:

> There seems to be no punishment of white males that quite equals the ridicule and personal viciousness reserved for women who rebel. Attractive or young women who act forcefully are assumed to be either unnatural or male-controlled. If they succeed, it can only have been sexually, through men. Old women or women considered unattractive by male standards are accused of acting out of bitterness because they could not get a man. Any woman who chooses to behave like a full human being should be warned that the armies of the status quo will treat her as something of a dirty joke. Ridicule is their natural and first weapon, with more serious opposition to follow. She will *need* sisterhood.[56]

When Billie Jean King took to the court at Houston, Title IX of the 1972 Education Act, which promised to withdraw federal funding from sex-discriminatory school programmes, was still facing serious opposition from sports departments resisting the call to increase the female presence in school athletics beyond its dismal 7 per cent. Schulman is correct in arguing that 'King's victory swept away resistance to Title IX' along with the belief that 'women lacked the desire and the ability to compete in interscholastic athletics'.[57] But, given that unequal pay for women in professional athletics would still be an issue in the twenty-first century, it was indeed apparent that, in the 1970s, King and her fellow activists would '*need* sisterhood'.

Certainly Bobby Riggs and other chauvinists had their own 'brotherhood' of sorts, one of whose most articulate spokesmen was Mailer. He had written the classic World War II novel, *The Naked and the Dead* (1948); he would soon write *The Fight*, and his noted machismo, both in life and in print, drew immense firepower from a number of feminist writers beginning with Germaine Greer. In *The Female Eunuch* (1970), Greer wrote that Mailer's writing about women had descended to 'the lowest levels of illiteracy – the schoolboy writing about "bloody girls"'.[58] Like Riggs, Mailer took great delight in baiting feminists and their male allies, bemoaning 'the womanizing of America' and the women who, as he claimed in *Cannibals and Christians* (1966), had become 'more selfish, more greedy, less warm, more lusty, and filled with hate'.[59] Slander such as this brought into the ring not only Greer but also Kate Millett, whose groundbreaking treatise, *Sexual Politics* (1970), sparked one of the most intense literary exchanges and one of the most bizarre public debates of the American 1970s.

The Town Hall Debate (1971)

Millett's *Sexual Politics*, one of the key texts of second-wave feminism, set out to establish 'a theory of patriarchy' demonstrating that 'sex is a status category with political implications'.[60] Her comprehensive analysis of ideological, biological, sociological, anthropological and psychological constructions of male dominance in western culture carried one ultimate aim: the elimination of 'the most pernicious of our systems of oppression . . . the sexual politic and its sick delirium of power and violence'.[61] Millett's treatise was divided into three overarching sections: theoretical, historical and literary. It was her attention to the third area that brought Mailer on to the battleground, for Millett devoted over twenty pages to critiquing his misogyny alongside that of D. H. Lawrence and Henry Miller. Beginning with the sexual violence of Mailer's *An American Dream* (1964) which she called 'an exercise in how to kill your wife and be happy ever after', Millett saw such work as 'a rallying cry for a sexual politics in which diplomacy has failed and war is the last political resort of a ruling caste that feels its position in deadly peril'.[62] Mailer, she argued, had been fighting a rearguard action on the part of all men recoiling from the feminist advances of the past two centuries:

> It is vaguely depressing to see a literary man vending the same trash as those hundreds of psychologues and quacks whose jeremiads confound the public with such titles as 'The Feminization of the American Male' [Patricia Sexton, 1969], 'The Disappearing Sexes' [Robert Oldenwald, 1965], and 'The Flight from Woman' [Karl Stern, 1965], zealous tracts which thrash away at the cliché of overbearing modern woman, deplore the rising threat of homosexuality, and glamorize the blunter male supremacist style which the middle class is fond of patronizing as proletarian, or good-old-days.[63]

As for Mailer in particular, Millett observed that 'his obsession' with machismo brought to mind 'a certain curio sold in Coney Island and called a Peter Meter, a quaint bit of folk art, stamped out in the shape of a ruler with printed inches and appropriate epithets to equate excellence with size'.[64]

Mailer quickly rose to the bait in return, firstly by reiterating his anti-feminist stance in 'The Prisoner of Sex', a provocative essay in the March 1971 issue of *Harper's* magazine. His section titles indicate his self-conferred stances: in 'The Prizewinner', he takes up the championship fight against the rising feminist tide; 'The Acolyte' derides feminist theory as vain and unnatural; 'The Advocate' defends at length the two other male writers, Lawrence and Miller, condemned by Millett alongside himself; and 'The Prisoner' mournfully depicts heroic males and lady-like, feminine women at the mercy both of biology and corrupt socialisation (read 'feminism').[65]

Not content with his published riposte, Mailer threw down the gauntlet to the most prominent feminists of the day, challenging them to a public debate at New York's Town Hall. He also contacted his friend, the filmmaker D. A. Pennebaker, perhaps best known for his 1967 documentary on Bob Dylan, *Don't Look Back*. As Pennebaker recalled: 'I knew Norman well . . . Had known him for years. He came to me [before the Town Hall gathering] and asked if I was going to film it. I think he gave me $3,000 to buy the film stock. Like buying your own funeral.'[66] Millett refused to take part, as did Steinem, who dismissed the debate format as macho posturing. Finally, on 30 April 1971, the event was staged, officially billed as 'A Dialogue on Women's Liberation with Norman Mailer, Germaine Greer, Diana Trilling, Jacqueline Ceballos and Jill Johnston.' (Trilling was a leading literary critic, Ceballos was the president of the National Organization of Women and Johnston was a lesbian activist and writer for *The Village Voice*.)

Mailer introduced himself to the audience, which included prominent public intellectuals such as Susan Sontag, Cynthia Ozick, Betty Friedan and Anatole Broyard. He began:

> The evening was billed at one time as 'Normal Mailer versus' the four ladies who are listed. I may say that was done almost over my dead body. I may have vanity, but I do not have the vanity to think that one man can take on four women.[67]

Such demurring notwithstanding, however, it was clear that this was to be a gladiatorial contest with Mailer as the lone champion of male supremacy, fully in keeping with his commitment (if not addiction) to public spectacle. The 'ladies', he said, would make their statements and he would respond.

Ceballos began with a demand for 'overworked and underpaid' women to 'have a voice in changing the world that is changing them' before attacking advertisers who depicted women as 'stupid, servile creatures' who 'get an orgasm whenever the kitchen floor is waxed'. Her call for payment for 'women's work' was a direct challenge to Mailer's position in 'The Prisoner of Sex' that the primary responsibility of women was to bear children and perpetuate the race. Mailer brushed her aside. The greatest 'performance art piece' of the evening, according to Millett, came next, from Johnston, who 'wasn't going to debate anything'.[68] Instead, she launched into a ten-minute stream-of-consciousness poem, beginning: 'The title of this episode is "New Approach". All women are lesbians except those who don't know it, naturally – just the way all men of course are homosexuals. They are, but don't know it yet. I am a woman and therefore a lesbian. I am a woman who is a lesbian because I am a woman.' When two women from the audience jumped onstage and joined Johnston in a bout of simulated lesbian sex (with Johnston proclaiming, 'We're going down on Women's Lib!'), Mailer urged Johnston, 'Come on, Jill, be a lady', inviting a taunt from a woman in the audience, 'Whatsamatter, Mailer, you threatened because you've found a woman you can't fuck?'

If this circus marked the lowest point of the 'debate', such as it was, its high point came with the arrival of Mailer's ultimate vanquisher, Greer. Glamorous, composed and strategically rhetorical, she began by positioning herself as the underdog: 'For me, the significance of this moment is that I am having to confront one of the most powerful figures in my own imagination – the being I think most privileged in male elitist society, namely, the masculine artist, the pinnacle of the masculine elite.' Her handicap, she claimed, was as much psychologically as culturally inflicted: 'Bred as I have been and educated as I have been, most of my life has been most powerfully influenced by the culture for which he stands, so that I am caught in a basic conflict between inculcated cultural values and my own deep conception of an injustice.' Sigmund Freud's corrosive influence, his automatic assumption of the artist as a 'he' whose aim was the acquisition of 'riches, fame, power and the love of women', also contributed to the handicap:

As an eccentric little girl who thought it might be worthwhile after all to be a poet, coming across these words for the first time was a severe check. The blandness of Freud's assumption that the artist was a man sent me back into myself to consider whether or not the proposition was reversible. Could a female artist be driven by the desire for riches, fame and the love of men? And all too soon it was very clear that the female artist's own achievements will disqualify her for the love of man – that no woman yet has been loved for her poetry.

Finally, the western artistic heritage itself imposed a handicap: 'We were either low, sloppy creatures or menials, or we were goddesses, or worst of all we were meant to be both, which meant that we broke our hearts trying to keep our aprons clean.'

Attempting to dismiss Greer's position as 'diaper Marxism', Mailer raised a point that was perhaps inevitable in a debate that was long on spectacle, high in temperature and short on detail: 'Why do you women keep saying – *without having done the analysis* – why [are you] so certain it's entirely the male's fault?' It was part of Greer's rhetorical strength that she could diffuse the tension of combat by muddying the distinctions between culprit and victim:

I didn't know that any women *were* certain it's 'entirely the male's fault' . . . And if the fact is that men have been unconsciously tyrannical – and I think it probably is the case – then it's certain also that they were debauched by their own tyranny and degraded by it and confused by it almost as much as the people they tyrannized over.

The crowning point of this historic debate was Greer's implication that it was not in the power of men to confer or deny women's liberation. Asked from the audience by Anatole Broyard, in echo of Freud, 'What do women want?', Greer sealed her evening's victory by dismissing both Broyard and Freud in the same breath: 'Don't worry, honey. No one wants anything from you.'

Turning the Tide: The Conservative Backlash

Boddy is quite right in observing that 'Mailer's versions of American masculinity are elaborately constructed masquerades' and that 'even as he asserts a hyper-masculinity, Mailer's deadpan humour underlines its anxieties'.[69] These 'anxieties' came to the fore decades after the Town Hall debate, when Mailer looked back at his bruising defeat and confessed: 'I was sort of asinine . . . You know, I have many mixed feelings about the woman's [*sic*] movement, but what I don't forgive myself for is being so retrograde in understanding that this was truly a powerful movement starting, and it had immense momentum behind it.'[70]

But, as one further series of gladiatorial battles indicates, opposition to feminist advances in the 1970s did not come only from men. The

Equal Rights Amendment, first introduced to Congress in 1920, had been championed by the National Organization of Women from the moment of its founding in 1966, most vocally by NOW's first president, Betty Friedan, author of *The Feminine Mystique* (1963). Fifty years to the day from the adoption of the Nineteenth Amendment guaranteeing the vote for women, on 26 August 1970, Friedan declared at a mass New York rally, 'This is not a bedroom war, this is a political movement.'[71] But as the debate over ERA ratification intensified in the 1970s, its most vocal and energetic opponent emerged from the grass roots of conservative antifeminism: Phyllis Schlafly, organiser of the 'Stop the ERA' movement (or STOP). Schlafly, called 'the Sweetheart of the Silent Majority' for her high-profile lecturing, writing and campaigning against the ERA, barnstormed the country condemning the amendment as a threat both to the privileges of women and the stability of the American family. In the spring of 1973, Schlafly and Friedan went head to head in a debate at Illinois State University. Friedan called Schlafly 'a traitor' to women and 'an Aunt Tom' before snarling: 'I'd like to burn you at the stake.'[72] As Donald Critchlow argues, this bitter personal contest was a distillation of a much larger and more momentous political struggle, one that ultimately heralded the ascendancy of the Radical Right in the next decade:

> When Friedan and Schlafly met onstage at Illinois State University in 1973, their arguments and the political forces they represented were already being felt in politics, but few people sensed that reverberations of their clash and what it symbolized were about to shake both main political parties from their moorings. Feminists gained many of their goals through legislation and shifting the Democratic party to the left. Yet, feminists lost the battle for the ERA, and that struggle enabled conservatism to emerge victorious.[73]

Another gladiator working tirelessly to hasten the day of victorious conservatism was the singer, former beauty-pageant queen and fundamentalist Christian, Anita Bryant, to most Americans the wholesome face of the Florida Citrus Commission on a series of television commercials (her chirpy tag line: 'Breakfast without orange juice is like a day without sunshine'). In 1977, the city of Miami, Florida, adopted a measure outlawing discrimination on the grounds of sexual orientation. Launching a 'Save Our Children' campaign to repeal the measure, Bryant vowed: 'The ordinance condones immorality and discriminates against my children's rights to grow up in a healthy, decent community. . . Before I yield to this insidious attack on God and His laws I will lead such a crusade to stop it as this country has not seen before.'[74] True to her word, under Bryant's inspiration the backlash against anti-discriminatory legislation spread like a wave across American cities, pitching the National Gay and Lesbian Task Force into a retaliatory campaign against Bryant, marking the anniversary of the Stonewall uprising with a series of rallies at which they proclaimed, 'No more Miamis . . . Anita, we would rather fight than switch.'[75] The iconic televised moment of the campaign occurred in October 1977, when a protester hit Bryant in the face with a pie during a press conference in Des Moines, Iowa. (The 'pieing' of politicians was fast developing into a tradition: New York mayor Abe Beame had been hit two months before.) Wiping her face, Bryant quipped, 'At least it's a fruit pie.'[76]

There is a sufficiently serious dimension to this farcical episode. As Fred C. Pincus notes, 'When directly pressed to give logical arguments for her position, [Bryant] would rise and sing "The Battle Hymn of the Republic" in an attempt to play on the patriotic sympathies of her audience; reason had no impact on her views.'[77] With such dynamics contributing to, if not driving, the visibility of the contest, Bryant's

Figure 5.4 President Carter and Ronald Reagan shake hands during debates (1980). © Bettmann/CORBIS.

opponents obviously felt the need to combat her ridiculous pathos with equally ridiculous farce.

But it remained to be seen who would have the last laugh, for the neoconservative ground-swell had gathered its force and there would be no stopping it before the presidential election of 1980. That election would bring a former Hollywood actor out from the domestic wings on to the global stage and bring down the curtain on the 1970s.

Rethinking the 1970s

In the early sixteenth century, the Italian Mannerist, Parmigianino, revolutionised painting with his 'Self-Portrait in a Convex Mirror' which was intended to present a wider visual frame around the subject than had been habitually presented. The convex mirror, which deliberately diminished the prominence of the subject's face even as it centred it, was intended to emphasise that there was more in the frame than just the subject himself. In Wolfgang Zucker's words, 'the convex mirror is of a higher reality, a deeper clarity, and a fuller concentration than the world it reflects'; it is, in post-medieval sensibility, 'the analogy of the Divine Order' whose 'precision was more than real'.[1] In 1975, the poet John Ashbery chose Parmigianino's concept – and his title – to engage in an extended reflection *upon* reflection. The experience of viewing the portrait, intended in its original aesthetics to secure clarity and precision, leads in the 1970s to a sense of distortion and erasure:

> So that you could be fooled for a moment
> Before you realize the reflection
> Isn't yours. You feel then like one of those
> Hoffmann characters who have been deprived
> Of a reflection, except that the whole of me
> Is seen to be supplanted by the strict
> Otherness of the painter in his
> Other room.[2]

Stephen Paul Miller seizes on Ashbery's poem as a signal indicator of the distorted perception of a society obsessed with 'surveillance' and – to a highly narcissistic extent – 'self-surveillance'.[3] Popular culture of the 1970s offers an even more dramatic indicator of this distortion and the potential threat to a viewer's subjectivity. It also offers, however, scope for a reading *against* narcissism as the decade's characteristic mode of perception.

Interrogating Narcissism

In Martin Scorsese's *Taxi Driver*, Travis Bickle prepares for his climactic massacre, staring into the mirror (and into the camera lens): 'You talkin' to me? You talkin' to me? You talkin' to me? Then who the hell else are you talkin' – you talkin' to me? Well, I'm the only one here.'[4] In this scene, as Leighton Grist observes, 'we share Travis's contemplation of self' even as 'the mirror shots uphold identification'; consequently, 'as Travis speaks to and threatens himself, he also speaks to and threatens us, proffering a possible estrangement'.[5]

The ambiguity of this scene, in which subject and object are confused, mirrors – reflects – the ambiguity with which the decade has been critically analysed on the one hand as the narcissistic 'Me Decade' and on the other hand as a decade of great collective advancement in which momentous strides were taken across a range of social and political landscapes. Exploring this ambiguity must force a rethinking of the 'culture of narcissism' presumed by Christopher Lasch, Tom Wolfe, Daniel Bell and others. Cultural depictions of narcissism, after all, can also be the most effective *critiques* of narcissism, and it is not difficult to see how such critiques can be misread. When film reviewer Jack Kroll damned 'the Catholic Scorsese and the Calvinist Schrader' for having 'flubbed their ending' in *Taxi Driver*, he assumed that the ending was the film's final statement: 'It's meant to slay you with irony, but it's simply incredible when Travis is hailed as a hero after the slaughter.'[6] Yet, as Lesley Stern observes, the concluding bloodbath 'is not presented narratively as a resolution; rather, it . . . is inscribed as an obsessive repetition, in a narrative that is profoundly disturbed in its frequent veering into aimlessly compulsive trajectories'.[7] Thus, 'the ending of the film . . . in which Travis lives and is hailed as a hero and which has provoked perplexity and criticism, is perfectly consistent with a certain demented and terrifying logic'.[8] In a close-up gesture that concludes the massacre (though not the film itself), the bloodied Travis raises his forefinger to his own temple and imitates the firing of a gun. Stern argues that this particular gesture 'signals . . . the compulsive repetition of obsession' and that 'Travis will be resurrected to continue in his deadly dementia'.[9] It is the implied circular ending that enables the critique of narcissism, which is to be found neither in the massacre nor in Travis's (temporary) celebrity, but rather in his most significant gestures – particularly the final gesture of the aforementioned mirror scene, when he points his gun at the mirror, at the camera, at the viewer, at himself, and declares: 'You're dead.'

It must be recognised that the film's complexity, its ambiguity and irony, do indeed allow the critique of narcissism to be read as a celebration of it. Other cultural expressions and moments have enabled similar readings, giving ammunition to the most resounding condemnations of seventies culture. Yet, to repeat Peter Carroll, 'The times were not narcissistic; only certain people were. And by using them as the benchmark of the decade, writers like Wolfe [and, as we have seen, Lasch and Bell] diminished the value of those who lived otherwise.'[10] Rethinking the 'culture of narcissism' leads to a re-evaluation of the markers that these critics use to identify narcissism, such as nostalgia, irony and individualism.

1970s Nostalgia: Not What It Used to Be

For Lasch, the close of the decade indicated that no significant social or historical lessons had been learned – only styles, stances and evasions: 'Americans seem to wish to forget not only the sixties, the riots, the new left, the disruptions on college campuses, Vietnam, Watergate, and the Nixon presidency, but their entire collective past, even in the antiseptic form in which it was celebrated during the Bicentennial.'[11] The corruption of history into 'nostalgia', Lasch lamented, was yet another symptom of American narcissism:

> In a narcissistic society – a society that gives increasing prominence and encouragement to narcissistic traits – the cultural devaluation of the past reflects not only the poverty of the prevailing ideologies, which have lost their grip on reality and abandoned the attempt to master it, but the poverty of the narcissist's inner life. A society that has made 'nostalgia' a marketable commodity on the cultural exchange quickly repudiates the suggestion that life in the past was in any important way better than life today.[12]

With the Reaganite ascendancy of 1980, Lasch was at least partially vindicated. Ronald Reagan offered to the American people a benign vision relying distinctly upon negative comparisons with the decade they had just left. That decade had begun in the thick of the Vietnam War, with over fifty thousand American soldiers having gone to their

graves and nearly two thousand having disappeared into the jungle
prison camps. At the close of the decade, fifty-three American prison-
ers were being held in the second year of their captivity by Iranian fun-
damentalists who had revealed before the world the impotence of the
Carter administration and, by extension, the United States at large.
Working Americans had felt themselves held hostage by OPEC
through two oil embargos; held hostage by a battered economy and the
twin demons of inflation and unemployment – 'stagflation'. America
may have won the race to the Moon in 1969 but a decade later – in July
1979 – the Skylab space station plunged dramatically out of the sky and
people the world over panicked about where it might crash (it eventually scattered debris over Western Australia and the Indian Ocean).
Punctuating the end of the decade, Miller notes, was not only the fall
of Jimmy Carter and Skylab, but also the death of disco, which 'suddenly fell off the charts' in 1979: a downward trajectory seemed to
characterise an entire decade 'held hostage by fear, cynicism and uncertainty', particularly in the post-Watergate, post-Vietnam years.[13]

This vacuum of hopelessness, Lasch perceived, was countered, at
least in part, by a collective appeal to an ersatz historical sense, namely
nostalgia, which Mark Twain had long before damned as 'mental and
moral masturbation'.[14] As it has been argued throughout this book,
however, the decade was in fact an immensely fertile period whose
capacity for generating cultural energy has only recently been critically acknowledged. It is true that one of the most significant aspects
of this body of cultural production is its entanglement with the workings of nostalgia, but those workings are surely more complex than
Lasch was willing to admit. Nostalgia was not only a significant cultural factor *in* the 1970s but it has since had an impact upon cultural
representations *of* the 1970s, as demonstrated by television sitcoms
such as *That Seventies Show* (1998–2006), films such as *Spirit of '76*
(Lucas Reiner, 1990), *Dazed and Confused* (Richard Linklater, 1993),
Boogie Nights (Paul Thomas Anderson, 1997), *The Last Days of Disco*
(Whit Stillman, 1998), *Almost Famous* (Cameron Crowe, 2000) and
big-screen treatments of the iconic seventies television shows *Starsky
and Hutch* (Todd Phillips, 2004) and *The Brady Bunch* (Betty Thomas,
1995). Carroll is partially correct in observing: 'Nearly all contemporary references to the 1970s represent our own nostalgia for the past,
which ironically often mimics the nostalgia that existed in the seventies about earlier decades.'[15] There are, however, significant exceptions
to such wistful representations of the 1970s, such as John Adams's
opera, *Nixon in China* (1987), which situates Nixon's historic visit to

Figure C.1 *That Seventies Show* (1998). Twentieth Century-Fox/The Kobal Collection/Michael Lavine.

Beijing in the context of tragedy and self-delusion – a combination that returns with violent overtones in Sean Penn's 2004 film, *The Assassination of Richard Nixon*. In fiction, Rick Moody's novel, *The Ice Storm* (1994), uses the 1973 break-up of a Connecticut family as a metaphor for a much wider social crisis (the novel was filmed by Ang Lee in 1997). Of all cultural texts working against the grain of seventies nostalgia, Spike Lee's film, *Summer of Sam* (1999) is perhaps the most harrowing, focusing on the terrorisation of New York in the summer of 1977 by the serial killer, David Berkowitz, the '.44 Calibre Killer' who also went by the name, 'Son of Sam'.

The pattern of ambivalent nostalgia was also a part of seventies culture, when nostalgia for the 1950s (as witnessed in the television series *Happy Days* and the films *American Graffiti* and *Grease*) was countered by such bleak representations as Robert Coover's *The Public Burning* (1977) and Kurt Vonnegut's *Jailbird* (1979), both of which link the seventies to the nightmare of the fifties through what Donald Morse pointedly calls 'the McCarthy–Nixon witchhunts'.[16] Even George Lucas's *American Graffiti* is not so rosy as some would argue. Howard Sounes, for one, appears to reduce the film's impact to warm memories of cruising the small-town strip to an evergreen rock-and-roll soundtrack,

> its pre-Vietnam innocence offering welcome escapism in the year that the US signed the cease-fire agreement in Paris, effectively admitting defeat in the Far East; also, coming out at a time when an embargo by oil-producing countries in the Middle East meant Americans were being forced to think about driving smaller, more fuel-efficient cars for the first time. *American Graffiti* helped create nostalgia for the gas-guzzling automobiles of the past and the apparently better world that that represented.[17]

Yet inscribed within the film's nostalgic frame are counter-currents of unease, through which, as David Wyatt notes, 'the young are prematurely old with regret', the characters sense that '"the whole strip is shrinking"' and they 'not so much enjoy their last night together as they remember or anticipate better ones'.[18] A critique of the seductions of nostalgia is thus inscribed into *American Graffiti* just as the critique of narcissism is inscribed into *Taxi Driver*. Once again the dual coding, the ambiguity, bedevil the interpretation.

Irony and Commitment

In similar fashion, dual coding and ambiguity have exasperated those critics who have not come to grips with the problem of irony in seventies culture. This interpretive problem was hardly new to the 1970s. When, in the mid-nineteenth century, Herman Melville put the words 'something Satanic about irony' and 'God defend me from Irony' into the mouth of his Confidence-Man,[19] he (himself a master ironist) was voicing an acknowledgement of what I have elsewhere called 'irony fatigue' – the inability to maintain the tension between serious criticism and playful utterance.[20] As far as Lasch was concerned, irony was everywhere in the seventies. It was not the playful, cheerful irony that Robert Venturi hoped would smooth the reception of postmodern disharmony in architecture; rather, it was a bitter, sardonic irony largely bound up with the occupational malaise of the post-industrial society:

> When jobs consist of little more than meaningless motions, and when social routines, formerly dignified as ritual, degenerate into role playing, the worker – whether he toils on an assembly line or holds down a high-paying job in a large bureaucracy – seeks to escape from the resulting sense of inauthenticity by creating an ironic distance from his daily life. He takes refuge in jokes, mockery, and cynicism.[21]

While some of the examples explored in the previous chapters do indeed lend credence to Lasch's observation (in particular the network sitcoms), this can also be challenged as a generalisation, readily confounded through reference to other cultural examples (Carver, Morrison, Gaines, Haley, Shange, Springsteen). Moreover, as I argued in Chapter 3, the interpretive crisis imposed by irony enables a given expression to be read both ways, with any side ignored at one's peril. Hence the Reaganite appropriation of the rhetoric of *Star Wars* for political purposes, apparently reflecting an earnest appeal to implausible binaries with no acknowledgement of their ironic potential. Reagan's appropriation of *Star Wars* and the trope of 'the Evil Empire' gives the lie to Irving Kristol's well-worn definition of neoconservatives as liberals who have been 'mugged by reality'.[22] If the *Star Wars* episode is anything to go by, Reagan – the former New Deal Democrat and trade union leader (one of whose first acts as president was to break the Professional Air Traffic Controllers' union in 1981) – would appear to have been less 'mugged by reality' than by 1970s irony.

At any rate, Lasch and other critics have overemphasised the controlling dynamics of irony in 1970s culture. There were numerous outgrowths of seventies culture, as we have seen, driven less by irony than by earnest endeavour and political commitment. These include, it must be said, the resurgence of post-sixties conservatism, which was more of a seventies phenomenon than the Reaganite eighties phenomenon that it is conventionally styled. Bruce J. Schulman describes the anchoring in the early 1970s of the 'new strain of conservative thought . . . that would help smooth the edges of conservatism and sell its worldview'.[23] At work 'smoothing the edges' were cultural phenomena such as the revival of Christian evangelism that tinged so much of American culture, infecting not only political and social debate but also the airwaves, which hosted popular Christian anthems as though they were secular hits. What were American Jews, Muslims and atheists to think of Norman Greenbaum's 1969–70 hit, 'Spirit in the Sky'? They might well consider it an ironic musical exercise but the growing social force of Christian evangelism would suggest otherwise. While it cannot be denied that the born-again President Jimmy Carter's relatively progressive administration was itself driven by an evangelical fervour, it was in the 1970s that evangelism fuelled the determined – and hardly playful – campaigns against the decade's most progressive social movements. Regardless of one's own political leanings, few could deny the earnest messianic force with which conservatives in the 1970s built up a following, embarked on their reactionary campaigns against women's liberation, the Equal Rights Amendment, gay rights and other movements associated with the 'liberal consensus', and prepared the ground for the Reaganite revolution.

The seventies, however, was a battleground upon which progressive forces took their stand with equal determination. Lasch may well have concluded mournfully:

> The disparity between romance and reality, the world of the beautiful people and the workaday world, gives rise to an ironic detachment that dulls pain but also cripples the will to change social conditions, to make even modest improvements in work and play, and to restore meaning and dignity to everyday life.[24]

But the impact of progressive activism in the 1970s suggests that Lasch was far too sweeping in his denunciations of 'ironic detachment' as the defining seventies stance. One example of seventies activism – the environmental movement – deserves particular acknowledgement for its impact upon subsequent decades.

Ecological Urgency

'Look at Mother Nature on the run in the 1970s': so sang Neil Young in 'After the Gold Rush' (1970), reflecting a heightened awareness of impending ecological disaster in the first year of the decade.[25] We can look back from the vantage point of the early twenty-first century to a particular day in 1970 to see the embedding of a progressive movement that, equally as determined as the neoconservative movement, has survived the swings of the political pendulum. On 22 April 1970, a national day of consciousness raising – dubbed 'Earth Day' – kick started the modern environmental movement. To some degree Earth Day was itself sparked by a particular viewpoint that had been finally enabled on 21 July 1969, as Carroll describes:

> It was the supreme irony of American technology that at the moment of its greatest achievement – the pinpoint landing of astronauts on the moon – human beings glimpsed just how unique and how vulnerable was the condition of the planet Earth. Seen against the dusty summits of the moon, the blue planet reaffirmed the limited horizons of the remainder of mankind trapped by inexorable, but ultimately friendly forces of gravitation. The world 'ecology', derived from the Greek *oikos*, meaning 'house', quickly entered the American vocabulary. The Earth, the Apollo space program reported, was mankind's only home.[26]

One cultural example of this new perception was the publication of Stewart Brand's *The Last Whole Earth Catalog* (1971–4), the popularity of which reflected a mass desire to alter modes of American living in the hope of securing a sustainable future. As Apple Computer founder Steve Jobs recalled in his 2005 commencement address at Stanford University, the Catalog 'was one of the bibles of my generation. . . It was sort of like Google in paperback form, 35 years before Google came along: it was idealistic, and overflowing with neat tools and great notions' to enable alternative practices in land and shelter use, craft and industry, nomadic living and community.[27] Andrew G. Kirk describes the phenomenon by which the Catalog earned 'a place in American cultural history', becoming the only catalogue to earn the National Book Award (1972): 'The solidly packed *Last Catalog* topped out at almost four hundred and fifty pages, with a durable squared binding that ensured that the catalogs could pass through many hands and move off and on many a commune bookshelf for years without disintegrating.'[28]

It is all too easy to dismiss the cult status of *The Last Whole Earth Catalog* and other aspects of 1970s environmentalism as post-sixties faddism. Schulman appears to do this as he recalls: 'After the disappointments of 1968, ecology emerged as a "fresh oppositional alternative". . . Hippies traded in the Day-Glo colors, groovy plastics, and mod fashions that had defined the Haight–Ashbury Summer of Love for muted earth tones, Apache headbands, and Indian shawls.'[29] Indeed, a certain scepticism about the seriousness of the environmental movement – with its 'long-haired greens' and 'new ecology action groups in communes, college towns, hip neighborhoods, and minority communities'[30] – may well have prompted President Nixon's Secretary of the Interior, Walter Hickel, to commemorate Earth Day 'by announcing approval of the eight-hundred-mile Alaska [oil] pipeline'.[31] And indeed, dismissive recollections of President Carter's sobering attention to America's limitations – including, as he reminded his fellow citizens, 'the limits of manipulation without harm to ourselves or to a delicate and balanced natural environment' – may well have ensured that 'the 1980 election of Ronald Reagan rejected limits on everything but social spending'.[32]

Yet, embedded in our recollections of the 1970s must be three particularly sinister environmental and biological wake-up calls. In July 1976, in the midst of the bicentennial celebrations, thirty-four delegates to an American Legion convention in Philadelphia died from – and consequently gave their name to – the infectious disease spread by bacteria in contaminated air and water systems: *Legionellosis*, or Legionnaire's Disease. In 1978, the residents of Love Canal in the town of Niagara Falls, New York, woke up to a potentially lethal environmental catastrophe: 'A peculiar stench filled the air, trees turned black, children detonated multicoloured sparks by crashing stones against the pavement, and the number of miscarriages and babies born with birth defects soared ominously.'[33] Love Canal – its homes, schools, parks and playgrounds – had been built upon a leaking toxic chemical dump, its name destined to become, in Murray Levine's words, 'a synonym for environmental pollutants of all kinds, the effluvia of an advanced industrial and technological machine that has created hitherto undreamed-of marvels and wealth, but which now, paradoxically, threatens our very existence'.[34] Finally, on 30 March 1979, the plot of James Bridges's newly released thriller, *The*

China Syndrome – about a disaster at an American nuclear power plant – came perilously close to realisation at the Three Mile Island nuclear plant in Harrisburg, Pennsylvania, from where over a million citizens were evacuated or fled. With pre-Chernobyl innocence, anchorman Walter Cronkite intoned on the CBS Evening News: 'The world has never known a day like today. It faced the considerable uncertainties and dangers of the worst nuclear power plant accident of the atomic age. And the horror tonight is that it could get much worse.' He then introduced a new phrase into modern apocalyptic vocabulary: 'The potential is there for the ultimate risk of meltdown at Three Mile Island.'[35]

The awareness of such disasters and near disasters, and the consequent cultural and political activism associated with them, must be considered as one of the most enduring legacies of 1970s environmentalism. Grass-roots endeavours, such as the campaign led by Lois Marie Gibbs of Love Canal to compel corporations to take legal responsibility for their pollution were highly inspirational, leading in a direct line to the massive 'No Nukes' rallies and concerts of the 1980s, Al Gore's *An Inconvenient Truth* (2006) and the global rock concerts of the twenty-first century drawing attention to the perils of climate change. There can be no more powerful example than the environmental movement to counter the assessment of the seventies as a hollowed-out decade mired in its own narcissism.

Narcissism, Individualism and Activism

Running through the negative critiques of seventies culture is a frequent equation of narcissism with individualism. Daniel Bell, for instance, lamented 'rampant individualism' and 'the idea of the untrammelled self' as narcissistic tendencies normally encouraged by any 'laissez-faire economy' but brought to dangerous extremes in the post-industrial society.[36] Lasch saw in the seventies 'the apotheosis of individualism', a 'dying' mode of life 'which in its decadence has carried the logic of individualism to the extreme of a war of all against all, the pursuit of happiness to the dead end of a narcissistic preoccupation with the self'.[37] Tom Wolfe argued that, 'historically', people 'have lived as if they are living their ancestors' lives and their offspring's lives and perhaps their neighbors' lives as well. They have seen themselves as inseparable from the great tide of chromosomes of which they are created and which they pass on' – in short, they have thought of themselves as part of a collective, 'their people, their race, their community'.[38] But now, in the midst of the 'Me Decade', collective awareness had all but evaporated:

> No matter whether you managed to renovate your personality through encounter sessions or not, you had finally focused your attention and your energies on the most fascinating subject on earth: *Me*. Not only that, you also put *Me* onstage before a live audience. [. . .] Just imagine . . . *Me and My Hemorrhoids* . . . moving an entire hall to the most profound outpouring of emotion! Just imagine . . . *my life* becoming a drama with universal significance . . . analyzed, like Hamlet's, for what it signifies for the rest of mankind. . .[39]

The problem, of course, is that is precisely what individual characterisations do, Wolfe's mockery notwithstanding: they 'signify' for the rest of us. They also raise the implicit question: when does self-expression or self-fashioning slip into outright narcissism? In reviewing the Laurel Canyon music scene, Michael Walker makes an important observation:

> Even at their commercial zenith in the '70s, when their self-absorption was at its most annoying, the canyon singer–songwriters had a nodding acquaintance with emotional intimacy and, in the Eagles, a journalist-like fetish for chronicling the times in which they were living.[40]

Granted, Walker gives – at best – two muted cheers for the Eagles; but he establishes that wholesale narcissism is hardly an appropriate charge to level at the culture of an entire decade, let alone its more 'annoying' cases.

If, indeed, the culture of the seventies was self-focused, it first begs the question whether it was any more so than the culture of other decades (all caricatures, like Wolfe's mockery, notwithstanding). More to the point, it raises questions over the communal value of individualism, an admittedly thorny problem arising more often in debates on 'enlightened self-interest' in ethics and economics. Shelton Waldrep, for one, places the individualistic focus within the broader frame of creativity and experimentation. He considers 'the seventies' ability to provide for an experimentation with self as 'one of the strengths of its cultural production'.[41] Hence, for instance, the case of the New York Dolls and other glitter bands, in which the emphasis on individual role play carried socially (as well as sexually) liberating potential that extended beyond a band's apparently narcissistic posturing, to the benefit of an oppressed group. To repeat Van Cagle, the opportunity afforded by the glitter subculture for people to 'try on roles' brought 'queerness from subtext to text' and made it 'unashamed, playful, and decoded for mass consumption'. [42]

Elsewhere, in one of the decade's most high-profile obscenity cases, the stand-up comedian, George Carlin, took it upon himself to test the limits of permissible public speech. His routine, 'Seven Words You Can Never Say on Television', resulted in his arrest for obscenity at a Milwaukee festival in 1973 (the case was subsequently dismissed). The first recorded version, on the album *Class Clown* (1972), was immediately popular among high school and college students across the country. A second version, on the album *Occupation: Foole* (1973), was broadcast on New York's WBAI radio station, resulting, through a listener's complaint, in the 1978 Supreme Court case, *FCC v. Pacifica Foundation* (the owners of the station). The seven offending words, Carlin taunted in the routine, were 'the ones that will curve your spine, grow hair on your hands and maybe even bring us, God help us, peace without honour'. [43] As Carroll notes, there was something highly rich in 'the crusade against obscenity' in which Carlin was caught up, given the revelations gleaned from the transcripts of Nixon's White House Tapes, peppered with what soon became a Watergate-era catch-phrase, 'expletive deleted':

> Inside the White House, the President felt no need to silence, much less to criticize, such expressions as —— (expletive deleted), —— (expletive deleted), or even —— (expletive deleted). But in his fiery speeches against antiwar protesters, [Vice-President Spiro] Agnew commonly denounced the use of street language and 'gutter obscenities'.
>
> This attack on dirty words served an important political purpose. Within the antiwar movement – and the burgeoning youth culture in general – the continuation of technological warfare in Vietnam itself appeared obscene, far more grievous than words like ——, ——, or ——. [44]

Like his mentor, Lenny Bruce, in the previous decade, Carlin was accused of narcissistic self-indulgence by his detractors and applauded as a martyr to free speech by his champions, who argued that he had revealed language as 'a live grenade to be inspected'. [45] Thus was one person's narcissist another person's activist, however quixotic – an individual doing what little he could, wherever he could, however he could, in order to widen the cage of restricted speech. In the end, he did very little indeed: the Supreme Court eventually ruled in favour of the Federal Communications Commission (FCC), the government body that had brought the charge against the radio station. As the First Amendment rights activist, Marjorie Heins, points out: 'In the famous "seven dirty words" case . . . [the FCC] announced the indecency definition that it still uses today: any depiction or description of "sexual or excretory activities or organs" in a manner that it deems "patently offensive as measured by contemporary community standards for the broadcast medium".'[46] In the wake of this ruling, Heins observes, the FCC have flexed their muscles in a host of politically driven censorship cases against radio talk shows and rap artists of both sexes in this century:

> The FCC's censorship of call-in radio shows that dwell on the far side of sexual invention may not generate widespread outrage. But giving any government agency unbridled power to censor whatever it deems 'patently offensive' or 'indecent' – depending on the political climate – is a dangerous proposition. Historically, FCC censorship has often targeted the radical or counter-cultural voices that – as one dissenting commissioner said years ago in protesting an indecency ruling against Jerry Garcia of the Grateful Dead – the commission 'fears because it does not understand'.[47]

Conclusion

The case of George Carlin, the lone comedian caught in the spotlight of notoriety, is useful in highlighting one of the dilemmas in assessing the culture of the 1970s, that final decade before the neoconservative triumph. Carlin's activism in defence of free speech can, it is true, be read ultimately as a narcissistic gesture akin to the rebellious 'posturing' that the playwright Tom Stoppard has recently assigned to the anti-war youth movement of the late sixties.[48] Stoppard's denunciation of the movement's 'street theatre' echoes precisely that of Lasch, who dismissed the movement's professed shift 'from dissent to resistance' in 1967: ' "It will be bloody," said one radical in defense of a particularly futile protest, "but blood makes the liberals mad". Far from provoking a liberal reaction, however, the politics of street theatre solidified opposition to the left and created a mounting demand for law and order.'[49]

But what was the alternative to such gestures on the part of committed activists? Joan Didion, in her essay 'On the Morning after the Sixties' (1970), confessed to a drained sense of futility at the start of the seventies: 'If I could believe that going to a barricade would affect man's fate in the slightest I would go to that barricade, and quite often I wish that I could, but it would be less than honest to say that I expect to happen upon such a happy ending.'[50] There is no telling what Didion would have written had she been looking back from 1980 instead of 1970. But this book has explored some examples of what she *might* have seen amid the cultural landscape. She might have seen that, culturally at least, not all the barricades had been dismantled. It is true, she might have seen some harrowing representations of cultural deple-tion, such as that offered by Kurt Vonnegut in his *cri de cœur* from *Breakfast of Champions* (1973), which presents contemporary culture as 'a sidewalk strewn with junk': 'I have no culture, no humane harmony in my brains. I can't live without a culture anymore.'[51] She might have seen the corporate-driven evasiveness of television sitcoms as well as the galvanising impact of *Roots*; dismissed the disco dance as mindless gyration or applauded its multicultural, multi-sexual promis-cuity; seen what Waldrep calls the 'experimentation . . . with the borders between genres and forms'[52] that allowed Toni Morrison to attempt expressing through fiction 'something that has probably been only fully expressed in music'.[53] She might have seen George Carlin taking the mantle from Lenny Bruce in a doomed attempt to speak frankly; or picked up and wrestled with the ambiguous signals from Scorsese's *Taxi Driver*.

In short, Didion might have seen what those of us on the other side of the eighties – and the nineties, for that matter – are also able to see when we look back at the mass of contradictory cultural expressions of the seventies. Like the subjects of Diane Arbus's photographs (as Arbus herself said in 1971), you cannot dismiss them: 'You can turn away but when you come back they'll still be there looking at you.'[54] They are not merely 'looking', but positively begging for ever-renewed interpretation.

Notes

Introduction

1. Bruce J. Schulman, *The Seventies: The Great Shift in American Culture, Society and Politics* (Cambridge, MA: Da Capo Press, 2001), p. xvi.
2. Stephen Rachman, 'The Wayne's Worlding of America: Performing the Seventies in the Nineties', in Shelton Waldrep (ed.), *The Seventies: The Age of Glitter in Popular Culture* (London: Routledge, 2000): 41–53 (p. 52).
3. Greil Marcus, 'Self Portrait No. 25', in Waldrep (ed.), *The Seventies*: 293–307 (p. 307).
4. Stephen Paul Miller, *The Seventies Now: Culture as Surveillance* (Durham: Duke University Press, 1999), p. 28.
5. Schulman, *The Seventies*, pp. xvi–xvii.
6. Ibid., pp. xii, xiv.
7. Edward D. Berkowitz, *Something Happened: A Political and Cultural Overview of the Seventies* (New York: Columbia University Press, 2006).
8. Mark Hamilton Lytle, *America's Uncivil Wars: The Sixties Era from Elvis to the Fall of Richard Nixon* (New York: Oxford University Press, 2006).
9. Philip Jenkins, *Decade of Nightmares: The End of the Sixties and the Making of Eighties America* (New York: Oxford University Press, 2006), p. 4.
10. J. David Hoeveler Jr, *The Postmodernist Turn: American Thought and Culture in the 1970s* (New York: Twayne, 1996), pp. xiii–xiv.
11. Daniel Bell, *The Coming of Post-Industrial Society: A Venture in Social Forecasting* (London: Heinemann, 1974), p. 477.
12. Ibid., p. 477.
13. Daniel Bell, *The Cultural Contradictions of Capitalism* (London: Heinemann, 1976), p. 37.

14. Ibid., p. 22.
15. Miller, *The Seventies Now*, p. 2.
16. Graham Thompson, *American Culture in the 1980s* (Edinburgh: Edinburgh University Press, 2007), p. 3.
17. Schulman, *The Seventies*, p. xii.
18. Quoted in Van M. Cagle, 'Trudging through the Glitter Trenches: The Case of the New York Dolls', in Waldrep (ed.), *The Seventies*: 125–51 (p. 136).
19. Miller, *The Seventies Now*, pp. 12, 20.
20. Schulman, *The Seventies*, p. xi.
21. Sherrie A. Inness, 'Strange Feverish Years: The 1970s and Women's Changing Roles', in Inness (ed.), *Disco Divas: Women and Popular Culture in the 1970s* (Philadelphia: University of Pennsylvania Press, 2003): 1–12 (p. 2).
22. Derek Kompare, *Rerun Nation: How Repeats Invented American Television* (New York: Routledge, 2005), p. 8.
23. Shelton Waldrep, 'Introducing the Seventies', in Waldrep (ed.), *The Seventies*: 1–15 (p. 14, n. 4).
24. Schulman, *The Seventies*, p. 98.
25. Cyra McFadden, *The Serial* (London: Picador, [1977] 1980), pp. 68–9.
26. Tom Wolfe, 'The Me Decade and the Third Great Awakening' [1976], in *The Purple Decades* (London: Vintage, 2005): 265–96 (p. 277).
27. Jim Hougan, *Decadence: Radical Nostalgia, Narcissism, and Decline in the Seventies* (New York: Morrow, 1975); Peter Marin, 'The New Narcissism', *Harper's* 251, no. 1 (October 1975): 45–56; Edwin Schur, *The Awareness Trap: Self-Absorption instead of Social Change* (New York: Quadrangle–New York Times, 1976); Richard Sennett, *The Fall of Public Man* (New York: Knopf, 1977).
28. Christopher Lasch, *The Culture of Narcissism: American Life in an Age of Diminishing Expectations* (London: W. W. Norton, [1978] 1991), p. 31. Further page references in parentheses are from this edition.
29. David A. Cook, *Lost Illusions: American Cinema in the Shadow of Watergate and Vietnam, 1970–1979* (New York: Charles Scribner's Sons, 2000), p. 5.
30. Peter N. Carroll, *It Seemed Like Nothing Happened: America in the 1970s* (New Brunswick, NJ: Rutgers University Press, [1982] 2000), p. xviii.
31. Miller, *The Seventies Now*, p. 1.
32. Ibid., p. 35.
33. David Wyatt, *Out of the Sixties: Storytelling and the Vietnam Generation* (Cambridge: Cambridge University Press, 1993), p. 1.

34. Howard Sounes, *Seventies: The Sights, Sounds and Ideas of a Brilliant Decade* (London: Simon and Schuster, 2006), p. 217.
35. Schulman, *The Seventies*, p. 8.
36. Bell, *Cultural Contradictions of Capitalism*, p. 28.
37. Ibid., p. 28.
38. Edward Said,*Orientalism*(London: Penguin, [1978] 1991), p. 1. Further page references in parentheses are from this edition.
39. 'Jimmy Carter on the Energy Crisis – February 1, 1977'. Broadcast available on *Global Public Media: Public Service Broadcasting for a Post-Carbon World* <http://globalpublicmedia.com/lectures/425>.
40. 'Primary Sources: The "Crisis of Confidence" Speech'. *American Experience*, PBS Online <http://www.pbs.org/wgbh/amex/carter/film-more/ps_crisis.html>.
41. Ibid.
42. Title IX of the Education Amendments 1972, 20 U.S.C. § 1681 <http://www.usdoj.gov/crt/cor/coord/titleixstat.htm>.
43. Equal Rights Amendment, H.J. Res. 40 <http://thomas.loc.gov/cgibin/query/z?c110:H.J.RES.40:>.
44. United States Supreme Court, Roe v. Wade, 410 U.S. 113 <http://caselaw.lp.findlaw.com/scripts/getcase.pl?navby=CASE&court=US&vol=410&page=113>.
45. Robin Morgan, 'Introduction', in Morgan (ed.), *Sisterhood Is Powerful: An Anthology of Writings from the Women's Liberation Movement* (New York: Vintage Books, 1970), p. xxix.
46. Miller, *The Seventies Now*, p. 7.
47. Boston Women's Health Book Collective, *Our Bodies, Ourselves: A Book by and for Women* (New York: Simon and Schuster, [1973] 1976), p. 11. Further page references in parentheses are from this edition.
48. Carroll, *It Seemed Like Nothing Happened*, p. 275.
49. Miller, *The Seventies Now*, p. 209.
50. Michael Bronski, *Culture Clash: The Making of Gay Sensibility* (Boston: South End Press, 1984), p. 5.
51. Ibid., p. 2.
52. Schulman, *The Seventies*, pp. 177, 183.
53. Tom Wolfe, 'These Radical Chic Evenings' [1970], in *The Purple Decades*: 181–97 (p. 190).
54. Michael E. Staub, 'Setting Up the Seventies: Black Panthers, New Journalism and the Rewriting of the Sixties', in Waldrep (ed.), *The Seventies*: 19–40 (p. 25).
55. Ibid., p. 21.

56. Hal Lindsay, *The Late, Great Planet Earth* (Grand Rapids, MI: Zondervan, 1970), p. 42.

57. 'Zion's Christian Soldiers', CBS News Online, 8 June 2003 <http://www.cbsnews.com/stories/2002/10/03/60minutes/main52426 8.shtml>.

58. Schulman, *The Seventies*, p. 93.

59. Sounes, *Seventies*, p. 373.

60. Jerome L. Himmelstein, *To the Right: The Transformation of American Conservatism* (Berkeley: University of California Press, 1990), p. 90.

61. Schulman, *The Seventies*, p. 8.

1. Fiction and Poetry

1. Quoted in Lewis P. Simpson, 'Southern Fiction', in Daniel Hoffman (ed.), *Harvard Guide to Contemporary American Writing* (Cambridge, MA: Belknap Press of the Harvard University Press, 1979): 153–90 (pp. 173–4).

2. A. Walton Litz, 'Literary Criticism', in Hoffman, *Harvard Guide*: 51–83 (p. 83).

3. Richard Bach, *Jonathan Livingston Seagull* (London: HarperElement, [1970] 2003), p. 26.

4. Zhu Hong, 'Will the "Super Culture" Catch On in China?' *Australian Journal of Chinese Affairs*, 5 (January 1981): 91–5 (p. 92).

5. Philip Slater, *Earthwalk* (New York: Anchor Press, 1974), p. 187.

6. Robert Pirsig, *Zen and the Art of Motorcycle Maintenance* (New York: Bantam, [1974] 1975), p. 18.

7. J. David Hoeveler Jr, *The Postmodern Turn: American Thought and Culture in the 1970s* (New York: Twayne, 1996), p. 15.

8. Richard Ruland and Malcolm Bradbury, *From Puritanism to Postmodernism: A History of American Literature* (New York: Penguin, 1992), pp. 420–1.

9. Stephen Paul Miller, *The Seventies Now: Culture as Surveillance* (Durham: Duke University Press, 1999), p. 11.

10. Ruland and Bradbury, *From Puritanism to Postmodernism*, p. 421.

11. Stanley Fish, 'Interpreting the *Variorum*', *Critical Inquiry* 2 (spring 1976): 465–85; Geoffrey Hartman, 'Toward Literary History', *Daedalus* 99, no. 2 (spring 1970): 355–83; Harold Bloom, *The Anxiety of Influence: A Theory of Poetry* (New York: Oxford University Press, 1973); Harold Bloom, *Poetry and Repression: Revisionism from Blake to Stevens* (New Haven: Yale University Press, 1976).

12. Litz, 'Literary Criticism', p. 74.

13. Ruland and Bradbury, *From Puritanism to Postmodernism*, p. 426.
14. Earl Rovit, 'Some Shapes in Recent American Fiction', *Contemporary Literature* 15, no. 4 (autumn 1974): 539–61 (pp. 542–3).
15. Bob Perelman, 'Dance', in Perelman, *Braille* (Ithaca, NY: Ithaca House, 1975), p. 33. Online at <http://english.utah.edu/eclipse/projects/BRAILLE>.
16. Paul Mann, *The Theory-Death of the Avant-Garde* (Bloomington: Indiana University Press, 1991), p. 32.
17. Lee Bartlett, 'What is "Language Poetry"?' *Critical Inquiry* 12, no. 4 (summer 1986): 741–52 (p. 742).
18. Geoff Ward, *Language Poetry and the American Avant-Garde* (Keele: Ryburn Press/British Association for American Studies, 1993), pp. 6–7.
19. Quoted in Craig Dworkin, 'Language Poetry', in Jeffrey Gray et al. (eds), *The Greenwood Encyclopedia of American Poets and Poetry*, vol. 3 (Westport, CT: Greenwood Press, 2006): 880–3 (p. 881).
20. Ward, *Language Poetry*, p. 15.
21. Bob Perelman, *The Marginalization of Poetry* (Princeton: Princeton University Press, 1996), pp. 12–13.
22. Ward, *Language Poetry*, pp. 6, 15.
23. Quoted in Marjorie Perloff, 'The Word as Such: L=A=N=G =U=A=G=E Poetry in the Eighties', *American Poetry Review* 13 (May–June 1984): 15–22. Online at <http://www.writing.upenn.edu/library/Perloff-Marjorie_Word-as-Such.html>.
24. Bob Perelman, 'The First Person', *Hills*, nos 6/7 (spring 1980): 156.
25. Ron Silliman, *The Age of Huts* (New York: Roof, 1986), p. 32.
26. Ward, p. 30; Barrett Watten, 'The Secret History of the Equal Sign: L=A=N=G=U=A=G=E between Discourse and Text', *Poetics Today* 20, no. 4 (winter 1999): 581–627 (p. 603).
27. Ward, 'Language Poetry', pp. 11, 30.
28. Stephen Fredman, *Poet's Prose: The Crisis in American Verse* (Cambridge: Cambridge University Press, 1983), p. 135.
29. Quoted in Bartlett, 'What is "Language Poetry"?', p. 745.
30. Fredman, *Poet's Prose*, p. 135.
31. Bruce Andrews and Charles Bernstein, 'Repossessing the Word', in Andrews and Bernstein (eds), *The L=A=N=G=U=A=G=E Book* (Carbondale: Southern Illinois University Press, 1984), p. ix.
32. Ward, 'Language Poetry', pp. 12, 14.
33. Perelman, *The Marginalization of Poetry*, p. 13.
34. Ron Silliman, 'Disappearance of the Word, Appearance of the World', in Andrews and Bernstein, *The L=A=N=G=U=A=G=E Book*, p. 131.

35. Steve McCaffery, 'From the Notebooks', in Andrews and Bernstein, *The L=A=N=G=U=A=G=E Book*, p. 160.
36. Andrews and Bernstein, 'Repossessing the Word', p. x.
37. Ward, 'Language Poetry', p. 16.
38. Ibid., p. 22.
39. Kathryn Hume, *American Dream, American Nightmare: Fiction since 1960* (Urbana: University of Illinois Press, 2002), p. 120.
40. Kim A. Hertzinger, 'Introduction: On the New Fiction', *Mississippi Review*, nos 40–1 (1985): 7–22 (p. 11).
41. William L. Stull, 'Raymond Carver', in J. M. Brook (ed.), *Dictionary of Literary Biography: Yearbook, 1988* (Detroit: Gale, 1988): 199–213 (pp. 199–200).
42. Kasia Boddy, 'Companion–Souls of the Short Story: Anton Chekhov and Raymond Carver', *Scottish Slavonic Review: An International Journal Promoting East–West Contacts* 18 (1992): 105–13.
43. Raymond Carver, 'Errand', *The New Yorker*, 1 June 1987. Reprinted in Carver, *Where I'm Calling From: Selected Stories* (New York: Atlantic Monthly Press, [1988] 1991): 419–32.
44. Bill Buford, 'Editorial', *Granta 8: Dirty Realism: New Writing from America* (Harmondsworth: Penguin, 1983): 4.
45. Kay Bonetti, 'Ray Carver: Keeping It Short', in Marshall Bruce Gentry and William L. Stull (eds), *Conversations with Raymond Carver* (Jackson: University Press of Mississippi, 1990): 53–61 (p. 60).
46. Raymond Carver, 'They're Not Your Husband', in Carver, *Will You Please Be Quiet, Please?* (London: Vintage, [1976] 1993): 16–22 (p. 16).
47. Raymond Carver, 'What's in Alaska?', *Will You Please Be Quiet, Please?*: 58–69 (p. 58).
48. Raymond Carver, 'Night School', *Will You Please Be Quiet, Please?*: 70–5 (p. 70).
49. Raymond Carver, 'Collectors', *Will You Please Be Quiet, Please?*: 76–81 (p. 76).
50. John Alton, 'What We Talk About When We Talk About Literature: An Interview with Raymond Carver', in Gentry and Stull (eds), *Conversations with Raymond Carver*: 151–68 (p. 161).
51. Ibid., p. 161.
52. Alan Wilde, *Middle Grounds: Studies in Contemporary American Fiction* (Philadelphia: University of Pennsylvania Press, 1987), p. 112.
53. Kirk Nesset, ' "This Word Love": Sexual Politics and Silence in Early Raymond Carver', *American Literature* 63, no. 2 (June 1991): 292–313 (pp. 293–4).
54. Ibid., p. 294.

55. Raymond Carver, 'Will You Please Be Quiet, Please?', *Will You Please Be Quiet, Please?*: 164–81 (p. 167).
56. Nesset, ' "This Word Love" ', p. 294.
57. Raymond Carver, 'Fat', *Will You Please Be Quiet, Please?*: 1–5 (p. 5).
58. Arthur F. Berthea, *Technique and Sensibility in the Fiction and Poetry of Raymond Carver* (New York: Routledge, 2001), p. 8.
59. Nesset, ' "This Word Love" ', p. 294.
60. Carol Hanish, 'The Personal Is Political', in Shulamith Firestone and Anne Koedt (eds), *Notes from the Second Year: Women's Liberation: Major Writings of the Radical Feminists* (New York: Radical Feminism, 1970): 76–8.
61. Walter Abish, *Alphabetical Africa* (New York: New Directions, 1974), pp. 1–2.
62. Marc Chénetier, *Beyond Suspicion: New American Fiction since 1960*, trans. Elizabeth A. Houlding (Philadelphia: University of Pennsylvania Press, 1996), p. 94.
63. Ronald Sukenick, *Out* (Chicago: Swallow Press, 1973). Online at <http://www.altx.com/out/table.html>.
64. Brian McHale, *Postmodern Fiction* (London: Routledge, [1987] 1996), p. 183.
65. John Johnston, *Information Multiplicity: American Fiction in the Age of Media Saturation* (Baltimore: Johns Hopkins University Press, 1998), p. 121.
66. John Barth, 'The Literature of Exhaustion', in Barth, *The Friday Book* (Baltimore: Johns Hopkins University Press, [1984] 1997): 62–76 (p. 64).
67. Jerome Klinkowitz, 'The Extra-Literary in Contemporary American Fiction', in Malcolm Bradbury and Sigmund Ro (eds), *Contemporary American Fiction* (London: Edward Arnold, 1987): 19–37 (p. 23).
68. Gilbert Sorrentino, *Mulligan Stew* (New York: Grove, 1979), p. 224.
69. Klinkowitz, 'The Extra-Literary', p. 31.
70. William H. Gass 'The Artist in Society' in Gass, *Fiction and the Figures of Life* (Boston: Godine, [1970] 1979): 276–88 (p. 282).
71. Federman quoted in Ruland and Bradbury, *From Puritanism to Post-Modernism*, p. 390.
72. Federman quoted in Peter Currie, 'The Eccentric Self: Anti-Characterization and the Problem of the Subject in American Postmodernist Fiction', in Bradbury and Ro, *Contemporary American Fiction*, 53–69 (p. 55).
73. Daniel Bell, *The Cultural Contradictions of Capitalism* (London: Heinemann, 1976), p. 95.
74. Ruland and Bradbury, *From Puritanism to Post-Modernism*, p. 391.

75. Leo Braudy, 'Realists, Naturalists and Novelists of Manners', in Hoffman, *Harvard Guide*: 84–152 (p. 118).
76. Kurt Vonnegut, *Jailbird* (London: Vintage, 1992 [1979]), p. 209.
77. Richard Nixon to H. R. Haldeman, White House Tapes, 23 June 1972. Audio version online at University of Virginia, Miller Center of Public Affairs, White House Tapes Project <www.whitehousetapes.org>.
78. Bell, *The Cultural Contradictions*, p. 118.
79. Miller, *The Seventies Now*, p. 19.
80. Peter N. Carroll, *It Seemed Like Nothing Happened: America in the 1970s* (New Brunswick, NJ: Rutgers University Press, [1982] 2000), pp. xii–xiii.
81. Bell, *The Cultural Contradictions*, p. 95.
82. Joseph Heller, *Something Happened* (New York: Knopf, 1974), p. 340.
83. Joseph Heller, *Good as Gold* (New York: Pocket Books, [1979] 1980), p. 205.
84. Gilbert H. Muller, *New Strangers in Paradise: The Immigrant Experience and Contemporary American Fiction* (Lexington: University Press of Kentucky, 1999), p. 31.
85. Carroll, *It Seemed Like Nothing Happened*, p. xv.
86. Addison Gayle Jr, *The Black Aesthetic* (Garden City, NY: Doubleday, 1972);Claudia Tate, 'On White Critics and Black Aestheticians',*College Language Association Journal* 22 (June 1979): 383–9.
87. Toni Cade Bambara, 'Black English', *Curriculum Approaches from a Black Perspective*, ed. The Black Child Development Institute (Atlanta: The Black Child Development Institute, 1972): n.p.; Sherley Ann Williams, *Give Birth to Brightness: A Thematic Study of Neo-Black Literature* (New York: Doubleday, 1972).
88. Bobby Seale, *Seize the Time* (New York: Random House, 1970); George Jackson, *Soledad Brother* (New York: Bantam, 1970); Donald Reeve, *Notes of a Processed Brother* (New York: Pantheon Books, 1971); Angela Davis, *Autobiography* (New York: Bantam Books, 1974).
89. Robert B. Stepto, 'After the 1960s: The Boom in Afro-American Fiction', in Bradbury and Ro, *Contemporary American Fiction*: 89–105 (p. 89).
90. Toni Morrison, *Song of Solomon* (London: Picador, [1977] 1989), p. 3. Further parenthetical page references are from this edition.
91. Michael Awkward, ' "Unruly and Let Loose": Myth, Ideology and Gender in *Song of Solomon*', *Callaloo* 13, no. 3 (summer 1990): 482–98 (p. 483).
92. Michael Rothberg, 'Dead Letter Office: Conspiracy, Trauma and *Song of Solomon*'s Posthumous Communication', *African American Review* 37, no. 4 (winter 2003): 501–16 (pp. 502–3).

93. Joyce Irene Middleton, 'From Orality to Literacy: Oral Memory in Toni Morrison's *Song of Solomon*', in Valerie Smith (ed.), *New Essays on* Song of Solomon (Cambridge: Cambridge University Press, 1995): 19–40 (p. 36).

94. Thomas LeClair, 'The Language Must Not Sweat: A Conversation with Toni Morrison', in Danille Taylor-Guthrie (ed.), *Conversations with Toni Morrison* (Jackson: University Press of Mississippi, 1994): 119–28 (p. 121).

95. Ibid., p. 121.

96. Sämi Ludwig, 'Toni Morrison's Social Criticism', in Justine Tally (ed.), *The Cambridge Companion to Toni Morrison* (Cambridge: Cambridge University Press, 2007): 125–38 (p. 136).

2. Television and Drama

1. John Fiske, *Reading Television* (London: Routledge, 2004), p. 11.

2. James Roman, *Love, Light and a Dream: Television's Past, Present and Future* (Westport, CT: Praeger, 1996), pp. 59–60.

3. William Keough, *Punchlines: The Violence of American Humor* (New York: Paragon House, 1990), p. 226.

4. Darrell Y. Hamamoto, *Nervous Laughter: Television Situation Comedy and Liberal Democratic Ideology* (New York: Praeger, 1991), p. 59.

5. David Marc, *Comic Visions; Television Comedy and American Culture* (Oxford: Blackwell, [1989] 1997), pp. 156–7.

6. Steve Neale and Frank Krutnik, *Popular Film and Television Comedy* (London: Routledge, [1990] 1995), p. 19.

7. Marc, *Comic Visions*, p. 157.

8. John Ozersky, *Archie Bunker's America: TV in an Era of Change, 1968–1978* (Carbondale: Southern Illinois University Press, 2003), p. 81.

9. Ibid., p. 81.

10. Marc, *Comic Visions*, p. 158.

11. Ozersky, *Archie Bunker's America*, pp. 81–2.

12. Keough, *Punchlines*, p. 227.

13. Lee Siegel, *Not Remotely Controlled: Notes on Television* (New York: Basic Books, 2007), p. 187.

14. Neale and Krutnik, *Popular Film and Television Comedy*, p. 244.

15. 'Our Finest Hour' [1978)]. *M*A*S*H – Collector's Edition, Season Seven*. Twentieth Century-Fox DVD, 2004.

16. Mike Budd and Clay Steinman, '*M.A.S.H.* Mystified: Capitalization, Dematerialization, Idealization', *Cultural Critique* 10 (autumn 1988): 59–75 (p. 62).

17. Keough, *Punchlines*, p. 227.
18. Quoted ibid., p. 228.
19. Yanek Mieczkowski, *Gerald Ford and the Challenges of the 1970s* (Lexington: University Press of Kentucky, 2005), p. 38.
20. Miller, *The Seventies Now*, p. 10.
21. Marc, *Comic Visions*, p. 130.
22. Peter N. Carroll, *It Seemed Like Nothing Happened: America in the 1970s* (New Brunswick: Rutgers University Press, 2000), p. 63.
23. Quoted in Gerard Jones, *Honey, I'm Home! Sitcoms: Selling the American Dream* (New York: St. Martin's Press, 1993), p. 220.
24. Ozersky, *Archie Bunker's America*, p. 65.
25. James B. Gilbert, 'Popular Culture', *American Quarterly* 35, nos 1–2 (spring–summer 1983): 141–54 (p. 141).
26. Jones, *Honey, I'm Home!*, p. 206.
27. Thomas Alan Holmes, review of Mallory Wober and Barry Gunter's *Television and Social Control*, in *South Atlantic Review* 56, no. 3 (September 1991): 146–8 (p. 147).
28. 'Sammy's Visit' [1972]. *All in the Family: The Complete Second Season*. Sony Pictures DVD, 2003.
29. Jones, *Honey, I'm Home!*, p. 160.
30. Ozersky, *Archie Bunker's America*, p. 66.
31. Carroll, *It Seemed Like Nothing Happened*, p. 62.
32. Stephen Paul Miller, *The Seventies Now: Culture as Surveillance* (Durham: Duke University Press, 1999), p. 59.
33. Michael Lang, *Gentrification amid Urban Decline* (Boston: Ballinger Publishing Co., 1982), pp. 18–19.
34. Fiske, *Reading Television*, p. 11.
35. MarcWeingarten, *Station to Station: The Secret History of Rock and Roll on Television* (New York: Simon and Schuster, 2000), p. 236.
36. Hamamoto, *Nervous Laughter*, passim.
37. Weingarten, *Station to Station*, p. 236.
38. John Korty (dir.), *The Autobiography of Miss Jane Pittman* [1974]. Classic Media DVD, 2003.
39. Ernest J. Gaines, 'Miss Jane and I', *Callaloo*, no. 3 (May 1978): 23–38 (p. 23).
40. Bruce J. Schulman, *The Seventies: The Great Shift in American Culture, Society, and Politics* (Cambridge, MA: Da Capo Press, 2001), p. 77.
41. Carroll, *It Seemed Like Nothing Happened*, pp. 297–8.
42. Ibid., p. 299.
43. See, for instance, Halford H. Fairchild et al., 'Impact of *Roots*: Evidence from the National Survey of Black Americans', *Journal of Black Studies* 16, no. 3 (March 1986): 307–18.

44. Carroll, *It Seemed Like Nothing Happened*, pp. 143–4.
45. Daniel Bell, *The Cultural Contradictions of Capitalism* (London: Heinemann, 1976), p. 108.
46. Fred Emery, *Watergate* (New York: Touchstone Books, 1995), p. 467.
47. Carroll, *It Seemed Like Nothing Happened*, p. 76.
48. Nixon to Haldeman, White House Tapes, 23 June 1972. Audio version online at the University of Virginia, Miller Center of Public Affairs, White House Tapes Project <www.whitehousetapes.org>.
49. Christopher Bigsby, *A Critical Introduction to Twentieth-Century American Drama* (Cambridge: Cambridge University Press, 1984), p. 119.
50. Susan Harris Smith, *American Drama: The Bastard Art* (Cambridge: Cambridge University Press, 1997), p. 186.
51. David Krasner, *American Drama 1945–2000* (Oxford: Blackwell, 2006), p. 101.
52. Marcia Siegel, 'Virtual Criticism and the Dance of Death', in Peggy Phelan and Jill Lane (eds), *The Ends of Performance* (New York: New York University Press, 1998): 247–61 (p. 249).
53. Susan C. W. Abbotson, *Masterpieces of Twentieth-Century American Drama* (Westport, CT: Greenwood Press, 2005), p. 41.
54. Bigsby, *A Critical Introduction*, p. 116.
55. Ibid., pp. 242–3.
56. Krasner, *American Drama*, p. 101.
57. Johan Callens, 'The 1970s', in Christopher Bigsby (ed.), *The Cambridge Companion to David Mamet* (Cambridge: Cambridge University Press, 2004), 41–56 (p. 41).
58. Anne Deane, *David Mamet: Language as Dramatic Action* (Madison, NJ: Fairleigh Dickinson University Press, 1990), p. 51.
59. David Mamet, *Plays: 1* (London: Methuen Drama, 1996), p. 313. Further page numbers in parentheses are from this edition.
60. David Mamet, *Three Uses of the Knife: On the Nature and Purpose of Drama* (New York: Vintage, [1998] 2000), p. 26.
61. Carla J. McDonough, 'Every Fear Hides a Wish: Unstable Masculinity in Mamet's Drama', *Theatre Journal* 44, no. 2 (May 1992): 195–205.
62. Ibid., p. 196.
63. Deane, *David Mamet*, p. 52.
64. Callens, 'The 1970s', p. 46.
65. Toby Silverman Zinman, 'Jewish Aporia: The Rhythm of Talking in Mamet', *Theatre Journal* 44, no. 2 (May 1992): 207–15 (p. 209).
66. Marc Silverstein, ' "We're Just Human": *Oleanna* and Cultural Crisis', *South Atlantic Review* 60, no. 2 (May 1995): 103–20 (p. 103).

67. McDonough, 'Every Fear Hides a Wish', p. 205.

68. Christopher Bigsby, *The Cambridge Companion to David Mamet* (Cambridge: Cambridge University Press, 2004), p. 1.

69. Luther S. Luedtke, 'From Fission to Fusion: Sam Shepard's Nuclear Families', in Gilbert Debusscher and Henry I. Schvey (eds), *New Essays in American Drama* (Amsterdam: Rodopi, 1989): 143–66 (p. 145).

70. Dinah Luise Leavitt, *Feminist Theater Groups* (Jefferson, NC: McFarland and Co., 1980), p. 4.

71. Ntozake Shange, *for colored girls who have considered suicide/when the rainbow is enuf* (New York: Simon and Schuster, [1975] 1997), pp. 5–6.

72. Erroll G. Hill and James V. Hatch, *A History of African American Theatre* (Cambridge: Cambridge University Press, 2003), p. 394.

73. Mae G. Henderson, 'Ghosts, Monsters, and Magic: The Ritual Drama of Larry Neal', *Callaloo* 23 (Larry Neal Special Issue, winter 1985): 195–214 (p. 195).

74. Samuel A. Hay, *African American Theatre: An Historical and Critical Analysis* (Cambridge: Cambridge University Press, 1994), p. 113.

75. Smith, *American Drama*, p. 74.

76. Misha Berson, *Between Worlds: Contemporary Asian American Plays* (New York: Theatre Communications Group, 1990), p. 9.

3. Film and Visual Culture

1. Daniel Bell, *The Cultural Contradictions of Capitalism* (London: Heinemann, 1976), p. 110.

2. Ibid., p. 107.

3. Ibid., pp. 106–7, 108.

4. Ibid., p. 67.

5. David A. Cook, *Lost Illusions: American Cinema in the Shadow of Watergate and Vietnam, 1970–1979* (New York: Charles Scribner's Sons, 2000), p. 6.

6. Ibid., pp. 6–7.

7. Geoff King, *New Hollywood Cinema* (New York: Columbia University Press, 2002), *passim*.

8. Cook, *Lost Illusions*, p. 32.

9. Quoted in Howard Sounes, *Seventies: The Sights, Sounds and Ideas of a Brilliant Decade* (London: Simon and Schuster, 2006), p. 15.

10. Quoted in Peter N. Carroll, *It Seemed Like Nothing Happened: America in the 1970s* (New Brunswick, NJ: Rutgers University Press, 2000), p. 244.

11. Marilyn Beck, 'The King of Comedy', New York *Daily News*, 2 February 1983, p. 37.
12. Laurent Beauzereau (dir.), *Making 'Taxi Driver'*. Columbia/Tristar Home Video, 1999.
13. Ibid.
14. Lesley Stern, *The Scorsese Connection* (Bloomington and London: Indiana University Press/British Film Institute, 1995), p. 33.
15. Leighton Grist, *The Films of Martin Scorsese, 1963–77* (London: Macmillan, 2000), p. 126.
16. Beauzereau, *Making 'Taxi Driver'* and David Thompson and Ian Christie (eds), *Scorsese on Scorsese* (London: Faber and Faber, 1996), p. 54.
17. Robin Wood, 'The Incoherent Text: Narrative in the 70s', *Movie*, no. 27–28 (1980): 24–42 (p. 28).
18. Thompson and Christie (eds), *Scorsese on Scorsese*, pp. 54, 60.
19. Beauzereau, *Making 'Taxi Driver'*.
20. Emanuel Levy, *Cinema of Outsiders: The Rise of American Independent Film* (New York: New York University Press, 1999) p. 119.
21. Grist, *The Films of Martin Scorsese*, p. 131.
22. Martin Scorsese (dir.), *Taxi Driver* [1976]. Columbia/Tristar Home Video, 1999. All dialogue quotations are from this source.
23. Richard Maltby, *Harmless Entertainment: Hollywood and the Ideology of Consensus* (London: Scarecrow Press, 1983), p. 348.
24. Stern, p. 53.
25. Thompson and Christie, p. 60.
26. Stern, *The Scorsese Connection*, p. 51.
27. Beauzereau, *Making 'Taxi Driver'*.
28. Thompson and Christie (eds), *Scorsese on Scorsese*, p. 66.
29. Grist, *The Films of Martin Scorsese*, p. 134.
30. Beauzereau, *Making 'Taxi Driver'*.
31. Maltby, *Harmless Entertainment*, p. 355.
32. Grist, *The Films of Martin Scorsese*, p. 133; Maltby, *Harmless Entertainment*, p. 348.
33. Maltby, *Harmless Entertainment*, p. 355.
34. Thompson and Christie (eds), *Scorsese on Scorsese*, p. 62.
35. Beauzereau, *Making 'Taxi Driver'*.
36. F. Scott Fitzgerald, *The Great Gatsby* (London: Penguin, [1926] 1990), p. 167.
37. Woody Allen (dir.), *Manhattan*. MGM DVD, [1979] 2000.
38. Cook, *Lost Illusions*, p. xvii.
39. Bruce J. Schulman, *The Seventies: The Great Shift in American Culture, Society and Politics* (Cambridge, MA: Da Capo Press, 2001), p. 150.

40. Cook, *Lost Illusions*, pp. xvi, 15.
41. Stephen Paul Miller, *The Seventies Now: Culture as Surveillance* (Durham: Duke University Press, 1999), p. 93.
42. Sounes, *Seventies*, p. 231.
43. Carroll, *It Seemed Like Nothing Happened*, pp. 183–4.
44. Maltby, *Harmless Entertainment*, p. 322.
45. David Wyatt, *Out of the Sixties: Storytelling and the Vietnam Generation* (Cambridge: Cambridge University Press, 1993), p. 24.
46. Fredric Jameson, 'Postmodernism and Consumer Society', in Philip Simpson et al. (eds), *Film Theory: Critical Concepts in Media and Cultural Studies* (London: Taylor and Francis, 2003): 192–208 (p. 197).
47. Sounes, *Seventies*, pp. 254–5.
48. George Lucas (dir.), *Star Wars* [1977]. Lucasfilm/Twentieth Century-FoxHome EntertainmentDVD, 1997. All dialogue quotations are from this source.
49. Miller, *The Seventies Now*, pp. 98, 99.
50. Wyatt, *Out of the Sixties*, p. 21.
51. Cook, *Lost Illusions*, p. xvi.
52. Miller, *The Seventies Now*, p. 98.
53. George Lucas (dir.), *Star Wars, Episode III: Revenge of the Sith* [2005]. Lucasfilm/Twentieth Century-Fox Home Entertainment DVD, 2006.
54. Wyatt, *Out of the Sixties*, p. 22.
55. Cook, *Lost Illusions*, p. 299.
56. Schulman, *The Seventies*, p. 157.
57. Robin Wood, *Hollywood from Vietnam to Reagan . . . And Beyond* (New York: Columbia University Press, 2003), p. 63.
58. Cook, *Lost Illusions*, p. 197.
59. Carroll, *It Seemed Like Nothing Happened*, p. 244.
60. Schulman, *The Seventies*, p. 80.
61. Ibid., p. 83.
62. Vera Dika, 'The Representation of Ethnicity in *The Godfather*', in Nick Browne (ed.), *Francis Ford Coppola's* The Godfather *Trilogy* (Cambridge: Cambridge University Press, 2000): 76–108 (p. 95).
63. Quoted in Peter Biskind, *Easy Riders, Raging Bulls: How the Sex-Drugs-and-Rock 'n' Roll Generation Saved Hollywood* (New York: Simon and Schuster, 1999), p. 164.
64. Ibid., p. 164.
65. Dika, 'The Representation of Ethnicity', p. 96.
66. Cook, *Lost Illusions*, p. 265.
67. Carroll, *It Seemed Like Nothing Happened*, p. 111.

68. Jennifer Devere Brody, 'The Returns of Cleopatra Jones', in Shelton Waldrep (ed.), *The Seventies: The Age of Glitter in Popular Culture* (London: Routledge, 2000): 225–47 (p. 237).
69. Ibid., p. 228.
70. Ibid., p. 240.
71. Quoted in Cook, *Lost Illusions*, p. 263.
72. Charles Kronengold, 'Identity, Value and the Work of Genre: Black Action Films', in Waldrep (ed.), *The Seventies*: 79–123 (p. 100).
73. Ibid., p. 101.
74. Wyatt, *Out of the Sixties*, p. 177.
75. Miller, *The Seventies Now*, p. 69.
76. Carroll, *It Seemed Like Nothing Happened*, p. 15.
77. Wyatt, *Out of the Sixties*, p. 178.
78. Michael Anderegg, 'Hollywood and Vietnam: John Wayne and Jane Fonda as Discourse', in Anderegg (ed.), *Inventing Vietnam: The War in Film and Television* (Philadelphia: Temple University Press, 1991): 15–32 (p. 15).
79. David Pye, 'Ulzana's Raid', in I. Cameron and D. Pye (eds), *The Movie Book of the Western* (London: Studio Vista, 1996): 262–8 (p. 263).
80. Michael Coyne, *The Crowded Prairie: American National Identity in the Hollywood Western* (London: I. B. Tauris, 1998), p. 161.
81. Bell, *Cultural Contradictions*, p. 117.
82. Ibid., p. 112.
83. J. David Hoeveler, *The Postmodernist Turn: American Thought and Culture in the 1970s* (New York: Twayne, 1996), p. 54.
84. Schulman, *The Seventies*, p. 28.
85. Hoeveler, *The Postmodernist Turn*, p. 75.
86. Ibid., p. 66.
87. Bell, *Cultural Contradictions*, p. 72.
88. Linda Hutcheon, *The Politics of Postmodernism* (New York: Routledge, 1989), p. 93.
89. Ibid., p. 101.
90. Hoeveler, *The Postmodernist Turn*, p. 70.
91. Hutcheon, *Politics of Postmodernism*, pp. 1, 106.
92. Ibid., pp. 1–2.
93. Sounes, *Seventies*, p. 332.
94. Miller, *The Seventies Now*, p. 240.
95. Geoff Ward, *Language Poetry and the American Avant-garde* (Keele: Ryburn Press/British Association for American Studies, 1993), p. 13.
96. Quoted in Carroll, *It Seemed Like Nothing Happened*, p. 258.

97. Leslie Fiedler, *Freaks: Myths and Images of the Secret Self* (London: Penguin, 1981), p. 318.

98. Diane Arbus, 'American Rites, Manners and Customs', in Diane Arbus, *Diane Arbus Revelations* (London: Jonathan Cape, 2003), p. 41.

99. Ibid., p. 41.

100. Sandra S. Phillips, 'The Question of Belief', in Arbus, *Diane Arbus Revelations*, 50–67 (p. 62).

101. Ibid., p. 50.

102. Elisabeth Sussman and Doon Arbus, 'A Chronology: 1923–1971', in Arbus, *Diane Arbus Revelations*, 121–225 (p. 153).

103. Fiedler, *Freaks*, p. 318.

104. Cath Carroll, *Tom Waits* (New York: Thunder's Mouth Press, 2000), p. 129.

105. Phillips, 'Question of Belief', pp. 54, 64.

106. Sussman and Arbus, 'A Chronology', p. 148 (italics in original).

107. Phillips, 'Question of Belief', p. 50.

108. Quoted in Sounes, *Seventies*, p. 91.

109. Ibid., p. 93.

110. Quoted in Patricia Bosworth, *Diane Arbus: A Biography* (New York: W. W. Norton, 2005), pp. 314–15.

111. Quoted in Sussman and Arbus, 'A Chronology', p. 220.

112. John Szarkowski, *Mirrors and Windows: American Photography since 1960* (New York: Museum of Modern Art, 1978), p. 13.

4. Popular Music and Style

1. *Jimi Hendrix: Wild Blue Angel (Live at the Isle of Wight)*. Experience Hendrix DVD, 2002.

2. Peter N. Carroll, *It Seemed Like Nothing Happened: America in the 1970s* (New Brunswick: Rutgers University Press, 2000), p. 71.

3. Howard Sounes, *Seventies: The Sights, Sounds and Ideas of a Brilliant Decade* (London: Simon and Schuster, 2006), p. 234.

4. Carroll, *It Seemed Like Nothing Happened*, p. 71.

5. Greil Marcus, 'Self Portrait No. 25', in Shelton Waldrep (ed.), *The Seventies: The Age of Glitter in Popular Culture* (London: Routledge, 2000): 293–307 (p. 293). First published in *Rolling Stone*, 23 July 1970.

6. Kurt Loder, 'Bob Dylan: *The Rolling Stone* Interview', *Rolling Stone* no. 424 (21 June 1984). Online at <http://www.rollingstone.com/news/story/5938701/bob_dylan_the_rolling_stone_interview>.

7. Bruce J. Schulman, *The Seventies: The Great Shift in American Culture, Society, and Politics* (Cambridge, MA: Da Capo Press, 2001), pp. 100–1.

8. Ibid., pp. 115–16.
9. Richard Carlin, *The Big Book of Country Music* (London: Penguin, 1995), pp. 339–40.
10. Schulman, *The Seventies*, p. 115.
11. *Bob Edwards Weekend Show*, KPLU Radio (Tacoma, WA), broadcast 11 February 2006.
12. Gordon Friesen, 'Editorial', *Broadside* 107 (June 1970), p. 10.
13. Jens Lund and R. Serge Denisoff, 'The Folk Music Revival and the Counterculture: Contributions and Contradictions', *Journal of American Folklore* 84, no. 334 (October–December 1971): 394–405 (p. 404).
14. Barbara Ching, 'Country Music', in Richard Gray and Owen Robinson (eds), *A Companion to the Literature and Culture of the American South* (Oxford: Blackwell, 2004): 203–20 (p. 214).
15. Jim Cullen, *The Civil War in Popular Culture* (Washington, DC: Smithsonian Institution Press, 1995), p. 125.
16. Schulman, *The Seventies*, p. xiv.
17. Sounes, *Seventies*, p. 373.
18. Gary Herman, *Rock 'n' Roll Babylon* (London: Plexus, 1994), p. 63.
19. Quoted in Barney Hoskyns, *Hotel California: The True Life Adventures of Crosby, Stills, Nash, Young, Mitchell, Taylor, Browne, Ronstadt, Geffen, the Eagles, and their Many Friends* (Hoboken, NJ: John Wiley and Sons, 2006), p. 150.
20. Michael Walker, *Laurel Canyon: The Inside Story of Rock-and-Roll's Legendary Neighborhood* (New York: Faber and Faber, 2007), p. 214.
21. Hoskyns, *Hotel California*, p. 73.
22. Quoted in Mark Brend, *American Troubadours: Groundbreaking Singer-Songwriters of the 60s* (San Francisco: Backbeat Books, 2001), p. 8.
23. Ibid., p. 8.
24. Walker, *Laurel Canyon*, p. 142.
25. Quoted ibid., p. 111.
26. John Einarson, *Desperados: The Roots of Country Rock* (New York: Cooper Square Press, 2001), p. 1.
27. Quoted in Peter Doggett, *Are You Ready for the Country: Elvis, Dylan, Parsons and the Roots of Country Rock* (London: Penguin, 2000), p. 49.
28. Quoted in Hoskyns, *Hotel California*, p. 151.
29. Quoted in Doggett, *Are You Ready*, p. 157.
30. Quoted in Hoskyns, *Hotel California*, p. 195.
31. Quoted in Doggett, *Are You Ready*, p. 373.
32. Walker, *Laurel Canyon*, p. 213.

33. Sam Shepard, *Rolling Thunder Logbook* (New York: Viking Press, 1978), p. 1.
34. Ibid., p. 132.
35. Ibid., pp. 132–3.
36. Quoted in James Miller, *Flowers in the Dustbin: The Rise of Rock and Roll, 1947–1977* (New York: Fireside, 2000), p. 320.
37. Sounes, *Seventies*, p. 249.
38. David Wyatt, *Out of the Sixties: Storytelling and the Vietnam Generation* (Cambridge: Cambridge University Press, 1993), pp. 29, 34.
39. Dave Marsh, *Bruce Springsteen: Two Hearts: The Definitive Biography, 1972–2003* (London: Routledge, 2004), p. 187.
40. Ibid., p. 187.
41. Bryan K. Garman, 'The Ghost of History: Bruce Springsteen, Woody Guthrie, and the Hurt Song', in June Skinner Sawyers (ed.), *Racing in the Street: The Bruce Springsteen Reader* (London: Penguin, 2004): 221–30 (p. 223).
42. Ibid., p. 221.
43. Michael Denning, *The Cultural Front: The Laboring of American Culture in the Twentieth Century* (London: Verso, 1988), pp. xvi, 73.
44. Marsh, *Bruce Springsteen*, p. 195.
45. Ibid., p. 195.
46. Jim Cullen, *Born in the USA: Bruce Springsteen and the American Tradition* (Middletown, CT: Wesleyan University Press, 2005), p. 112.
47. Quoted in Larry David Smith, *Bob Dylan, Bruce Springsteen and American Song* (Westport, CT: Praeger, 2002), p. 149.
48. Quoted in Marsh, *Bruce Springsteen*, p. 197.
49. Martin Scorsese, 'Foreword', in Sawyers (ed.), *Racing in the Street*, p. xiii.
50. Ibid., p. xiii.
51. Quoted in Daniel Cavicci, *Tramps Like Us: Music and Meaning among Springsteen Fans* (New York: Oxford University Press, 1998), p. 130.
52. Quoted in Smith, *Bob Dylan*, p. 149.
53. Sounes, *Seventies*, p. 257.
54. Herman, *Rock 'n' Roll Babylon*, p. 71.
55. Van M. Cagle, 'Trudging through the Glitter Trenches: The Case of the New York Dolls', in Shelton Waldrep (ed.), *The Seventies: The Age of Glitter in Popular Culture* (London: Routledge, 2000): 125–51 (pp. 126–7).
56. Ibid., p. 126.
57. Katrina Irving, 'Rock Music and the State: Dissonance or Counterpoint?', *Cultural Critique* 10 (autumn 1988): 151–70 (pp. 168–9).

58. Leerom Medovoi, 'Mapping the Rebel Image: Postmodernism and the Masculinist Politics of Rock in the USA', *Cultural Critique* 20 (winter 1991–2): 153–88 (pp. 181–2).

59. Dave Laing, 'Essay Review', *PopularMusic* 16, no. 2 (May 1997): 223–6 (p. 226).

60. Cagle, 'Glitter Trenches', p. 295.

61. Schulman, *The Seventies*, p. 153

62. Carroll, *It Seemed Like Nothing Happened*, p. 267.

63. Schulman, *The Seventies*, p. 154.

64. Cagle, 'Glitter Trenches', p. 125.

65. Ibid., pp. 154–5.

66. Stephen Paul Miller, *The Seventies Now: Culture as Surveillance* (Durham: Duke University Press, 1999), p. 237.

67. Ibid., p. 237.

68. Schulman, *The Seventies*, p. 73.

69. Quoted in Vince Aletti, 'The Dancing Machine: An Oral History', in Waldrep (ed.), *The Seventies*: 273–81 (p. 275).

70. Sounes, *Seventies*, p. 340.

71. Carroll, *It Seemed Like Nothing Happened*, p. 266.

72. Ibid., p. 266.

73. David A. Cook, *Lost Illusions: American Cinema in the Shadow of Watergate and Vietnam, 1970–1979* (New York: Charles Scribner's Sons, 2000), p. 56.

74. Miller, *The Seventies Now*, p. 204.

75. Schulman, *The Seventies*, pp. 73–4.

76. Ibid., p. 73.

77. Miller, *The Seventies Now*, p. 208.

78. Schulman, *The Seventies*, p. 74.

79. Ibid., p. 73.

80. Daniel Bell, *The Cultural Contradictions of Capitalism* (London: Heinemann, 1976), p. 116.

81. Sounes, *Seventies*, p. 121.

82. Ibid., pp. 122–3, 130.

83. Quoted in Aletti, 'The Dancing Machine', p. 275.

84. Anne-Lise François, ' "These Boots Were Made for Walkin' "': Fashion as "Compulsive Artifice" ', in Waldrep (ed.), *The Seventies*: 155–75 (p. 168).

85. Ibid., p. 155.

86. Carroll, *It Seemed Like Nothing Happened*, p. 296.

87. François, ' "These Boots" ', p. 168.

88. Miller, *The Seventies Now*, p. 45.

89. Carroll, *It Seemed Like Nothing Happened*, pp. 272–3.
90. François, ' "These Boots" ', p. 174, n. 5.
91. Ibid., p. 156.

5. Public Space and Spectacle

1. Erving Goffman, *Relations in Public: Microstudies of the Public Order* (New York: Basic Books, 1971), p. ix.
2. Erving Goffman, *The Presentation of the Self in Everyday Life* (New York: Doubleday, 1959), p. 22.
3. Ibid., p. 22.
4. William Butler Yeats, *Memoirs*, ed. Denis Donoghue (London: Macmillan, 1972), p. 51.
5. Elin Diamond, 'Introduction', in Diamond (ed.), *Performance and Cultural Politics* (London: Routledge, 1996): 1–12 (p. 2).
6. Peggy Phelan, 'Playing Dead in Stone, Or, When Is a Rose Not a Rose?', in Diamond (ed.), *Performance and Cultural Politics*: 65–88 (pp. 72–3).
7. Vivian M. Patraka, 'Spectacles of Suffering', in Diamond (ed.), *Performance and Cultural Politics*: 89–107 (p. 99).
8. Ibid., p. 100.
9. Ron Dick and Dan Patterson, *Wings of Change* (Erin, ON: Boston Mills Press, 2005), pp. 58–9.
10. Howard Sounes, *Seventies: The Sights, Sounds and Ideas of a Brilliant Decade* (London: Simon and Schuster, 2006), pp. 322–3.
11. Virginia Woolf, 'Mr Bennett and Mrs Brown', in Mitchell A. Leaska (ed.), *The Virginia Woolf Reader* (New York: Harvest/Harcourt, 1984): 192–212 (p. 194).
12. Charles Jencks, *The Language of Post-Modern Architecture* (New York: Rizzoli, [1977] 1991), p. 23.
13. J. David Hoeveler Jr, *The Postmodernist Turn: American Thought and Culture in the 1970s* (New York: Twayne, 1996), p. 91.
14. Robert Venturi, *Complexity and Contradiction in Architecture* (New York: Museum of Modern Art, 1966), p. 17.
15. Robert Venturi, Denise Scott Brown and Steven Izenour, *Learning from Las Vegas* (Cambridge, MA: MIT Press, [1972] 1977) p. 76. Further page citations are from this edition.
16. Sounes, *Seventies*, pp. 61, 66.
17. Daniel Bell, *The Cultural Contradictions of Capitalism* (London: Heinemann, 1976), pp. 105–6.
18. Bruce J. Schulman, *The Seventies: The Great Shift in American Culture, Society and Politics* (Cambridge, MA: Da Capo Press, 2001), pp. 15, 17.

19. Melvin Small and William D. Hoover, 'Preface', in Small and Hoover (eds), *Give Peace a Chance: Exploring the Vietnam Antiwar Movement* (Syracuse, NY: Syracuse University Press, 1992): xv–xvii (p. xv).

20. Melvin Small, 'The Impact of the Antiwar Movement', in Robert J. McMahon (ed.), *Major Problems in the History of the Vietnam War* (Lexington, MA: D. C. Heath and Co., 1995): 487–94 (p. 489).

21. Rhodri Jeffreys-Jones, *Peace Now! American Society and the Ending of the Vietnam War* (New Haven: Yale University Press, 1999), p. 3.

22. Nora M. Alter, *Vietnam Protest Theatre: The Television War on Stage* (Bloomington: Indiana University Press, 1996), p. xiii. Italics in the original.

23. Ibid, pp. xii, xiii, xix. Italics in the original.

24. Murray Edelman, *Constructing the Political Spectacle* (Chicago: University of Chicago Press, 1988): pp. 1–2.

25. Guy Debord, *The Society of the Spectacle*, trans. Ken Knabb (Oakland: AK Press, 2006), pp. 10–11. Italics in the original.

26. Norman Mailer, *Armies of the Night* (London: Weidenfeld and Nicolson, 1968), pp. 91–2.

27. Ibid., p. 108.

28. Jeffreys-Jones, *Peace Now!*, p. 52.

29. David Farber, 'The Counterculture and the Antiwar Movement', in Small and Hoover (eds), *Give Peace a Chance*: 7–21 (p. 19).

30. Ibid., p. 18.

31. David E. James, 'The Vietnam War and American Music', in Rick Berg and John Carlos Rowe (eds), *The Vietnam War and American Culture* (New York: Columbia University Press, 1991): 226–54 (p. 245).

32. Quoted in John Storey, 'Rockin' Hegemony: West Coast Rock and Amerika's War in Vietnam', in Alf Louvre and Jeffrey Walsh (eds), *Tell Me Lies about Vietnam* (Milton Keynes: Open University Press, 1988): 181–9 (p. 191).

33. Jeffreys-Jones, *Peace Now!*, pp. 83–4.

34. Quoted in Philip Caputo, *13 Seconds: A Look Back at the Kent State Shootings* (New York: Penguin, 2005), p. 105.

35. Quoted ibid., p. 105.

36. Tom Wells, *The War Within: America's Battle over Vietnam* (Berkeley: University of California Press, 1994), p. 426.

37. Ibid., p. 447.

38. Jeffreys-Jones, *Peace Now!*, p. 43.

39. George W. Hopkins, ' "May Day" 1971', in Small and Hoover (eds), *Give Peace a Chance*: 71–88 (p. 72).

40. Michael E. Staub, 'Setting Up the Seventies: Black Panthers, New Journalism and the Rewriting of the Sixties', in Shelton Waldrep (ed.), *The Seventies: The Age of Glitter in Popular Culture* (London: Routledge, 2000): 19–40 (p. 30).

41. Carroll, *It Seemed Like Nothing Happened*, pp. 105–6.

42. Schulman, *The Seventies*, pp. 11–12.

43. Hoeveler, *The Postmodernist Turn*, p. 64.

44. Rebecca Schneider, 'After Us the Savage Goddess', in Diamond (ed.), *Performance and Cultural Politics*: 157–78 (p. 166).

45. Stephen Paul Miller, *The Seventies Now: Culture as Surveillance* (Durham: Duke University Press, 1999), pp. 63–4.

46. Ibid., p. 10.

47. Quoted in Kasia Boddy, *Boxing: A Cultural History* (London: Reaktion Books, 2008), pp. 346–7.

48. Ibid., p. 10.

49. Mark Kriegel, *Namath: A Biography* (New York: Penguin, 2004), p. 248.

50. Boddy, *Boxing*, p. 333.

51. Miller, *The Seventies Now*, p. 10.

52. Norman Mailer, *The Fight* (New York: Vintage [1975], 1997), p. 3.

53. Charles Maher, 'Riggs Butchered by Mrs King as Promoters Score a Million' [1973], in Jean O'Reilley and Susan K. Kahn (eds), *Women and Sports in the United States: A Documentary Reader* (Lebanon, NH: Northeastern University Press, 2007): 41–5 (pp. 41–2).

54. Quoted in Jay Jennings, ' "A Necessary Spectacle": 6–4, 6–3, 6–3', *New York Times*, 21 August 2005. Online at <http://www.nytimes.com/2005/08/21/books/review/21JENNING.html>.

55. Ibid., p. 161.

56. Gloria Steinem, *Outrageous Acts and Everyday Rebellions* (New York: Henry Holt/Owlet Books, [1984] 1995), p. 126.

57. Schulman, *The Seventies*, p. 161.

58. Germaine Greer, *The Female Eunuch* (New York: Farrar, Straus and Giroux, [1970] 2001), p. 119.

59. Norman Mailer, *Cannibals and Christians* (New York: Dial Press, 1966), pp. 199, 201.

60. Kate Millett, *Sexual Politics* (Urbana:University of Illinois Press, [1970] 2000), p. 24.

61. Ibid., p. 22.

62. Ibid., pp. 15, 16.

63. Ibid., p. 330.

64. Ibid., p. 330.

65. Norman Mailer, 'The Prisoner of Sex', *Harper's Magazine*, March 1971: 41–92.
66. Quoted in Jerry Tallmer, 'A Bloody Township in the War of the Sexes, Caught on Film', *The Villager* (New York) 77, no. 4 (27 June–3 July 2007). Online at <http://www.thevillager.com/villager_217/abloody townshipinthewar.html>.
67. In Chris Hedegus and D. A. Pennebaker (dirs), *Town Bloody Hall*. Pennebaker Hedegus Films, 1979. All quotes from the debate are from this source.
68. Quoted in Christine Wallace, *Germaine Greer: Untamed Shrew* (London: Metro Books, 2000), p. 183.
69. Boddy, *Boxing*, p. 351.
70. Quoted in Sounes, *Seventies*, p. 97.
71. Quoted in Carroll, *It Seemed Like Nothing Happened*, p. 34.
72. Quoted in Donald T. Critchlow, *Phyllis Schlafly and Grassroots Conservatism* (Princeton: Princeton University Press, 2005), p. 226.
73. Ibid., p. 14.
74. Quoted in Carroll, *It Seemed Like Nothing Happened*, 290.
75. Ibid., p. 291.
76. Michael Bronski, 'Shove, the Second Time Around', *The Phoenix* (Boston), 12–19 September 2002. Online at <http://72.166.46.24/ boston/news_features/other_stories/documents/02433435.htm>.
77. Fred C. Pincus, 'Discrimination Comes in Many Forms: Individual, Institutional and Structural', in Maurianne Adams et al. (eds), *Readings for Diversity and Social Justice* (London: Routledge, 2000): 21–30 (pp. 27–8).

Conclusion

1. Wolfgang M. Zucker, 'Reflections on Reflections', *Journal of Aesthetics and Art Criticism* 20, no. 3 (1962): 239–50 (pp. 242, 244).
2. John Ashbery, *Self-Portrait in a Convex Mirror* (London: Penguin, [1975] 1976), p. 74.
3. Stephen Paul Miller, *The Seventies Now: Culture as Surveillance* (Durham: Duke University Press, 1999), p. 2.
4. Martin Scorsese (dir.), *Taxi Driver*. Columbia/Tristar Home Video, [1976] 1999.
5. Leighton Grist, *The Films of Martin Scorsese, 1963–77* (London: Macmillan, 2000), p. 138.
6. Quoted in Mary Pat Kelly, *Martin Scorsese: The First Decade* (Pleasantville, NY: Redgrave, 1980), p. 187.

7. Lesley Stern, *The Scorsese Connection* (Bloomington and London: Indiana University Press/British Film Institute, 1995), p. 42.

8. Ibid., p. 57.

9. Ibid., p. 57.

10. Peter N. Carroll, *It Seemed Like Nothing Happened: America in the 1970s* (New Brunswick, NJ: Rutgers University Press, [1982] 2000), p. xviii.

11. Christopher Lasch, *The Culture of Narcissism: American Life in an Age of Diminishing Expectations* (London: W. W. Norton, [1978] 1991), p. 5.

12. Ibid., p. xvii.

13. Miller, *The Seventies Now*, pp. 63, 126.

14. Mark Twain, letter to William Bowen, 31 August 1876. Online at the Mark Twain Project, University of California <http://www.marktwain-project.org>.

15. Carroll, *It Seemed Like Nothing Happened*, p. ix.

16. Donald E. Morse, *The Novels of Kurt Vonnegut: Imagining Being an American* (Westport, CT: Praeger, 2003), p. 117.

17. Howard Sounes, *Seventies: The Sights, Sounds and Ideas of a Brilliant Decade* (London: Simon and Schuster, 2006), p. 168.

18. David Wyatt, *Out of the Sixties: Storytelling and the Vietnam Generation* (Cambridge: Cambridge University Press, 1993), p. 13.

19. Herman Melville, *The Confidence-Man* [1857], in Melville, *Pierre, Israel Potter, The Confidence-Man, Tales, and Billy Budd* (New York: Literary Classics of the United States, Inc., 1984), p. 986.

20. Will Kaufman, *The Comedian as Confidence Man: Studies in Irony Fatigue* (Detroit: Wayne State University Press, 1997).

21. Lasch, pp. 94–5.

22. Joseph Dorman, *Arguing the World: The New York Intellectuals in Their Own Words* (Chicago: University of Chicago Press, 2001), p. 167.

23. Bruce J. Schulman, *The Seventies: The Great Shift in American Culture, Society and Politics* (Cambridge, MA: Da Capo Press, 2001), p. 203.

24. Lasch, *The Culture of Narcissism*, p. 96.

25. Neil Young, 'After the Gold Rush', on Young, *After the Gold Rush*. Reprise/Wea CD, [1970] 1990.

26. Carroll, *It Seemed Like Nothing Happened*, p. 124.

27. Steve Jobs, 'You've Got to Find What You Love', Commencement Address, Stanford University, 12 June 2005. Stanford News Service Online <http://news-service.stanford.edu/news/2005/june15/jobs-061 505.html>.

28. Andrew G. Kirk, *Counterculture Green: The Whole Earth Catalog and American Environmentalism* (Lawrence: University Press of Kansas, 2007), p. 111.

29. Schulman, *The Seventies*, pp. 89–90.

30. Ibid., p. 91.

31. Carroll, *It Seemed Like Nothing Happened*, p. 126.

32. Miller, *The Seventies Now*, p. 7.

33. Carroll, *It Seemed Like Nothing Happened*, p. 304.

34. Murray Levine, 'Introduction', in Lois Marie Gibbs, *Love Canal: My Story* (Buffalo: SUNY Press, 1982), p. xiii.

35. Chana Gazit and David Steward (prod.), *Meltdown at Three Mile Island*. Steward/Gazit Productions for PBS, 'The American Experience', 1999.

36. Daniel Bell, *The Cultural Contradictions of Capitalism* (London: Heinemann, 1976), p. 16.

37. Lasch, *The Culture of Narcissism*, pp. xv, 66.

38. Tom Wolfe, 'The Me Decade and the Third Great Awakening' [1976], in *The Purple Decades* (London: Vintage, 2005): 265–96 (p. 292).

39. Ibid., p. 279.

40. Michael Walker, *Laurel Canyon: The Inside Story of Rock-and-Roll's Legendary Neighborhood* (New York: Faber and Faber, 2007), p. 240.

41. Shelton Waldrep, 'Introducing the Seventies', in Waldrep (ed.), *The Seventies: The Age of Glitter in Popular Culture* (London: Routledge, 2000): 1–15 (p. 9).

42. Van M. Cagle, 'Trudging through the Glitter Trenches: The Case of the New York Dolls', in Waldrep (ed.), *The Seventies*: 125–51 (pp. 126–7).

43. George Carlin, 'Filthy Words', on *Occupation: Foole* [1973], Atlantic/Wea CD, 2000.

44. Carroll, *It Seemed Like Nothing Happened*, p. 8.

45. William Keough, *Punchlines: The Violence of American Humor* (New York: Paragon House, 1990), p. 193.

46. Marjorie Heins, 'More than Seven Dirty Words', *The Free Expression Policy Project: A Think-Tank on Intellectual and Artistic Freedom* (4 August 2003). Online at <http://www.fepproject.org/commentaries/rustytrombone.html>.

47. Ibid.

48. Tom Stoppard, '1968: The Year of the Posturing Rebel', *Sunday Times* (London), 16 March 2008. *Times Online* <http://www.timesonline.co.uk/tol/news/uk/article3558639.ece>.

49. Lasch, *The Culture of Narcissism*, p. 82.

50. Joan Didion, 'On the Morning after the Sixties', in Didion, *The White Album* (New York: Farrar, Straus and Giroux, [1979] 2001): 205–8 (p. 208).

51. Kurt Vonnegut, *Breakfast of Champions* (New York: Dell, [1973] 1999), p. 5.
52. Waldrep (ed.), *The Seventies*, p. 9.
53. Nellie McKay, 'An Interview with Toni Morrison', *Contemporary Literature* 24, no. 4 (1983): 413–29 (p. 426).
54. Diane Arbus, *Diane Arbus Revelations* (London: Jonathan Cape, 2003), p. 226.

Bibliography

General

Daniel Bell, *The Coming of Post-Industrial Society: A Venture in Social Forecasting* (London: Heinemann, 1974).

Daniel Bell, *The Cultural Contradictions of Capitalism* (London: Heinemann, 1976).

Edward D. Berkowitz, *Something Happened: A Political and Cultural Overview of the Seventies* (New York: Columbia University Press, 2006).

Boston Women's Health Book Collective, *Our Bodies, Ourselves: A Book by and for Women* (New York: Simon and Schuster, [1973] 1976).

Michael Bronski, *Culture Clash: The Making of Gay Sensibility* (Boston: South End Press, 1984).

Peter N. Carroll, *It Seemed Like Nothing Happened: America in the 1970s* (New Brunswick, NJ: Rutgers University Press, [1982] 2000).

David A. Cook, *Lost Illusions: American Cinema in the Shadow of Watergate and Vietnam, 1970–1979* (New York: Charles Scribner's Sons, 2000).

J. David Hoeveler Jr, *The Postmodernist Turn: American Thought and Culture in the 1970s* (New York: Twayne, 1996).

Jim Hougan, *Decadence: Radical Nostalgia, Narcissism, and Decline in the Seventies* (New York: Morrow, 1975).

Sherrie A. Inness, ed., *Disco Divas: Women and Popular Culture in the 1970s* (Philadelphia: University of Pennsylvania Press, 2003).

Philip Jenkins, *Decade of Nightmares: The End of the Sixties and the Making of Eighties America* (New York: Oxford University Press, 2006).

Derek Kompare, *Rerun Nation: How Repeats Invented American Television* (New York: Routledge, 2005).

Christopher Lasch, *The Culture of Narcissism: American Life in an Age of Diminishing Expectations* (London: W. W. Norton, [1978] 1991).

Hal Lindsay, *The Late, Great Planet Earth* (Grand Rapids, MI: Zondervan, 1970).

Mark Hamilton Lytle, *America's Uncivil Wars: The Sixties Era from Elvis to the Fall of Richard Nixon* (New York: Oxford University Press, 2006).

Jerome L. Himmelstein, *To the Right: The Transformation of American Conservatism* (Berkeley: University of California Press, 1990).

Cyra McFadden, *The Serial* (London: Picador, [1977] 1980).

Peter Marin, 'The New Narcissism', *Harper's* 251, no. 1 (October 1975): 45–56.

Stephen Paul Miller, *The Seventies Now: Culture as Surveillance* (Durham: Duke University Press, 1999).

Robin Morgan, ed., *Sisterhood Is Powerful: An Anthology of Writings from the Women's Liberation Movement* (New York: Vintage Books, 1970).

Edward Said, *Orientalism* (London: Penguin, [1978] 1991).

Bruce J. Schulman, *The Seventies: The Great Shift in American Culture, Society and Politics* (Cambridge, MA: Da Capo Press, 2001).

Edwin Schur, *The Awareness Trap: Self-Absorption instead of Social Change* (New York: Quadrangle-New York Times, 1976).

Richard Sennett, *The Fall of Public Man* (New York: Knopf, 1977).

Howard Sounes, *The Seventies: The Sights, Sounds and Ideas of a Brilliant Decade* (London: Simon and Schuster, 2006).

Graham Thompson, *American Culture in the 1980s* (Edinburgh: Edinburgh University Press, 2007).

Shelton Waldrep, ed., *The Seventies: The Age of Glitter in Popular Culture* (London: Routledge, 2000).

Tom Wolfe, 'These Radical Chic Evenings' [1970], in *The Purple Decades* (London: Vintage, 2005): 181–97.

Tom Wolfe, 'The Me Decade and the Third Great Awakening' [1976], in *The Purple Decades* (London: Vintage, 2005): 265–96.

David Wyatt, *Out of the Sixties: Storytelling and the Vietnam Generation* (Cambridge: Cambridge University Press, 1993).

Fiction and Poetry

Walter Abish, *Alphabetical Africa* (New York: New Directions, 1974).

Bruce Andrews and Charles Bernstein, eds, *The L=A=N=G=U=A=G=E Book* (Carbondale: Southern Illinois University Press, 1984).

Michael Awkward, ' "Unruly and Let Loose": Myth, Ideology and Gender in *Song of Solomon*', *Callaloo* 13, no. 3 (summer 1990): 482–98.

Richard Bach, *Jonathan Livingston Seagull* (London: HarperElement, [1970] 2003).

Toni Cade Bambara, 'Black English', *Curriculum Approaches from a Black Perspective*, ed. The Black Child Development Institute (Atlanta: The Black Child Development Institute, 1972).

John Barth, 'The Literature of Exhaustion', in Barth, *The Friday Book* (Baltimore: Johns Hopkins University Press, [1984] 1997): 62–76.

Lee Bartlett, 'What Is "Language Poetry"?' *Critical Inquiry* 12, no. 4 (summer 1986): 741–52.

Daniel Bell, *The Cultural Contradictions of Capitalism* (London: Heinemann, 1976).

Arthur F. Berthea, *Technique and Sensibility in the Fiction and Poetry of Raymond Carver* (New York: Routledge, 2001).

Harold Bloom, *The Anxiety of Influence: A Theory of Poetry* (New York: Oxford University Press, 1973).

Harold Bloom, *Poetry and Repression: Revisionism from Blake to Stevens* (New Haven: Yale University Press, 1976).

Kasia Boddy, 'Companion-Souls of the Short Story: Anton Chekhov and Raymond Carver', *Scottish Slavonic Review: An International Journal Promoting East-West Contacts* 18 (1992): 105–13.

Malcolm Bradbury and Sigmund Ro, eds, *Contemporary American Fiction* (London: Edward Arnold, 1987).

Bill Buford, 'Editorial', *Granta 8: Dirty Realism: New Writing from America* (Harmondsworth: Penguin, 1983): 4.

Peter N. Carroll, *It Seemed Like Nothing Happened: America in the 1970s* (New Brunswick, NJ: Rutgers University Press, [1982] 2000).

Raymond Carver, *Where I'm Calling From: Selected Stories* (New York: Atlantic Monthly Press, [1988] 1991).

Raymond Carver, *Will You Please Be Quiet, Please?* (London: Vintage, [1976] 1993).

Marc Chénetier, *Beyond Suspicion: New American Fiction since 1960*, trans. Elizabeth A. Houlding (Philadelphia: University of Pennsylvania Press, 1996).

Angela Davis, *Autobiography* (New York: Bantam Books, 1974).

Shulamith Firestone and Anne Koedt, eds, *Notes from the Second Year: Women's Liberation: Major Writings of the Radical Feminists* (New York: Radical Feminism, 1970).

Stanley Fish, 'Interpreting the *Variorum*', *Critical Inquiry* 2 (spring 1976): 465–85.

Stephen Fredman, *Poet's Prose: The Crisis in American Verse* (Cambridge: Cambridge University Press, 1983).

William H. Gass, *Fiction and the Figures of Life* (Boston: Godine, [1970] 1979).

Addison Gayle Jr, *The Black Aesthetic* (Garden City, NY: Doubleday, 1972).

Marshall Bruce Gentry and William L. Stull, eds, *Conversations with Raymond Carver* (Jackson: University Press of Mississippi, 1990).

Jeffrey Gray et al., eds, *The Greenwood Encyclopedia of American Poets and Poetry* (Westport, CT: Greenwood Press, 2006).

Geoffrey Hartman, 'Toward Literary History', *Daedalus* 99, no. 2 (spring 1970): 355–83.

Joseph Heller, *Something Happened* (New York: Knopf, 1974).

Joseph Heller, *Good as Gold* (New York: Pocket Books, [1979] 1980).

Kim A. Hertzinger, 'Introduction: On the New Fiction', *Mississippi Review* nos 40–1 (1985): 7–22.

J. David Hoeveler Jr, *The Postmodernist Turn: American Thought and Culture in the 1970s* (New York: Twayne, 1996).

Daniel Hoffman, ed., *Harvard Guide to Contemporary American Writing* (Cambridge, MA: Belknap Press of the Harvard University Press, 1979).

Zhu Hong, 'Will the "Super Culture" Catch On in China?' *Australian Journal of Chinese Affairs* 5 (January 1981): 91–5.

Kathryn Hume, *American Dream, American Nightmare: Fiction since 1960* (Urbana: University of Illinois Press, 2002).

George Jackson, *Soledad Brother* (New York: Bantam, 1970).

John Johnston, *Information Multiplicity: American Fiction in the Age of Media Saturation* (Baltimore: Johns Hopkins University Press, 1998).

Sämi Ludwig, 'Toni Morrison's Social Criticism', in Justine Tally, ed., *The Cambridge Companion to Toni Morrison* (Cambridge: Cambridge University Press, 2007): 125–38.

Brian McHale, *Postmodern Fiction* (London: Routledge, [1987] 1996).

Paul Mann, *The Theory-Death of the Avant-Garde* (Bloomington: Indiana University Press, 1991).

Stephen Paul Miller, *The Seventies Now: Culture as Surveillance* (Durham: Duke University Press, 1999).

Toni Morrison, *Song of Solomon* (London: Picador, [1977] 1989).

Gilbert H. Muller, *New Strangers in Paradise: The Immigrant Experience and Contemporary American Fiction* (Lexington: University Press of Kentucky, 1999).

Kirk Nesset, ' "This Word Love": Sexual Politics and Silence in Early Raymond Carver', *American Literature* 63, no. 2 (June 1991): 292–313.

Bob Perelman, *Braille* (Ithaca, NY: Ithaca House, 1975).

Bob Perelman, 'The First Person', *Hills*, nos 6–7 (spring 1980): 156.

Bob Perelman, *The Marginalization of Poetry* (Princeton: Princeton University Press, 1996).

Marjorie Perloff, 'The Word as Such: L=A=N=G=U=A=G=E Poetry in the Eighties', *American Poetry Review* 13 (May–June 1984): 15–22.

Robert Pirsig, *Zen and the Art of Motorcycle Maintenance* (New York: Bantam, [1974] 1975).

Donald Reeve, *Notes of a Processed Brother* (New York: Pantheon Books, 1971).

Michael Rothberg, 'Dead Letter Office: Conspiracy, Trauma and *Song of Solomon*'s Posthumous Communication', *African American Review* 37, no. 4 (winter 2003): 501–16.

Earl Rovit, 'Some Shapes in Recent American Fiction', *Contemporary Literature* 15, no. 4 (autumn 1974).

Richard Ruland and Malcolm Bradbury, *From Puritanism to Postmodernism: A History of American Literature* (New York: Penguin, 1992).

Bobby Seale, *Seize the Time* (New York: Random House, 1970).

Ron Silliman, *The Age of Huts* (New York: Roof, 1986).

Philip Slater, *Earthwalk* (New York: Anchor Press, 1974).

Valerie Smith, ed., *New Essays on* Song of Solomon (Cambridge: Cambridge University Press, 1995).

Gilbert Sorrentino, *Mulligan Stew* (New York: Grove, 1979).

William L. Stull, 'Raymond Carver', in J. M. Brook, ed., *Dictionary of Literary Biography: Yearbook, 1988* (Detroit: Gale, 1988).

Ronald Sukenick, *Out* (Chicago: Swallow Press, 1973).

Claudia Tate, 'On White Critics and Black Aestheticians', *College Language Association Journal* 22 (June 1979): 383–9.

Danille Taylor-Guthrie, ed., *Conversations with Toni Morrison* (Jackson: University Press of Mississippi, 1994).

Kurt Vonnegut, *Jailbird* (London: Vintage, 1992 [1979]).

Geoff Ward, *Language Poetry and the American Avant-Garde* (Keele: Ryburn Press/British Association for American Studies, 1993).

Barrett Watten, 'The Secret History of the Equal Sign: L=A=N=G=U=A=G=E between Discourse and Text', *Poetics Today* 20, no. 4 (winter 1999): 581–627.

Alan Wilde, *Middle Grounds: Studies in Contemporary American Fiction* (Philadelphia: University of Pennsylvania Press, 1987).

Sherley Ann Williams, *Give Birth to Brightness: A Thematic Study of Neo-Black Literature* (New York: Doubleday, 1972).

Television and Drama

Susan C. W. Abbotson, *Masterpieces of Twentieth-Century American Drama* (Westport, CT: Greenwood Press, 2005).

Daniel Bell, *The Cultural Contradictions of Capitalism* (London: Heinemann, 1976).

Misha Berson, *Between Worlds: Contemporary Asian American Plays* (New York: Theatre Communications Group, 1990).

Christopher Bigsby, *A Critical Introduction to Twentieth-Century American Drama* (Cambridge: Cambridge University Press, 1984).

Christopher Bigsby, *The Cambridge Companion to David Mamet* (Cambridge: Cambridge University Press, 2004).

Mike Budd and Clay Steinman, '*M.A.S.H.* Mystified: Capitalization, Dematerialization, Idealization', *Cultural Critique* 10 (autumn 1988): 59–75.

Johan Callens, 'The 1970s', in Christopher Bigsby, ed., *The Cambridge Companion to David Mamet* (Cambridge: Cambridge University Press, 2004): 41–56.

Peter N. Carroll, *It Seemed Like Nothing Happened: America in the 1970s* (New Brunswick: Rutgers University Press, 2000).

Anne Deane, *David Mamet: Language as Dramatic Action* (Madison, NJ: Fairleigh Dickinson University Press, 1990).

Fred Emery, *Watergate* (New York: Touchstone Books, 1995).

Halford H. Fairchild et al., 'Impact of *Roots*: Evidence from the National Survey of Black Americans', *Journal of Black Studies* 16, no. 3 (March 1986): 307–18.

John Fiske, *Reading Television* (London: Routledge, 2004).

Ernest J. Gaines, 'Miss Jane and I', *Callaloo*, no. 3 (May 1978): 23–38.

James B. Gilbert, 'Popular Culture', *American Quarterly* 35, nos 1–2 (spring-summer 1983): 141–54.

Darrell Y. Hamamoto, *Nervous Laughter: Television Situation Comedy and Liberal Democratic Ideology* (New York: Praeger, 1991).

Samuel A. Hay, *African American Theatre: An Historical and Critical Analysis* (Cambridge: Cambridge University Press, 1994).

Mae G. Henderson, 'Ghosts, Monsters, and Magic: The Ritual Drama of Larry Neal', *Callaloo* 23 (Larry Neal Special Issue, winter 1985): 195–214.

Erroll G. Hill and James V. Hatch, *A History of African American Theatre* (Cambridge: Cambridge University Press, 2003).

Thomas Alan Holmes, review of Mallory Wober and Barry Gunter's *Television and Social Control*, in *South Atlantic Review* 56, no. 3 (Sept. 1991): 146–8.

Gerard Jones, *Honey, I'm Home! Sitcoms: Selling the American Dream* (New York: St. Martin's Press, 1993).

William Keough, *Punchlines: The Violence of American Humor* (New York: Paragon House, 1990).

John Korty (dir.), *The Autobiography of Miss Jane Pittman* [1974]. Classic Media DVD, 2003.

David Krasner, *American Drama 1945–2000* (Oxford: Blackwell, 2006).

Michael Lang, *Gentrification amid Urban Decline* (Boston: Ballinger Publishing Co., 1982).

Dinah Luise Leavitt, *Feminist Theater Groups* (Jefferson, NC: McFarland and Co., 1980).

Luther S. Luedtke, 'From Fission to Fusion: Sam Shepard's Nuclear Families', in Gilbert Debusscher and Henry I. Schvey, eds, *New Essays in American Drama* (Amsterdam: Rodopi, 1989): 143–66.

Carla J. McDonough, 'Every Fear Hides a Wish: Unstable Masculinity in Mamet's Drama', *Theatre Journal* 44, no. 2 (May 1992): 195–205.

David Mamet, *Plays: 1* (London: Methuen Drama, 1996).

David Mamet, *Three Uses of the Knife: On the Nature and Purpose of Drama* (New York: Vintage, [1998] 2000).

David Marc, *Comic Visions: Television Comedy and American Culture* (Oxford: Blackwell, [1989] 1997).

Yanek Mieczkowski, *Gerald Ford and the Challenges of the 1970s* (Lexington: University Press of Kentucky, 2005).

Stephen Paul Miller, *The Seventies Now: Culture as Surveillance* (Durham: Duke University Press, 1999).

Steve Neale and Frank Krutnik, *Popular Film and Television Comedy* (London: Routledge, [1990] 1995).

'Our Finest Hour' [1978]. *M*A*S*H – Collector's Edition, Season Seven*. Twentieth Century-Fox DVD, 2004.

John Ozersky, *Archie Bunker's America: TV in an Era of Change, 1968–1978* (Carbondale: Southern Illinois University Press, 2003).

James Roman, *Love, Light and a Dream: Television's Past, Present and Future* (Westport, CT: Praeger, 1996).

Annette Saddik, *Contemporary American Drama* (Edinburgh: Edinburgh University Press, 2007).

'Sammy's Visit' [1972]. *All in the Family: The Complete Second Season*. Sony Pictures DVD, 2003.

Bruce J. Schulman, *The Seventies: The Great Shift in American Culture, Society, and Politics* (Cambridge, MA: Da Capo Press, 2001).

Ntozake Shange, *for colored girls who have considered suicide/when the rainbow is enuf* (New York: Simon and Schuster, [1975] 1997).

Lee Siegel, *Not Remotely Controlled: Notes on Television* (New York: Basic Books, 2007).

Marcia Siegel, 'Virtual Criticism and the Dance of Death', in Peggy Phelan and Jill Lane, eds, *The Ends of Performance* (New York: New York University Press, 1998): 247–61.

Marc Silverstein, ' "We're Just Human": *Oleanna* and Cultural Crisis', *South Atlantic Review* 60, no. 2 (May 1995): 103–20.

Susan Harris Smith, *American Drama: The Bastard Art* (Cambridge: Cambridge University Press, 1997).

Marc Weingarten, *Station to Station: The Secret History of Rock and Roll on Television* (New York: Simon and Schuster, 2000).

Toby Silverman Zinman, 'Jewish Aporia: The Rhythm of Talking in Mamet', *Theatre Journal* 44, no. 2 (May 1992): 207–15.

Film and Visual Culture

Woody Allen (dir.), *Manhattan*. MGM DVD, [1979] 2000.

Michael Anderegg, 'Hollywood and Vietnam: John Wayne and Jane Fonda as Discourse', in Michael Anderegg, ed., *Inventing Vietnam: The War in Film and Television* (Philadelphia: Temple University Press, 1991): 15–32.

Diane Arbus, 'American Rites, Manners and Customs', in Diane Arbus, *Diane Arbus Revelations* (London: Jonathan Cape, 2003): 41.

Laurent Beauzereau (dir.), *Making 'Taxi Driver'*. Columbia/Tristar Home Video, 1999.

Marilyn Beck, 'The King of Comedy', New York *Daily News*, 2 February 1983, p. 37.

Daniel Bell, *The Cultural Contradictions of Capitalism* (London: Heinemann, 1976).

Peter Biskind, *Easy Riders, Raging Bulls: How the Sex-Drugs-and-Rock 'n' Roll Generation Saved Hollywood* (New York: Simon and Schuster, 1999).

Patricia Bosworth, *Diane Arbus: A Biography* (New York: W. W. Norton, 2005).

Jennifer Devere Brody, 'The Returns of Cleopatra Jones', in Shelton Waldrep, ed., *The Seventies: The Age of Glitter in Popular Culture* (London: Routledge, 2000): 225–47.

Cath Carroll, *Tom Waits* (New York: Thunder's Mouth Press, 2000).

Peter N. Carroll, *It Seemed Like Nothing Happened: America in the 1970s* (New Brunswick, NJ: Rutgers University Press, 2000).

David A. Cook, *Lost Illusions: American Cinema in the Shadow of Watergate and Vietnam, 1970–1979* (New York: Charles Scribner's Sons, 2000).

Michael Coyne, *The Crowded Prairie: American National Identity in the Hollywood Western* (London: I. B. Tauris, 1998).

Vera Dika, 'The Representation of Ethnicity in *The Godfather*', in Nick Browne, ed., *Francis Ford Coppola's* The Godfather *Trilogy* (Cambridge: Cambridge University Press, 2000): 76–108.

Leslie Fiedler, *Freaks: Myths and Images of the Secret Self* (London: Penguin, 1981).

F. Scott Fitzgerald, *The Great Gatsby* (London: Penguin, [1926] 1990).

Leighton Grist, *The Films of Martin Scorsese, 1963–77* (London: Macmillan, 2000).

J. David Hoeveler Jr, *The Postmodernist Turn: American Thought and Culture in the 1970s* (New York: Twayne, 1996).

Linda Hutcheon, *The Politics of Postmodernism* (New York: Routledge, 1989).

Fredric Jameson, 'Postmodernism and Consumer Society', in Philip Simpson et al., eds, *Film Theory: Critical Concepts in Media and Cultural Studies* (London: Taylor and Francis, 2003): 192–208.

Geoff King, *New Hollywood Cinema* (New York: Columbia University Press, 2002).

Charles Kronengold, 'Identity, Value and the Work of Genre: Black Action Films', in Shelton Waldrep, ed., *The Seventies: The Age of Glitter in Popular Culture* (London: Routledge, 2000): 79–123.

Emanuel Levy, *Cinema of Outsiders: The Rise of American Independent Film* (New York: New York University Press, 1999).

George Lucas (dir.), *Star Wars* [1977]. Lucasfilm/Twentieth Century-Fox Home Entertainment DVD, 1997.

George Lucas (dir.), *Star Wars, Episode III: Revenge of the Sith* [2005]. Lucasfilm/Twentieth Century-Fox Home Entertainment DVD, 2006.

Richard Maltby, *Harmless Entertainment: Hollywood and the Ideology of Consensus* (London: Scarecrow Press, 1983).

Stephen Paul Miller, *The Seventies Now: Culture as Surveillance* (Durham: Duke University Press, 1999).

Sandra S. Phillips, 'The Question of Belief', in Diane Arbus, *Diane Arbus Revelations* (London: Jonathan Cape, 2003): 50–67.

David Pye, 'Ulzana's Raid', in I. Cameron and D. Pye, eds, *The Movie Book of the Western* (London: Studio Vista, 1996): 262–8.

Bruce J. Schulman, *The Seventies: The Great Shift in American Culture, Society and Politics* (Cambridge, MA: Da Capo Press, 2001).

Martin Scorsese (dir.), *Taxi Driver* [1976]. Columbia/Tristar Home Video, 1999.

Howard Sounes, *Seventies: The Sights, Sounds and Ideas of a Brilliant Decade* (London: Simon and Schuster, 2006).

Lesley Stern, *The Scorsese Connection* (Bloomington and London: Indiana University Press/British Film Institute, 1995).

Elisabeth Sussman and Doon Arbus, 'A Chronology: 1923–1971', in Diane Arbus, *Diane Arbus Revelations* (London: Jonathan Cape, 2003): 121–225.

John Szarkowski, *Mirrors and Windows: American Photography since 1960.* (New York: Museum of Modern Art, 1978).

David Thompson and Ian Christie, eds, *Scorsese on Scorsese* (London: Faber and Faber, 1996).

Geoff Ward, *Language Poetry and the American Avant-garde* (Keele: Ryburn Press/British Association for American Studies, 1993).

Robin Wood, 'The Incoherent Text: Narrative in the 70s', *Movie*, no. 27/28 (1980): 24–42.

Robin Wood, *Hollywood from Vietnam to Reagan . . . And Beyond* (New York: Columbia University Press, 2003).

David Wyatt, *Out of the Sixties: Storytelling and the Vietnam Generation* (Cambridge: Cambridge University Press, 1993).

Popular Music and Style

Vince Aletti, 'The Dancing Machine: An Oral History', in Shelton Waldrep, ed., *The Seventies: The Age of Glitter in Popular Culture* (London: Routledge, 2000): 273–81.

Daniel Bell, *The Cultural Contradictions of Capitalism* (London: Heinemann, 1976).

Bob Edwards Weekend Show, KPLU Radio (Tacoma, WA), broadcast 11 February 2006.

Mark Brend, *American Troubadours: Groundbreaking Singer-Songwriters of the 60s* (San Francisco: Backbeat Books, 2001).

Van M. Cagle, 'Trudging through the Glitter Trenches: The Case of the New York Dolls', in Shelton Waldrep, ed., *The Seventies: The Age of Glitter in Popular Culture* (London: Routledge, 2000): 125–51.

Richard Carlin, *The Big Book of Country Music* (London: Penguin, 1995).

Peter N. Carroll, *It Seemed Like Nothing Happened: America in the 1970s* (New Brunswick: Rutgers University Press, 2000).

Daniel Cavicci, *Tramps Like Us: Music and Meaning among Springsteen Fans* (New York: Oxford University Press, 1998).

Barbara Ching, 'Country Music', in Richard Gray and Owen Robinson, eds, *A Companion to the Literature and Culture of the American South* (Oxford: Blackwell, 2004): 203–20.

David A. Cook, *Lost Illusions: American Cinema in the Shadow of Watergate and Vietnam, 1970–1979* (New York: Charles Scribner's Sons, 2000).

Jim Cullen, *The Civil War in Popular Culture* (Washington, DC: Smithsonian Institution Press, 1995).

Jim Cullen, *Born in the USA: Bruce Springsteen and the American Tradition* (Middletown, CT: Wesleyan University Press, 2005).

Michael Denning, *The Cultural Front: The Laboring of American Culture in the Twentieth Century* (London: Verso, 1988).

Peter Doggett, *Are You Ready for the Country: Elvis, Dylan, Parsons and the Roots of Country Rock* (London: Penguin, 2000).

John Einarson, *Desperados: The Roots of Country Rock* (New York: Cooper Square Press, 2001).

Anne-Lise François, ' "These Boots Were Made for Walkin' " ': Fashion as "Compulsive Artifice" ', in Shelton Waldrep, ed., *The Seventies: The Age of Glitter in Popular Culture* (London: Routledge, 2000): 155–75.

Gordon Friesen, 'Editorial', *Broadside* 107 (June 1970): 10.

Bryan K. Garman, 'The Ghost of History: Bruce Springsteen, Woody Guthrie, and the Hurt Song', in June Skinner Sawyers, ed., *Racing in the Street: The Bruce Springsteen Reader* (London: Penguin, 2004): 221–30.

Gary Herman, *Rock'n'Roll Babylon* (London: Plexus, 1994).

Barney Hoskyns, *Hotel California: The True Life Adventures of Crosby, Stills, Nash, Young, Mitchell, Taylor, Browne, Ronstadt, Geffen, the Eagles, and Their Many Friends* (Hoboken, NJ: John Wiley and Sons, 2006).

Katrina Irving, 'Rock Music and the State: Dissonance or Counterpoint?', *Cultural Critique* 10 (autumn 1988): 151–70.

Jimi Hendrix: Wild Blue Angel (Live at the Isle of Wight). Experience Hendrix DVD, 2002.

Dave Laing, 'Essay Review', *Popular Music* 16, no. 2 (May 1997): 223–6.

Jens Lund and R. Serge Denisoff, 'The Folk Music Revival and the Counterculture: Contributions and Contradictions', *Journal of American Folklore* 84, no. 334 (Oct.–Dec. 1971): 394–405.

Greil Marcus, 'Self Portrait No. 25', in Shelton Waldrep, ed., *The Seventies: The Age of Glitter in Popular Culture* (London: Routledge, 2000): 293–307.

Dave Marsh, *Bruce Springsteen: Two Hearts: The Definitive Biography, 1972–2003* (London: Routledge, 2004).

Leerom Medovoi, 'Mapping the Rebel Image: Postmodernism and the Masculinist Politics of Rock in the USA', *Cultural Critique* 20 (winter 1991–2): 153–88.

James Miller, *Flowers in the Dustbin: The Rise of Rock and Roll, 1947–1977* (New York: Fireside, 2000).

Stephen Paul Miller, *The Seventies Now: Culture as Surveillance* (Durham: Duke University Press, 1999).

Bruce J. Schulman, *The Seventies: The Great Shift in American Culture, Society, and Politics* (Cambridge, MA: Da Capo Press, 2001).

Sam Shepard, *Rolling Thunder Logbook* (New York: Viking Press, 1978).

Larry David Smith, *Bob Dylan, Bruce Springsteen and American Song* (Westport, CT: Praeger, 2002).

Howard Sounes, *Seventies: The Sights, Sounds and Ideas of a Brilliant Decade* (London: Simon and Schuster, 2006).

Michael Walker, *Laurel Canyon: The Inside Story of Rock-and-Roll's Legendary Neighborhood* (New York: Faber and Faber, 2007).

David Wyatt, *Out of the Sixties: Storytelling and the Vietnam Generation* (Cambridge: Cambridge University Press, 1993).

Public Space and Spectacle

Nora M. Alter, *Vietnam Protest Theatre: The Television War on Stage* (Bloomington: Indiana University Press, 1996).

Daniel Bell, *The Cultural Contradictions of Capitalism* (London: Heinemann, 1976).

Kasia Boddy, *Boxing: A Cultural History* (London: Reaktion Books, 2008).

Philip Caputo, *13 Seconds: A Look Back at the Kent State Shootings* (New York: Penguin, 2005).

Donald T. Critchlow, *Phyllis Schlafly and Grassroots Conservatism* (Princeton: Princeton University Press, 2005).

Guy Debord, *The Society of the Spectacle*, trans. Ken Knabb (Oakland: AK Press, 2006).

Ron Dick and Dan Patterson, *Wings of Change* (Erin, ON: Boston Mills Press, 2005).

Murray Edelman, *Constructing the Political Spectacle* (Chicago: University of Chicago Press, 1988).

David Farber, 'The Counterculture and the Antiwar Movement', in Melvin Small and William D. Hoover, eds, *Give Peace a Chance: Exploring the Vietnam Antiwar Movement* (Syracuse: Syracuse University Press, 1992): 7–21.

Erving Goffman, *The Presentation of the Self in Everyday Life* (New York: Doubleday, 1959).

Erving Goffman, *Relations in Public: Microstudies of the Public Order* (New York: Basic Books, 1971).

Germaine Greer, *The Female Eunuch* (New York: Farrar, Straus and Giroux, [1970] 2001).

Chris Hedegus and D. A. Pennebaker (dirs), *Town Bloody Hall*. Pennebaker Hedegus Films, 1979.

J. David Hoeveler Jr, *The Postmodernist Turn: American Thought and Culture in the 1970s* (New York: Twayne, 1996).

George W. Hopkins, '"May Day" 1971', in Melvin Small and William D. Hoover, eds, *Give Peace a Chance: Exploring the Vietnam Antiwar Movement* (Syracuse, NY: Syracuse University Press, 1992): 71–88.

David E. James, 'The Vietnam War and American Music', in Rick Berg and John Carlos Rowe, eds, *The Vietnam War and American Culture* (New York: Columbia University Press, 1991): 226–54.

Rhodri Jeffreys-Jones, *Peace Now! American Society and the Ending of the Vietnam War* (New Haven: Yale University Press, 1999).

Charles Jencks, *The Language of Post-Modern Architecture* (New York: Rizzoli, [1977] 1991).

Mark Kriegel, *Namath: A Biography* (New York: Penguin, 2004).

Charles Maher, 'Riggs Butchered by Mrs King as Promoters Score a Million' [1973], in Jean O'Reilley and Susan K. Kahn, eds, *Women and Sports in the United States: A Documentary Reader* (Lebanon, NH: Northeastern University Press, 2007): 41–5.

Norman Mailer, *Cannibals and Christians* (New York: Dial Press, 1966).

Norman Mailer, *Armies of the Night* (London: Weidenfeld and Nicolson, 1968).

Norman Mailer, 'The Prisoner of Sex', *Harper's Magazine*, March 1971: 41–92.

Norman Mailer, *The Fight* (New York: Vintage [1975], 1997).

Stephen Paul Miller, *The Seventies Now: Culture as Surveillance* (Durham: Duke University Press, 1999).

Kate Millett, *Sexual Politics* (Urbana: University of Illinois Press, [1970] 2000).

Vivian M. Patraka, 'Spectacles of Suffering', in Elin Diamond, ed., *Performance and Cultural Politics* (London: Routledge, 1996): 89–107.

Peggy Phelan, 'Playing Dead in Stone, Or, When Is a Rose Not a Rose?', in Elin Diamond, ed., *Performance and Cultural Politics* (London: Routledge, 1996): 65–88.

Fred C. Pincus, 'Discrimination Comes in Many Forms: Individual, Institutional and Structural', in Maurianne Adams et al., eds, *Readings for Diversity and Social Justice* (London: Routledge, 2000): 21–30.

Rebecca Schneider, 'After Us the Savage Goddess', in Elin Diamond, ed., *Performance and Cultural Politics* (London: Routledge, 1996): 157–78.

Bruce J. Schulman, *The Seventies: The Great Shift in American Culture, Society and Politics* (Cambridge, MA: Da Capo Press, 2001).

Melvin Small, 'The Impact of the Antiwar Movement', in Robert J. McMahon, ed., *Major Problems in the History of the Vietnam War* (Lexington, MA: D. C. Heath and Co., 1995): 487–94.

Melvin Small and William D. Hoover, eds, *Give Peace a Chance: Exploring the Vietnam Antiwar Movement* (Syracuse: Syracuse University Press, 1992).

Howard Sounes, *Seventies: The Sights, Sounds and Ideas of a Brilliant Decade* (London: Simon and Schuster, 2006).

Michael E. Staub, 'Setting Up the Seventies: Black Panthers, New Journalism and the Rewriting of the Sixties', in Shelton Waldrep, ed., *The*

Seventies: The Age of Glitter in Popular Culture (London: Routledge, 2000): 19–40.

Gloria Steinem, *Outrageous Acts and Everyday Rebellions* (New York: Henry Holt/Owlet Books, [1984] 1995).

John Storey, 'Rockin' Hegemony: West Coast Rock and Amerika's War in Vietnam', in Alf Louvre and Jeffrey Walsh, eds, *Tell Me Lies about Vietnam* (Milton Keynes: Open University Press, 1988): 181–9.

Robert Venturi, *Complexity and Contradiction in Architecture* (New York: Museum of Modern Art, 1966).

Robert Venturi, Denise Scott Brown and Steven Izenour, *Learning from Las Vegas* (Cambridge, MA: MIT Press, [1972] 1977).

Christine Wallace, *Germaine Greer: Untamed Shrew* (London: Metro Books, 2000).

Tom Wells, *The War Within: America's Battle over Vietnam* (Berkeley: University of California Press, 1994).

Virginia Woolf, 'Mr Bennett and Mrs Brown', in Mitchell A. Leaska, ed., *The Virginia Woolf Reader* (New York: Harvest/Harcourt, 1984): 192–212.

William Butler Yeats, *Memoirs*, ed. Denis Donoghue (London: Macmillan, 1972).

Conclusion

Diane Arbus, *Diane Arbus Revelations* (London: Jonathan Cape, 2003).

John Ashbery, *Self-Portrait in a Convex Mirror* (London: Penguin [1975], 1976).

Daniel Bell, *The Cultural Contradictions of Capitalism* (London: Heinemann, 1976).

Van M. Cagle, 'Trudging through the Glitter Trenches: The Case of the New York Dolls', in Shelton Waldrep, ed., *The Seventies: The Age of Glitter in Popular Culture* (London: Routledge, 2000): 125–51.

George Carlin, 'Filthy Words', on *Occupation: Foole* [1973], Atlantic/Wea CD, 2000.

Peter N. Carroll, *It Seemed Like Nothing Happened: America in the 1970s* (New Brunswick, NJ: Rutgers University Press, [1982] 2000).

Joan Didion, 'On the Morning after the Sixties', in Didion, *The White Album* (New York: Farrar, Straus and Giroux, [1979] 2001): 205–8.

Joseph Dorman, *Arguing the World: The New York Intellectuals in Their Own Words* (Chicago: University of Chicago Press, 2001).

Chana Gazit and David Steward (prod.), *Meltdown at Three Mile Island*. Steward/Gazit Productions for PBS, 'The American Experience', 1999.

Leighton Grist, *The Films of Martin Scorsese, 1963–77* (London: Macmillan, 2000).

Will Kaufman, *The Comedian as Confidence Man: Studies in Irony Fatigue* (Detroit: Wayne State University Press, 1997).

Mary Pat Kelly, *Martin Scorsese: The First Decade* (Pleasantville, NY: Redgrave, 1980).

William Keough, *Punchlines: The Violence of American Humor* (New York: Paragon House, 1990).

Andrew G. Kirk, *Counterculture Green: The Whole Earth Catalog and American Environmentalism* (Lawrence: University Press of Kansas, 2007).

Christopher Lasch, *The Culture of Narcissism: American Life in an Age of Diminishing Expectations* (London: W. W. Norton, [1978] 1991).

Murray Levine, 'Introduction', in Lois Marie Gibbs, *Love Canal: My Story* (Buffalo: SUNY Press, 1982): xiii.

Nellie McKay, 'An Interview with Toni Morrison', *Contemporary Literature* 24, no. 4 (1983): 413–29.

Herman Melville, *The Confidence-Man* [1857], in Melville, *Pierre, Israel Potter, The Confidence-Man, Tales, and Billy Budd* (New York: Literary Classics of the United States, Inc., 1984).

Stephen Paul Miller, *The Seventies Now: Culture as Surveillance* (Durham: Duke University Press, 1999).

Donald E. Morse, *The Novels of Kurt Vonnegut: Imagining Being an American* (Westport, CT: Praeger, 2003).

Bruce J. Schulman, *The Seventies: The Great Shift in American Culture, Society and Politics* (Cambridge, MA: Da Capo Press, 2001).

Martin Scorsese (dir.), *Taxi Driver*. Columbia/Tristar Home Video [1976], 1999.

Howard Sounes, *Seventies: The Sights, Sounds and Ideas of a Brilliant Decade* (London: Simon and Schuster, 2006).

Lesley Stern, *The Scorsese Connection* (Bloomington and London: Indiana University Press/British Film Institute, 1995).

Kurt Vonnegut, *Breakfast of Champions* (New York: Dell, [1973] 1999).

Shelton Waldrep, 'Introducing the Seventies', in Waldrep, ed., *The Seventies: The Age of Glitter in Popular Culture* (London: Routledge, 2000): 1–15.

Michael Walker, *Laurel Canyon: The Inside Story of Rock-and-Roll's Legendary Neighborhood* (New York: Faber and Faber, 2007).

Tom Wolfe, 'The Me Decade and the Third Great Awakening' [1976], in *The Purple Decades* (London: Vintage, 2005): 265–96.

David Wyatt, *Out of the Sixties: Storytelling and the Vietnam Generation* (Cambridge: Cambridge University Press, 1993).

Neil Young, 'After the Gold Rush', on Young, *After the Gold Rush*. Reprise/Wea CD, [1970] 1990.

Wolfgang M. Zucker, 'Reflections on Reflections', *Journal of Aesthetics and Art Criticism* 20, no. 3 (1962): 239–250.

Websites

Michael Bronski, 'Shove, the Second Time Around', *The Phoenix* (Boston), 12–19 September 2002 <http://72.166.46.24/boston/news_features/other_storiesdocuments/02433435/.htm>

Equal Rights Amendment, H.J. Res. 40 <http://thomas.loc.gov/cgi-bin/query/z?c110:H.J.RES.40:>

Marjorie Heins, 'More than Seven Dirty Words', *The Free Expression Policy Project: A Think-Tank on Intellectual and Artistic Freedom* (4 August 2003) <http://www.fepproject.org/commentaries/rustytrombone.html>

Jay Jennings, ' "A Necessary Spectacle": 6–4, 6–3, 6–3', *New York Times*, 21 August 2005 <http://www.nytimes.com/2005/08/21/books/review/21JENNING.html>

'Jimmy Carter on the Energy Crisis – February 1, 1977'. *Global Public Media: Public Service Broadcasting for a Post-Carbon World* <http://globalpublicmedia.com/lectures/425>

Steve Jobs, 'You've Got to Find What You Love', Commencement Address, Stanford University, 12 June 2005. Stanford News Service Online <http://news-service.stanford.edu/news/2005/june15/jobs-061505.html>

Kurt Loder, 'Bob Dylan: *The Rolling Stone* Interview', *Rolling Stone* no. 424 (21 June 1984) <http://www.rollingstone.com/news/story/5938701/bob_dylan_the_rolling_stone_interview>

Richard Nixon et al., White House Tapes. Audio version at University of Virginia, Miller Center of Public Affairs, White House Tapes Project <www.whitehousetapes.org>

Bob Perelman, 'Dance', in Perelman, *Braille* (Ithaca, NY: Ithaca House, 1975), p. 33 <http://english.utah.edu/eclipse/projects/BRAILLE>

Marjorie Perloff, 'The Word as Such: L=A=N=G=U=A=G=E Poetry in the Eighties', *American Poetry Review* 13 (May–June 1984): 15–22 <http://www.writing.upenn.edu/library/Perloff-Marjorie_Word-as-Such.html>

'Primary Sources: The "Crisis of Confidence" Speech [Jimmy Carter]'. *American Experience*, PBS Online <http://www.pbs.org/wgbh/amex/carter/filmmore/ps_crisis.html>

Tom Stoppard, '1968: The Year of the Posturing Rebel', *Sunday Times* (London), 16 March 2008. *Times Online* <http://www.timesonline.co.uk/tol/news/uk/article3558639.ece>

Ronald Sukenick, *Out* (Chicago: Swallow Press, 1973) <http://www.altx.com/out/table.html>

Jerry Tallmer, 'A Bloody Township in the War of the Sexes, Caught on Film', *The Villager* (New York) 77, no. 4 (27 June–3 July 2007) <http://www.thevillager.com/villager_217/abloodytownshipinthewar.html>

Title IX of the Education Amendments 1972, 20 U.S.C. § 1681 <http://www.usdoj.gov/crt/cor/coord/titleixstat.htm>

Mark Twain, letter to William Bowen, 31 August 1876. Mark Twain Project, University of California <http://www.marktwainproject.org>

U.S. Supreme Court, Roe v. Wade, 410 U.S. 113 <http://caselaw.lp.findlaw.com/scripts/getcase.pl?navby=CASE&court=US&vol=410&page=113>

'Zion's Christian Soldiers', CBS News Online, 8 June 2003 <http://www.cbsnews.com/stories/2002/10/03/60minutes/main524268.shtml>

Index